I started to count the assertions in this book with which I wholeheartedly agree, and there were so many I ran out of patience. Analytics are at the core of data science and AI and establishing an integrated support organization for them makes perfect sense. So do the people and process-related steps the authors recommend. Buy and read this book and do what it says to do. You have nothing to lose but your organization's bad decisions!

> – Thomas H. Davenport, Distinguished Professor, Babson College, Visiting Professor, Oxford Saïd Business School, Research Fellow, MIT Initiative on the Digital Economy, Author of *Competing on Analytics* and *The AI Advantage*

It's All Analytics – Part I provides a rich context on AI, data science, and analytics. Part II takes it to the next level and shows how to transform smart solutions to tremendous value for the business, and more importantly, how to do it in the right way.

As authors pointed out, a large percentage of corporate analytics efforts failed. This is not due to short of analytics talent, or lack of technology investment. The success requires a lot more – people and process, senior leadership commitment, re-organization, and culture of innovation, to name a few.

I am thrilled that Scott, David, and Gary continue to share their years of experience in Part II, and truly believe that it could not only help business executives save hundreds of millions of dollars of investment, but also achieve billions of dollars of value to the business and shareholders.

It's All Analytics – Part II continues to be a fun read with many practical examples and thought exercises and explains complex concepts in simple language. It's an incredible piece of work. If any business has the ambition to be smarter and stronger in the digital era, this is a must read for all its executives.

> – Xingchu Liu, PhD, Senior Vice President, Enterprise Data & Analytics, Macy's

I found the secret sauce in Scott Burk's new book *It's All Analytics*. I have found that every business stakeholder with whom I have engaged intrinsically understands the decisions that they need to make; they make them every day or every week. They also intrinsically understand the value of those decisions and – with a little help – can quickly attribute value to improving the effectiveness of those decisions.

Chapter 2 'The Anatomy of a Business Decision' does a marvelous job of articulating the importance of not only identifying and understanding the value of those key decisions, but also highlights how those key decisions provide a natural linkage between the business and data science teams. Powerful concept in its simplicity.

– Bill Schmarzo, Author, Professor, Data Monetization Consultant,
and Dean of Big Data

Analytics, whether it be in the form of data science, business intelligence, machine learning, or any other new and exciting application that's under development, is transforming the world at a speed unprecedented in human history. Most businesses know this and understand that embracing this change is not just a competitive advantage, but a requirement to remain competitive. However, many businesses don't know how to do this, and make the mistake of thinking that if they hire some data scientists and buy some data tools this will solve their problem. This is a recipe for failure, and potentially quite expensive failure. Data scientists and data tools are components of implementing change in how a business works, and without an understanding of these changes and a plan for how they will be implemented, the data scientists and data tools will do no good.

While there are many books and resources on both the concepts and the tools for data science, there aren't many books on how to make them work within a business. This book by Burk, Sweenor, and Miner fills this critical gap. Here, they walk through what organizations need to do, yesterday, to transition into an analytics first business, in terms of organizational, data, and analytics technology design. If you're in a business that wants to start this transition, or is struggling to make it happen, then you need to read this book and follow what it says. It's no exaggeration to say the future of your business depends on it.

– Dylan Zwick, PhD, Former Director of Data Science,
Overstock.com

There are a great many books that have been written about Analytics that focus on the technical side of the equation. We are now seeing more books that are focusing on the organizational and process side of the Analytics environment. And we are seeing more and more books written about how Analytics Teams should be organized and managed. All of these areas of focus are warranted and are helping practitioners, students, academics, researchers and others who are interested in the field to gain a more holistic view of how the Analytics field is rapidly evolving, growing and changing.

This new book is a unique combination of data, process, technology, organizational approaches and more. If you are seeking an overview of what you need to know about data and analytics, this book is a great place to start. I speak with a number of people who want to find a way to join the field, either as students about to leave university and begin their careers or people who want to make a change in their career paths or those who have left the workforce and are now ready to rejoin the day-to day-working world. For all of those people with all those varied viewpoints and perspectives, this book is a good place to start your journey.

– John Thompson, Global Head, Advanced Analytics and
AI, CSL Behring

Its All Analytics – Part II is particularly appropriate at this time. We stand at the juncture of a new revolution in business – Rise of the Business Ecosystem driven by analytics. The biggest challenge we face getting there is not technical but organizational. This book defines the pathway to get there.

– Robert Nisbet, PhD, Consulting Data Miner,
Goleta (Santa Barbara), California

It's All Analytics – Part II
Designing an Integrated AI, Analytics, and Data Science Architecture for Your Organization

Scott Burk, PhD

David E. Sweenor

Gary Miner, PhD

Routledge
Taylor & Francis Group

A PRODUCTIVITY PRESS BOOK

First published 2022
by Routledge
600 Broken Sound Parkway #300, Boca Raton FL, 33487

and by Routledge
2 Park Square, Milton Park, Abingdon, Oxon, OX14 4RN

Routledge is an imprint of the Taylor & Francis Group, an informa business

ISBN: 9780367359713 (hbk)
ISBN: 9781032066813 (pbk)
ISBN: 9780429343957 (ebk)

DOI: 10.4324/9780429343957

Typeset in Garamond
by codeMantra

To my wife Jackie, for her endearing support on all my endeavors.

Scott Burk

To my beautiful wife Erin, for her unwavering love and support.
To my two sons Andy and Chris, for their energy, inspiration, and curiosity.

David E. Sweenor

To my wife, Linda, for putting up with my book writing activities,
when we are "supposed" to be retired, doing what "retired people
usually do" – Travel and forget about their professional lives!!!....
But did I not say "this will be the last book?!?" … when in fact
we have 3 more to go, Linda herself being lead author on the
2nd Edition of our 'big medical book' with expected publication data
of 2022 or early 2023 – THEN we can REALLY RETIRE, right?

Gary Miner

Contents

SECTION III DESIGNING FOR ANALYTICS SUCCESS

Foreword and Tribute to the Authors

This book debunks the common notion that data are the foundation of any analysis. It shows that a much more basic foundation is needed before results of data analysis can be used in an organization effectively – appropriate business processes must be designed and built to accept them. The question is posed early in the book, "We have to change the way we work"? Yes, we must change the way we work. That has happened many times before. It happened during the Industrial Revolution to harness steam power to drive big machines. It happened during the Computer Revolution to move from typewriters to word processors and from paper ledgers to computer databases. This book stands firmly on the 2nd habit proposed by Steven Covey among his *7 Habits of Highly Effective People* – begin with the end in mind. We can't expect to "force-fit" new solutions into old business practices, any more than ancient people expected to store new wine in old wineskins. Wal-Mart followed this premise by re-engineering its entire business to function as a "business ecosystem", rather than a bunch of separate systems cobbled together with business process "band-aids". The System is the starting point, not any element of it. If you dare to read this book, be prepared to learn how to change the entire system in your organization to function as what Bill Gates called the "digital nervous system". The nerve pulse output of the corporate "brain" must be transmitted effectively through the proper communication channels to move the "muscles" of the organization appropriately to get things done. This happens in biological organisms via the nervous system and the blood stream. The groups of these "business organisms" can work effectively only through proper communication channels orchestrated to permit the entire organization to function as a business ecosystem driven not by steam, and not even by the data themselves, but by analytical products fueled by them."

Robert Nisbet, PhD
Consulting Data Miner
Goleta (Santa Barbara), California

Preface

More than 70% of corporate analytics efforts fail – even after these corporations have spent very large investments in time, talent, and digital systems. These expenditures were made with anticipation of great returns on investment. It is widely accepted that these projects should return great monetary or corporate benefits. While there are examples of such stories, AI and analytics projects and programs are coming up short. So why do some programs succeed and others fail?

Putting it very simply:

- Companies know they need to invest in AI and analytics.
- Many companies know they should see greater returns on their investments.
- What are the gaps? What is missing in most efforts? What should companies do differently?

This book is about answering those questions and more. It is about covering topics at a level rarely discussed in boardrooms and other books. Yet, these topics need to be understood and addressed.

Why Are Organizations Struggling with Analytics?

For many reasons, we will address those in detail, but let's start with the single biggest problem:

AI and analytics programs are considered something you "add to your business or organization" – a department, some data scientists, some software, and some training. Why doesn't this work? It is not a lack of investment. There is no lack of available tools and platforms in the market. It isn't for lack of trying. Some organizations have been trying to become more data driven for 20 years.

> Well that didn't work, but if we try harder, hire someone smarter to run the department, invest more then surely it will work!

But it doesn't. There are some things that have to be built into the fabric of the business; AI and analytics are one of those things. You might have some success taking an additive or modular approach. However, it will be limited and if your competitors do it more holistically they are going to run circles around you.

You don't need an analytics addition. You don't need an analytics evolution. **You need to reengineer your business around AI and analytics**. The people, the processes, the systems, and the procedures and protocols – all should be parts of this analytics fabric. This is the art and science of the analytics revolution.

One of the most successful corporate paradigm shifts in the United States was the quality revolution. It was only when companies tore out the old business models and paradigms, and then added quality control methods, that they were again able to compete globally. These programs were not short term in nature; they were not add-on programs. They permeated the entire enterprise. Everyone from the cleaning crew to the c-suite was re-educated and forced to adopt their work to a new way of thinking – or exit. It was a necessary mandate; people felt the immediate need to adapt, quickly.

This book is laid out in three parts. Successful analytics programs are built on three cornerstones:

1. Designing and aligning the message of an analytics culture to the people and systems within an organization. Tear down the cultural divide, establish an analytics Center of Excellence, and create an innovation-oriented culture. Understand how decisions should be constructed and made. We present these in Part 1:
   Designing for Organizational Success
2. No organizational plan, educational prowess, or analytics platform can be successful without meaningful data. Data have become complicated and there is much hype about platforms and technologies. We present data architecture considerations at an executive level. We survey data movement, storage, and consumption. Determining the data

infrastructure that will be necessary to support all enterprise initiatives for AI and analytics is essential. We present this in Part II:

   Designing for Data Success

3. Determining the AI platforms, functionality, and infrastructure that will be necessary to support all the enterprise initiatives for AI and analytics. Architectural considerations for the data scientist, understanding the differences of academic versus professional practice, and the analytic model maturity framework are all important aspects to success. Is it better to build, buy, or outsource analytics activities? We present this in Part 3:

   Designing for Analytics Technology Success

Some Key Takeaways

1. Understand the importance of culture for analytics success.
2. Understand why organizing people and processes is more important than the budget.
3. Understand the fundamental building blocks of data architectures and how to piece these blocks together for your particular organization.
4. Understand the fundamental building blocks of AI and analytics platforms and how to piece these blocks together for your particular organization.
5. Understanding how AI and analytics are evolving to support changes in society's views are demanding things such as Trustworthy AI, ethics, regulations, and more robust compliance measures.
6. Understand how to scale, sustain, and expand the advances you have made in data and analytics foundations with a meaningful governance infrastructure.

We need an analytics revolution. Be part of it.

Scott Burk
David E. Sweenor
Gary Miner

Authors

Scott Burk has been solving complex business and healthcare problems for 25 years through science, statistics, machine learning, and business acumen. Scott started his career—well actually in analytics—as an analytic chemist after graduating with a double major in biology and chemistry from Texas State University. He continued his education, going to school at night taking advanced courses in science and math at the University of Texas at Dallas (UTD). He then started programming at the toxicology lab where he was working and continued taking computer science (CS) and business courses until he graduated with a master's in business with a concentration in finance soon after from UTD.

Texas Instruments (TI) hired him as a financial systems analyst in its Semiconductor Group, but due to TI's needs and Scott's love of computers, he soon after became a systems analyst for corporate TI. He worked there for 3 years and started itching to get back to school (even though he continued to take courses at night (Operations Research and CS) through TI's generous educational program). TI granted him an educational leave of absence, and he went to Baylor University to teach in the business school and get a PhD in statistics. He joined Baylor as a nontenure track professor teaching quantitative business analysis (today=business analytics).

After graduating, Scott went back to TI as a decision support manager for the consumer arm of TI (today=consulting data scientist). He engaged in many functional areas – marketing and sales, finance, engineering, logistics, customer relations, the call center, and more. It was a dream job, but unfortunately, TI exited that business.

Shortly thereafter, he joined Baylor, Scott & White (BSW) Medical Center, a large integrated healthcare delivery system in Texas, as a consulting statistician. He moved into an executive role as an associate executive director,

Information Systems leading data warehousing, business intelligence, and quality organizations working with clinics, hospitals, and the health plan. At the same time, he received a faculty appointment and taught informatics at Texas A&M University. He left, but later came back to Baylor, Scott & White as the chief statistician for BSW Healthplan.

Scott continued his education, getting an advanced management certification from Southern Methodist University (SMU) and master's degree (MS) in data mining (machine learning) from Central Connecticut State University. Scott is a firm believer in life-long learning.

He also worked as the chief statistician at Overstock, reengineering the way they tested and evaluated marketing campaigns and other programs (analytics and statistics). He launched their "total customer value" program. He was a lead pricing scientist (analytics and optimization) for a B2B pricing optimization company (Zilliant) for a number of years. He thoroughly enjoyed working with a rich diverse, well-educated group that affected the way he looks at multidisciplinary methods of solving problems.

He was a risk manager for eBay/PayPal, identifying fraud and other risks on the platform and payment system. He has been working the last few years supporting software development, marketing, and sales, specifically data infrastructure, data science, and analytics platforms for Dell and now TIBCO. He supports his desire to learn and keep current by writing and teaching in the Masters of Data Science Program at City University of New York.

David E. Sweenor is an analytics thought leader, international speaker, and author, and has codeveloped several patents. David has over 20 years of hands-on business analytics experience spanning product marketing, strategy, product development, and data warehousing. He specializes in artificial intelligence, machine learning, data science, business intelligence, the internet of things, and manufacturing analytics.

In his current role as the senior director of product marketing at Alteryx, David is responsible for GTM strategy for the data science and machine learning portfolio. Prior to joining Alteryx, David has served in a variety of roles—including an Analytics Center of Competency solutions consultant, competitive intelligence analyst, semiconductor yield characterization engineer, and various advanced analytics roles for SAS, IBM, TIBCO, Dell, and Quest. David holds a BS in applied physics from Rensselaer Polytechnic Institute in Troy, NY, and an MBA from the University of Vermont.

Follow David on Twitter @DavidSweenor and connect with him on LinkedIn https://www.linkedin.com/in/davidsweenor/.

Gary Miner received his BS from Hamline University, St. Paul, Minnesota, with biology, chemistry, and education majors; MS in zoology and population genetics from the University of Wyoming; and PhD in biochemical genetics from the University of Kansas as the recipient of a NASA Pre-Doctoral Fellowship. During the doctoral study years, he also studied mammalian genetics at The Jackson Laboratory, Bar Harbor, ME, under a College Training Program on an NIH award; another College Training Program at the Bermuda Biological Station, St. George's West, Bermuda, in a Marine Developmental Embryology Course, on an NSF award; and a third College Training Program held at the University of California, San Diego, at the Molecular Techniques in Developmental Biology Institute, again on an NSF award.

Subsequently he did a postdoctoral in behavioral genetics at the University of Minnesota, where, along with research in schizophrenia and Alzheimer's disease (AD), he learned "how to write books" from assisting the edit of two book manuscripts by his mentor, Irving Gottesman, PhD (Dr. Gottesman returned the favor 41 years later by writing two tutorials for the 2012 book on *Practical Text Mining* book). After academic research and teaching positions, Dr. Miner did another two-year NIH-postdoctoral in psychiatric epidemiology and biostatistics at the University of Iowa, where he became thoroughly immersed in studying affective disorders and AD. All together he spent over 30 years researching and writing papers and books on the genetics of AD (Miner, G.D., Richter, R, Blass, J.P., Valentine, J.L, and Winters-Miner, Linda. *Familial Alzheimer's Disease: Molecular Genetics and Clinical Perspectives.* Dekker: NYC, 1989; and Miner, G.D., Winters-Miner, Linda, Blass, J.P., Richter, R, and Valentine, J.L. *Caring for Alzheimer's Patients: A Guide for Family & Healthcare Providers.* Plenum Press Insight Books: NYC. 1989).

Over the years he has held positions, including professor and department chairman, at various universities including the University of Kansas, The University of Minnesota, Northwest Nazarene University, Eastern Nazarene University, Southern Nazarene University, Oral Roberts University Medical School where he was an associate professor of pharmacology and the director of the Alzheimer Disease & Geriatric Disorders Research Laboratories, and even for a period of time in the 1990s he was a visiting clinical professor of psychology for Geriatrics at the Fuller Graduate School of Psychology & Fuller Theological Seminary in Pasadena, CA.

In 1985 he and his wife Dr. Linda Winters Miner (author of several tutorials in this book) founded The Familial Alzheimer's Disease Research Foundation (aka "The Alzheimer's Foundation"), which became a leading force in organizing both local and international scientific meetings and thus bringing together all the leaders in the field of genetics of AD from several countries, which then led to the writing of the first scientific book on the genetics of AD. This book included papers by over 100 scientists coming out of the First International Symposium on the Genetics of AD held in Tulsa, OK, in October 1987. During part of this time he was also an affiliate research scientist with the Oklahoma Medical Research Foundation located in Oklahoma City with the University of Oklahoma School of Medicine.

Dr. Miner was influential in bringing all of the world's leading scientists working on genetics of AD together at just the right time when various laboratories from Harvard to Duke University and University of California-San Diego to the University of Heidelberg, in Germany, and universities in Belgium, France, England, and Perth, Australia, were beginning to find "genes" which they thought were related to AD.

During the 1990s Dr. Miner was appointed to the Oklahoma Governor's Task Force on AD, and also as an associate editor for AD for *The Journal Of Geriatric Psychiatry & Neurology*, which he still serves on to this day. By 1995 most dominantly inherited genes for AD had been discovered, and the one on which Dr. Miner had been working since the mid-1980s with the University of Washington in Seattle—the gene on Chromosome 1 of the human genome—was the last of these initial five to be identified. At that time, having met the goal of finding out some of the genetics of AD, Dr. Miner decided to do something different—to find an area of the business world—and since he had been analyzing data for over 30 years, working for StatSoft, Inc. as a senior statistician and data mining consultant, it seemed to offer a perfect "semi-retirement" career. Interestingly (as his wife had predicted), he discovered that the "business world" was much more fun than the "academic world", and at a KDD-Data Mining meeting in 1999 in San Francisco, he decided that he would specialize in "data mining". Incidentally, he first met Bob Nisbet there who told him, "You just have to meet this bright young rising star John Elder!" and within minutes Bob found and introduced me to John, as he was also at this meeting; thus was born the union that resulted in major, bestselling books, on data mining and predictive analytics being produced during 2009–2018, some in their 2nd editions.

As Gary delved into this new "data mining" field and looked at statistics textbooks in general, he saw the need for "practical statistical books" and started writing chapters and organizing various outlines for different books. Gary, Bob, and John kept running into each other at KDD meetings and eventually at a breakfast meeting in Seattle in August 2005 decided they needed to write a book on data mining. Right then and there they reorganized Gary's outline which eventually became *Handbook of Statistical Analysis and Data Mining Applications*, 2009, published by Elsevier. In 2012, he was the lead author of *Practical Text Mining*, a second book from Elsevier/Academic Press, and in 2015, a third in this "series" *Practical Predictive Analytics* and *Decisioning Systems for Medicine*. All thanks go to Dr. Irving Gottesman, Gary's "mentor in book writing", who planted the seed back in 1970 while Gary was doing a postdoctoral with him at the University of Minnesota.

The second Edition of the 2009 book *Handbook of Statistical Analysis and Data Mining Applications* (https://www.amazon.com/Handbook-Statistical-Analysis-Mining-Applications/dp/0124166326/) was released in 2018, and a book written more for the layperson and decision maker, titled *Healthcare's Out Sick – Predicting A Cure – Solutions That Work!!!*, was released in 2019, published by Routledge/Taylor and Francis Group – "A Productivity Press Book" (https://www.amazon.com/HEALTHCAREs-OUT-SICK-PREDICTING-INNOVATIONS/dp/1138581097).

Dr. Miner is currently working on second and third books in a series with Scott Burk, PhD, along with a 2nd edition of the 2015 "big 1200 page book" on *Practical Predictive Analytics for Medicine*. He also periodically teaches courses on "Predictive Analytics and Healthcare Analytics" for the University of California-Irvine.

DESIGNING FOR ORGANIZATIONAL SUCCESS

Chapter 1

Some Say It Starts with Data—It Doesn't

But where were they going

Without ever knowing the way?

The Way, Fastball

Introduction

The philosopher Aristotle once exclaimed, *horror vacui* – which roughly translates to *nature abhors a vacuum*. In the business world, things are no different. Businesses abhor uncertainty and desire, among other things, stability and predictability. Since the beginning of the COVID pandemic in 2020, business models, norms, and business processes have been severely disrupted – which we have all experienced firsthand. From shortages in critical medicines, medical equipment, facilities, and staffing to not being able to find necessities like food, paper towels, and toilet paper in the supermarket, the impact has been devastating for many.

In order for organizations to build a more resilient business, leaders are accelerating investments in data and analytics technology. Many global business leaders understand that technologies such as artificial intelligence (AI), machine learning (ML), cloud, and data visualization are critical to the

DOI: 10.4324/9780429343957-2

success of organizations' strategic goals. Organizations that can redefine themselves and apply appropriate data and analytics technology to their business processes will be rewarded with a sustainable and resilient business. They will also be rewarded with a more predictable and stable future.

Organizations are keenly aware that data continues to be created at unprecedented rates. Business leaders are continually trying to capitalize on this data. But many organizations cannot analyze and act in any meaningful way on the events that create data. Sadly, as soon as data is generated, its information value that can be unlocked from the data begins to decay (Rozsnyai et al., 2009). In order to extract the maximum value and actionable insight from data, it is paramount to ensure that their organizational structure, business processes, and analytics technology are set up for success. What can organizations do to transform disruption into opportunity and align their people, processes, and technology into a competitive weapon?

Organizational Alignment

Start with the End in Mind

In 1989, Stephen R. Covey published the seminal book *The 7 Habits of Highly Effective People*. The second habit noted was to "Begin with the End in Mind" – and analytics and data science are no different. Many organizations are keenly aware that when aligned with business strategy, analytics and data science are critical for a sustainable, resilient, competitive advantage. But at the same time, they often treat it haphazardly and not as a part of the critical business infrastructure, nor do they treat data and analytic processes and output as a core strategic asset.

In order to use AI, analytics, and data science as a competitive weapon, business leaders need to step back and articulate a clear strategic direction for their organization. This business strategy is more than mere hyperbole; they should include strategic goals, business objectives, and key results often referred to as OKRs (objectives and key results). Each of the OKRs may give rise to one or more business initiatives that will be required to achieve those business objectives.

DON'T UNDERESTIMATE THE IMPORTANCE
OF CHANGE MANAGEMENT

A recent *Harvard Business Review* article noted that many companies are failing to become data driven despite an increase in technology spending (Bean & Davenport, 2019). The executive survey ("Big Data and AI Executive Survey 2019", 2019) yielded many interesting insights, a few of which are identified below:

- 77% of respondents say that "business adoption" of Big Data and AI initiatives continues to represent a challenge for their organizations.
- Only 7.5% of these executives cite technology as the challenge.
- **93% of respondents identify people and process issues as the obstacle.**
- 40.3% identify lack of organization alignment.
- 24% cite cultural resistance as the leading factors contributing to this lack of business adoption.

Now, entire volumes have been written on change management, and some of the most famous were researched by John P. Kotter (1995). Kotter's book *Leading Change* is widely considered one of the seminal works on change management. Although a detailed treatment of the change management process is beyond the scope of this work, Kotter identified an 8 Step Process for Leading Change (Kotter, 2014) as summarized below:

1. Create a Sense of Urgency
2. Build a Guiding Coalition
3. Form a Strategic Vision and Initiatives
4. Enlist a Volunteer Army
5. Enable Action by Removing Barriers
6. Generate Short-Term Wins
7. Sustain Acceleration
8. Institute Change

It is our hope that when you begin any data or analytic initiative within your business, you keep Kotter's 8 Step Process at the forefront of your discussions. This is one of the most critical elements for ensuring success of data, data science, ML, and AI projects.

In a recent discussion with the Global Head of AI at a global biopharmaceutical company, the following dialogue took place:

David Sweenor: When you consider the data science and ML projects that your team has worked on, what was the primary reason they may not have been successful as you hope? Is it a technology or people and process issue?

Global Head of AI: It's never been a technology issue. In one example, our AI team worked on a project for a year in constant collaboration with the business function that was to receive the application. However, when we went to embed the AI technology in their existing processes, the group manager said, "we have to change how we work?"

In the above dialogue, there was a misalignment between the data science team and business team. Everyone agreed that analytics and data science could help improve the business decisions but the teams did not think through organizational and process changes that would be required. Analytics would substantially change how the business team did their work and they were not quite ready to change their business process nor work behaviors.

To summarize this discussion: As an AI team, you need to be able to hand over the processes and analytic applications you have developed to the corporate project management office who are experienced in change management. The adopting (owning) group may also want to bring in the information technology (IT) team to handle and maintain any IT processes that the AI team developed.

Once the strategic goals, business objectives, OKRs, and business initiatives are established, the leadership and management teams will need to define, map, and prioritize specific projects for each of the initiatives. For the scope of this section, we will primarily limit our discussion to how data and analytics technology can help with those objectives, but other technologies may need to be considered. For example, there may be integration, networking, hardware, devices, applications, infrastructure, security, and other software required for the ultimate solution.

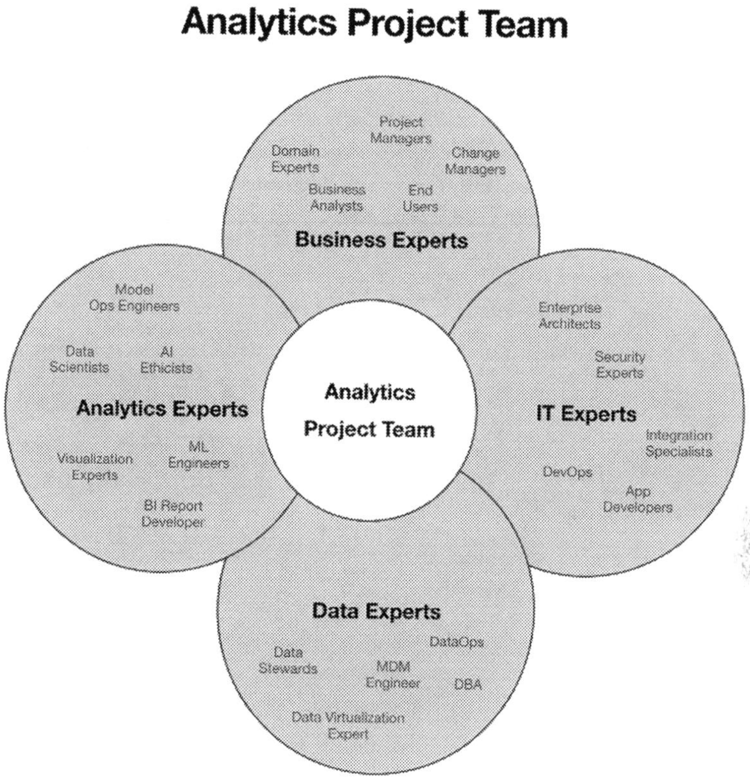

Analytics Project Team

Figure 1.1   Analytics project team – analytics, data, business, and IT roles are required for project success.

Now that we have prioritized and defined a series of projects to which we can apply data and analytics technology, the organization will then need to establish a cross-functional team to drive the project forward. This team should be composed of all the stakeholders involved in the solution. Some of the roles may include Business Analysts, Project Managers, Organizational Change Managers, IT Professionals, Data Scientists, Software Developers, DevOps Professionals, ML Engineers, Data Engineers, Visualization Experts, App Developers, Integration Specialists, Data and AI Ethicists, Governance Experts, Security Professionals, and so forth. A few of these roles are illustrated in Figure 1.1.

One of the most important roles that need to be heavily involved with the cross-functional team is the end users and domain experts. After all, most of these initiatives will require change in how the end users normally conduct their business. If you don't have buy-in from them, you are doomed to fail! Additionally, for each project, we need to ensure that the surrounding functional teams put project management plans and change management plans in place to achieve those objectives. As they say, it takes a village to bring an analytic project to fruition!

HELP! WHERE DO WE START?

Many organizations struggle on where to start with data and analytic initiatives. Industry thought leader Bernard Marr first suggests that businesses need to step back and understand if their business model is still relevant. Marr also recommends that 80% of your data should be used for the organization's biggest challenges, problems, and strategic initiatives. In his book *The Intelligence Revolution: Transforming Your Business with AI* (Marr, 2020) and recent conference talk (Marr, 2020b), Marr identifies the following areas where organizations can use data and analytics.

5 Key Areas Where We Can Use Data and Analytics

1. To improve decision-making within organizations
2. To better understand customers/markets
3. To deliver more intelligent services and products
4. To improve internal business processes
5. Use data as an asset that can be monetized

To get started, Marr suggests that organizations should pick two or three strategic projects and two or three quick wins as initial projects. He also recommends being maniacally focused on customers. Lastly, Marr advises companies to work on Point *5 – Use data as an asset that can be monetized* after the first four have been addressed.

Each of these projects may require a set of different capabilities to enable their achievement. Recently, the analyst firm Gartner Inc. has brought the notion of "composable apps" (Panetta, 2020) to the forefront of IT and analytics technology discussions. Essentially, "composable apps" are assembled from a set of modular technology building blocks that provide the functionality needed to achieve the stated goal of the application. We like to think of them as Lego blocks. With the right assortment of Legos, you can build almost anything – from cities, to cars, to hospitals, to farms, and to airplanes. These technologies often include integration technology, data management technology, and analytic technology. Data- and analytics-related integration technology is discussed in Chapter 8, data management capability is covered in Part 2, and the analytics capabilities will be discussed in Chapter 10.

In summary to realize the benefits of analytics within the organization, the following elements are a prerequisite:

1. Establish strategic business priorities and OKRs.
2. Define, map, and prioritize specific projects for each of the initiatives.
3. Establish cross-functional teams to understand how technology can help achieve stated business objectives.
4. Establish project management and change management processes and plans.
5. Understand data required to make decision.
6. Understand analytic techniques required to make decision.
7. Partner with end users, domain experts, and business stakeholders and iterate on a solution.
8. Track progress, learn from failures, and celebrate success.

Remove the Cultural Divide and Establish a Center of Excellence

One element that helps to create a sustainable data and analytic culture within an organization is to establish an Analytics Center of Excellence. In the first book, *It's All Analytics* (Burk & Miner, 2020), the authors discussed the different types of organizational structures which included:

- Centerized
- Decentralized
- Matrix or hybrid structures

Now, one important facet of the CoE is the reporting structure within the organization. In the book *Building Analytic Teams* (Thompson, 2020) by John K. Thompson, there is an interesting discussion on the CoE reporting structure. Thompson argues that the best organizational home for the CoE is reporting directly to the Chief Executive Officer (CEO) or the Chief Operating Officer (COO).

When a CoE reports to the CEO, this typically signifies the priority and importance of the CoE to the organization. Also, this would certainly create strong alignment between the organization's strategic objectives and the projects and initiatives that the CoE will undertake. Additionally, this helps with ensuring that the CoE has the appropriate amount of funding and that corporate project management and change management teams are appropriately involved.

Now, realizing that the CEO is extremely busy and may not have the appropriate amount of time to spend with the CoE, Thompson believes that reporting to the COO is the next best option since they have the corporate functions reporting to them. In addition to being able to help marshal the necessary resources for the CoE, they can help facilitate and promote collaboration between the CoE and the various business units as needed.

Now that we have explored the optimal reporting structure for a CoE, where is the worst corporate home for a CoE? We (and Thompson) feel that putting the CoE within an IT organization is probably the worst possible place for them. Why is this the case?

In order to address this, we must understand the differences between how an analytics team operates and how an IT team operates. For a review of the analytic process, please see Chapter 10. If we think about the analytics process, it is iterative in nature and takes a great amount of creativity and innovation to map specific analytic techniques to business problems. As the analytics team attempts to discover, explore, and investigate different analytic approaches, there may be successes and failures. The team will continue to iterate until a suitable approach is found. Then the team will refine and optimize that particular approach.

However, it should be noted that the business processes or decisions that the team is trying to model through mathematics may not be possible for either the analytic team or the decision team. There are many reasons for this which include lack of analytics literacy, lack of patience, lack of clear objectives, and lack of sponsorship. Additionally, one reason may be that the data needed to model the process, system, or behavior is simply not available or may not have been collected. The key point is that the analytics process is creative, iterative, and will have both wins and losses.

Now, if we consider how an IT organization operates, they are typically risk averse and do things in a very structured manner (and for good reason). The creative and interactive elements are, for the most part, nonexistent within an IT organization. So, if an analytics CoE reports to an IT function, they will, over time, pick up and start to emulate the norms and behaviors of the overall function. Additionally, IT management will tend to reward the CoE if they are behaving and acting similar to how the rest of the organization acts. In other words, the analytics CoE will begin to draw up detailed plans, change management processes, and, overall, will be more risk averse compared to if they were not reporting to an IT organization. The two paradigms comparing how an analytics team operates and how an IT team functions couldn't be more diametrically opposed.

I WANT TO BE SMART

Earlier in my career, I (David) worked in a Business Analytics Center of Excellence for a large multinational corporation. The stated goal of the group was to create a shared analytics infrastructure available to any business unit within the organization worldwide. The corporation had hundreds (if not thousands) of disparate servers which hosted various analytics, data science, and business intelligence applications around the globe and many more project teams and end users of that technology around the world. If the organization could decommission the disparate servers, it would result in substantial cost savings.

In addition to helping establish the business architecture of the solution, as a part of the initiative, one of my roles was to help adopting organizations migrate to the shared services (private cloud) model. Obviously, there were many adopting departments (over 120 different project teams upon launch) and business units that simply wanted to migrate their existing analytics and reports to the new infrastructure. Simple enough, we helped them through that process.

As the project progressed, more and more groups wanted to create new business applications on the shared infrastructure. Many of these groups did not have significant experience with business analytics technology at the time so it would begin with a discovery and brainstorming session on what could be possible with data analytics and how it could help them. Interestingly enough, many organizations stated "I wanted our department or business unit to become smarter". I would respond, "I would like to be smarter too. What are you trying to do"? Most of these groups, excited about the analytics technology and its potential, did not have a solid understanding of what they wanted to achieve and accomplish – they just wanted to be smarter.

This is where it would have been helpful to step back and align their objectives to the business strategy and then map and understand how technology (in this case analytics technology) could help support those decisions. Before embarking on any analytic initiative, they need to understand the objectives, goals, and implications of becoming smart.

Furthermore, since many of these efforts are truly transformative and will change the way the group operates, they need to understand the commitment required to achieve their objective.

Another interesting aspect of the Business Analytics Center of Excellence was that it reported up through the finance IT organization within the office of the CTO. Relating to our earlier discussion on optimal reporting structures, this may have been suboptimal. An IT organization is very different from how an analytics team should operate.

It has been stated that managing an analytics team is more like managing a team of creative people versus managing a team of IT professionals. An analytics team should be able to test and try different approaches and methodologies, they should be able to iterate rapidly, take risks, be innovative, fail, and learn from these failures. An IT organization is quite the opposite, they are risk averse (for good reason), generally follow strict processes and procedures and want things to run mechanistically.

Innovation-Oriented Cultures

As previously mentioned, analytics is unique from the perspective that there is a certain amount of creativity required and it is iterative. For an organization to move up the analytic maturity curve (see Chapter 10), it needs to understand risks and be receptive to experimentation and the occasional failure or setback. Assuming that the analytic investments are appropriately prioritized, your company can put formal programs together to foster innovation. In fact, here's one such example where an organization used the following process when projects failed:

Steps in this process were (Thompson, 2020):

1. Acknowledgment of the failure
2. A description of the failure
3. A description of the chance of recovery or remediation
4. A discussion of the best path forward
5. A decision on whether to regroup and work toward obtaining the original objective or to move onto the next challenge
6. Back to action

To be successful with AI initiatives, organizations need to establish a clear business strategy, start with the end in mind, create cross-functional project teams, promote an innovation-oriented culture, and have the right technology building blocks in place.

For anyone who has worked in a manufacturing environment, this is very similar to the plan do check act process.

CoE Team Structure

When designing the team structure, there are two approaches to staffing the CoE team. One approach is to hire full service team members and the other is to hire functionally oriented team members.

Some organizations may staff the team so that each team member can provide "Full Service" capability which means they may work on all of the various tasks and the other approach may be "Functionally Oriented". That is, there may be people who specialize in data pipelines, model building, model deployment, and so forth.

Full Service Team Members

With this approach, a CoE chooses to hire highly experienced data scientists (who tend to be more expensive) that can implement an end-to-end data science and ML solution. In other words, the data scientist can perform all of the data science and ML steps. The data scientist can:

- Access and integrate data from a wide variety of sources,
- Explore, prepare, and clean the data including:
  - Impute missing values,
  - Remove redundant variables,
  - Understand and handle outliers,
  - Transform variables,
  - Perform data reduction techniques,
  - Creating and selecting meaningful features from the data,
  - Format and put the data in the right shape and format for modeling.
- Create, train, and compare a wide variety of models types.
- Select the winning model for the analytic task at hand.
- Test and deploy the model to the target runtime environment.
- Monitor model performance and retrain, update, and remodel when appropriate.

Much of the literature refers to this type of person as a Data Scientist Unicorn with the insinuation being that unicorns do not exist and no one data scientist can be an expert at all of the steps.

Functionally Oriented Team Members

Functionally oriented approaches are different in that there is generally a team of people working together for the end-to-end process. As an example:

- **Data Engineer** – creates data pipelines for data scientist
- **Data Scientists** – creates data science workflow to prepare data for analytics and create models
- **ML Engineers** – create specialized deep learning ML models and optimize their performance
- **Model Ops Engineers** – create monitoring mechanisms for deployed models and update and retrain and remodel when needed
- **Dev Ops Engineers** – integrate modes within the runtime environment
- **IT professionals** – manage the overall IT infrastructure

Now, in many organizations, it's not so black and white but we hope this gives a sense of the two fundamentally different approaches that one can take.

Data and Analytic Project Team Roles

As previously mentioned, it takes a village to bring an analytics project to fruition. Some of the roles required for a successful data and analytics team include:

- Corporate/Leadership/Governance Roles
  - Chief Analytic Officer/Chief Data Officer
  - Project Manager
  - Change Manager
  - Data and AI Ethicists
  - Governance Experts
  - Security Experts
- Business Roles
  - Business Domain Expert or Subject Matter Expert
  - Business Analyst
- Data Roles
  - Data Engineer
  - Data Steward
  - MDM Engineer

- – Data Virtualization Engineer
- – DBA
- ■ Analytics Roles
  - – BI Report Developer
  - – Data Scientist
  - – ML Engineer
- ■ Hybrid Roles
  - – Model Ops Engineer
  - – DevOps Engineer
- ■ IT Roles
  - – Applications Developer
  - – Integration Specialists
  - – IT Architect

Now, we recognize that the roles identified above are the different skills that are needed in an "ideal world" and the skills or number of staff may not exist within many organizations. However, we list these roles so that the reader can gain a better sense of the different skills and capabilities that will be needed to bring an analytics project to fruition.

Data and Analytics Literacy

What Is Data Literacy? Data Literacy vs Analytics Literacy

The term data literacy has grown in popularity the last few years. There is no doubt this is a very important concept. In a narrow sense, data literacy has been defined as the ability to read, understand, create, and communicate data as information. With this narrow sense, you need to add "analytics literacy" to this definition to make it useful for any successful business application. That is why we added "analytics literacy" to this section's title. Alternatively, you can use the term data literacy in a broader sense.

For example, Valerie Logan uses the following definition for data literacy (*The Data Lodge*, n.d.):

> The ability to read, write and communicate with data in context and it includes the ability to understand that there's a language around how we are using data in the world. And there's different ways, I call them constructs, for how that language manifests in

your work or life. How do you think with data? Like, how do you process with data? How do you engage with other people with data? Like how do you communicate around reports and charts and analytics and artificial intelligence? And finally, how do you apply the outputs of data – how do you make data more useful in your work and in your life.

She adds an important comment on her website (*The Data Lodge*, n.d.):

> Data and analytics are the linchpin of digital transformation, yet culture is the hardest part. Data literacy is the missing link, and the key to cracking the culture code.

First, we will use the broad sense of the term data literacy for the rest of this section; this definition includes analytics literacy in the way Valerie describes it above. Second, we want to focus on the last sentence of her quote. We speak of digital transformation and technology in this book. But, that is not where most AI and analytics programs fail. They fail in "the softer side", the culture. **That is why weaving data literacy inside the culture is so important.**

> When AI and analytics programs fail, it's typically not a technology issue. But rather, the softer side, the culture.

Many mandatory corporate education programs sometimes considered the "flavor of the month program" lack any "sticking power"; they are "one and done". They are not part of the culture. Data literacy will be required for any organization that will survive in the private sector, and stakeholders will demand it in the public sector. Can you imagine an enterprise existing today without computer literacy? No.

Designing the Organization for Program Success

Education is a great place to start, but much more is needed. Education alone will not provide data literacy. You have to make it part of the culture from top to bottom, with patience over a long period of time. It is not the latest corporate initiative. It is a mandate. In the early days of the "computer revolution" when companies started adopting digital technology, there were difficult conversations. Some people that had been valuable had to go because they would or could not adapt. It will be the same in the "AI and analytics revolution". Some will survive, some will not, and some will have to reinvent themselves.

One of the most successful corporate paradigm shifts in the United States was the quality revolution. As global markets opened in the 70s and 80s it was clear that the United States had major problems. The quality of goods produced outside the United States were cheaper and superior. Market share was drastically dropping. Through programs initiated in the late 80s and 90s US quality rose and made up the gaps. A prime example was the Total Quality Management Program (TQM) introduced by Edward R. Deming (see "Additional Resources" at the end of this chapter). According to (Ciampa, 1996):

> **TQM** consists of organization-wide efforts to install and make permanent climate where employees continuously improve their ability to provide on demand products and services that customers will find of particular value. "**Total**" emphasizes that departments in addition to production (for example sales and marketing, accounting and finance, engineering and design) are obligated to improve their operations; "**Management**" emphasizes that executives are obligated to actively manage quality through funding, training, staffing, and goal setting. While there is no widely agreed-upon approach, TQM efforts typically draw heavily on the previously developed tools and techniques of quality control.
>
> *(Emphasis added)*

These programs were not short term in nature, they permeated the entire enterprise (Scott (author) was at Texas Instruments in the 90s and can attest to the success of these programs, stock in 1990 was $2, on 1/21/21 it was $175).

These quality programs have not gone away, they have morphed into new programs built on many of the same paradigms, just adapted for new pressures, technology, and changes organizations are facing.

Organizations that want to succeed with analytics should:

1. Commit at the highest level in the organization.
2. Commit to the long term. This is the long game.
3. Think carefully and strategically about their industry, their position in the industry, and how they can effectively compete with AI and Analytics.
4. Determine the role of analytics in every function of the organization.

5. Communicate the what, why, and how across the entire organization.
6. Commit to educate and support staff by role and individual responsibility.
7. Commit to change processes (where it makes sense) based on augmented decision-making and automation. Do not change process just to change process, but most can benefit with some form of a data-driven approach.
8. Support, reeducate, retrain, and relocate staff whenever possible. But, be willing to lose staff by attrition or cut staff if they cannot commit to the new culture.
9. Stay the course. Reiterate and adjust where necessary.

This is **designing and aligning** the organization for program success. The final step is execution.

Analytics Success Involves More than Technology

People and Process – Not Merely Technology

Organizations want to be data driven. They know that the right investments can set them apart in a very competitive and evolving world, and thus these organizations are accelerating investments in AI technology.

However, *leading corporations are failing in their efforts to become* "data driven" (Bean & Davenport, 2019). A survey conducted by NewVantage Partners polled very large corporations such as American Express, Ford Motor, General Electric, General Motors, and Johnson & Johnson. Results of the survey ("Big Data and AI Executive Survey 2019", 2019) included the following statistics:

- 72% of survey participants report that they **have yet to forge a data culture.**
- 69% report that they have **not created a data-driven organization.**
- 53% state that they are **not yet treating data as a business asset.**
- 52% admit that they are not competing on data and analytics.
- Further, the percentage of firms identifying themselves as being data driven **had declined in each of the past 3 years** – from 37.1% in 2017 to 32.4% in 2018 to 31.0% in 2019.

Why?

Because investments in technology and infrastructure is the easy part! The hard part **is a commitment to process, people, and culture**! Note the bolded bullets above. These gaps are not in technology. They are gaps in culture. Gaps in alignment of people and strategy – data and analytics literacy, we just discussed. It is *Design and Align* and that includes people, process, and technology.

You must tackle the hard part to gain all the rewards. **You must commit to the Analytics Revolution and that means a shift in culture.** Just as enterprises and agencies had to adapt to the computer revolution, major companies had to adapt to the quality revolution. Organizations now have to adapt to the analytics revolution or be wiped out.

Ethics

Analytics also starts with doing the right thing. Now, more than ever, employees want to be part of organizations that do not merely meet narrow needs of boards, elected officials, or investors; employees want more. They want to be part of organizations that are socially responsible and organizations that have a positive corporate social impact (see gray box, Millennials Have High Expectations). You cannot be socially responsible without ethics; it is a necessary condition. It does not ensure social responsibility. But it is virtually impossible to be socially responsible without ethics.

Ethical concerns are mentioned in several chapters of the book. We specifically address concerns in Chapter 3. We also address corporate responsibilities of analytics and data.

Millennials Have High Expectations for the Actions of Business When It Comes to Social Purpose and Accountability

For example, a 2016 Cone Communications study reveals:

- 75% of millennials would take a pay cut to work for a socially responsible company.
- 76% of millennials consider a company's social and environmental commitments before deciding where to work.
- 64% of millennials won't take a job if a potential employer doesn't have strong corporate responsibility practices.

According to a PricewaterhouseCoopers report titled "Millennials at work – Reshaping the workplace", corporate social values become more important to millennials when choosing an employer once their basic needs, like adequate pay and working conditions, are met. The report states that "millennials want their work to have a purpose, to contribute something to the world and they want to be proud of their employer".

Governance

Governance is sometimes undervalued by people outside of IT or a direct governance function. However, it is critical and should be part of the data literacy program to educate the importance and various roles of governance. It isn't about making jobs harder. It is about sustainability more than anything else. It is about securing and sustaining investments. If you are going to spend millions of dollars on people and technology you need a multi-tier governance strategy. You need human resource governance, data governance, and AI and analytics governance as part of a corporate governance umbrella.

Technology

Data and Analytics Platform Service Areas

In order for data and analytics platforms to effectively serve the business, the organization needs to consider the various domains that the platform needs to support. Broadly speaking, they will generally span four different functional areas: Enterprise Systems, Customer Experience Systems, IoT (Internet of Things) Platform, and Partner Ecosystems (Swanton, 2018) as illustrated in Figure 1.2.

Data and Analytics Architecture

To effectively meet the needs of Customer Experience, Partner Ecosystems, IoT Platforms, and the Enterprise, organizations need a robust data and analytics architecture. Figure 1.3 identifies some of the common components that will be in the data and analytics architecture. These functional areas span data management, analytics, and deployment of those analytic pipelines into business systems. Many of the data-related technologies will be discussed in Part 2 and analytics technology will be discussed in Part 3.

Data and Analytics Platform Service Areas

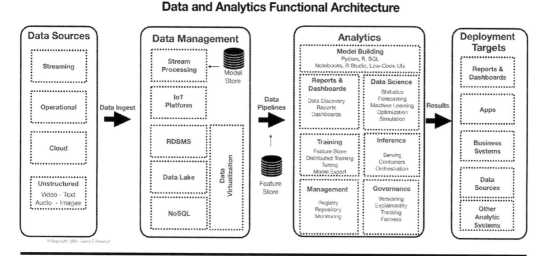

Seamless
Transitions

Hyper-
personalized

Customer
Engagement

Next-Best
Action

Customer Experience

Supplier
Networks

Connected
Services

Partner Ecosystem

**Data and Analytics
Platform**

Enterprise

CRM

MES

ERP

HR Systems

Alliances

Value-Added
Services

Supply Chain

Financial
Systems

IoT Platform

Enterprise

Cloud

Edge
Analytics

Things

Platform

Figure 1.2   Data and analytics platform service areas.

Data and Analytics Functional Architecture

Data Sources

Streaming

Operational

Cloud

Unstructured
Video · Text
Audio · Images

Data Ingest

Data Management

Stream
Processing

Model
Store

IoT
Platform

RDBMS

Data Lake

Data
Virtualization

NoSQL

Data
Pipelines

Feature
Store

Analytics

Model Building
Python, R, SQL
Notebooks, R Studio, Low-Code UIs

Reports &
Dashboards
Data Discovery
Reports
Dashboards

Data Science
Statistics
Forecasting
Machine Learning
Optimization
Simulation

Training
Feature Store
Distributed Training
Tuning
Model Export

Inference
Serving
Containers
Orchestration

Management
Registry
Repository
Monitoring

Governance
Versioning
Explainability
Tracking
Fairness

Results

**Deployment
Targets**

Reports &
Dashboards

Apps

Business
Systems

Data
Sources

Other
Analytic
Systems

Figure 1.3   Data and analytics functional architecture.

Summary

It is important to start with the end in mind when beginning any data and analytic initiative. Organizations need to understand the business decision to be made and then work backward from that. Then, to improve your odds of success, we recommend that organizations establish an analytics CoE and staff the CoE.

After the organization is aligned and committed to data and analytics, we discussed the importance of data and analytic literacy. We then briefly discussed the importance of people and processes as well as ethics and governance. Lastly, we discussed the service areas for data and analytics platforms as well as the components of the data and analytics architecture.

References

Bean, R., & Davenport, T. H. (2019, February 5). *Companies are failing in their efforts to become data-driven.* Harvard Business Review. https://hbr.org/2019/02/companies-are-failing-in-their-efforts-to-become-data-driven

Big Data and AI Executive Survey 2019. (2019). In *NewVantages Partners.* http://newvantage.com/wp-content/uploads/2018/12/Big-Data-Executive-Survey-2019-Findings-Updated-010219-1.pdf

Burk, S., & Miner, G. D. (2020). *It's All Analytics!: The Foundations of AI, Big Data, and Data Science Landscape for Professionals in Healthcare, Business, and Government.* CRC Press, Boca Raton, FL.

Ciampa, D. (1996). *Total Quality: A User's Guide for Implementation.* Addison-Wesley, Boston, MA.

Kotter, J. P. (1995). *Leading change: Why transformation efforts fail.* Harvard Business Review. https://hbr.org/1995/05/leading-change-why-transformation-efforts-fail-2.

Kotter, J. P. (2014). *The 8-Step Process for Leading Change - Kotter.* Kotter https://www.kotterinc.com/8-steps-process-for-leading-change/.

Marr, B. (2020a). *The Intelligence Revolution: Transforming Your Business with AI.* Kogan Page.

Marr, B. (2020b, November). *DATAcated Conference: Bernard Marr - How to develop a data strategy.* YouTube. https://youtu.be/e7QVnXDGVlw

Panetta, K. (2019, February 6). *A Data and Analytics Leader's Guide to Data Literacy.* Www.gartner.com. https://www.gartner.com/smarterwithgartner/a-data-and-analytics-leaders-guide-to-data-literacy/

Panetta, K. (2020, October 19). *Gartner Keynote: The Future of Business Is Composable.* Www.gartner.com. https://www.gartner.com/smarterwithgartner/gartner-keynote-the-future-of-business-is-composable

Rozsnyai, S., Schiefer, J., & Roth, H. (2009). SARI-SQL: Event query language for event analysis. *2009 IEEE Conference on Commerce and Enterprise Computing, CEC 2009,* 24–32. https://doi.org/10.1109/cec.2009.14.

The Data Lodge. (n.d.). Www.thedatalodge.com. Retrieved January 30, 2021, from https://www.thedatalodge.com/.

Thompson, J. K. (2020). *Building Analytics Teams: Harnessing Analytics and Artificial Intelligence for Business Improvement.* Packt Publishing Limited, Birmingham.

Additional Resources

Valerie Logan is on a mission to expand data/analytics literacy. She has participated in many webinars, podcasts, and events which are easy to find. Her website is https://www.thedatalodge.com/.

> Cobb, Charles G. *From Quality to Business Excellence: A Systems Approach to Management.* Milwaukee, Wis., Asq Quality Press, 3 Feb. 2003.

W. Edwards Deming was a foundational figure. There are dozens of books written by him or about him and everything we have experienced is worth reading. You can also find useful videos of his lessons such as those referring to 'The Red Bead Experiment' or 'Lessons from the Read Bead Experiment'. You can also check out the W. Edwards Deming Institute, https://deming.org/. Two seminal books to consider are, *The New Economics for Industry, Government, Education* (1991) by Deming and *The Essential Deming: Leadership Principles from the Father of Quality* (2012) by W. Edwards Deming, Joyce Orsini, and Diana Deming Cahill.

> Stephens, Kenneth S, and J M Juran. *Juran, Quality, and a Century of Improvement.* Milwaukee, Wis., Asq Quality Press, 1 Oct. 2004.

## Chapter 2

The Anatomy
of a Business Decision

Be wise today so you don't cry tomorrow.

E.A. Bucchianeri

The Anatomy of a Business Decision

Before we can understand how a business decision is made, it is important to understand how a business works. From a very high level, any business, corporation, or government is composed of a number of functional areas and departments. These different functional areas execute various business processes that are designed to achieve a specific set of tasks in support of organizational goals.

Some of these functional areas are identified below:

- Administration
- Clinical and Inpatient Operations
- Continuum of Care
- Pharmacy and Pharmacy Administration
- Bed and Resource Management
- Claims Processing
- Finance and Accounting
- Human Resources

DOI: 10.4324/9780429343957-3

- Production and Quality Control
- Research and Development
- Sales and Marketing
- Supply Chain and Distribution
- Service and Support

Now, each of these functional areas has a series of business processes associated with it. As an example, business process may include:

- Quote to Cash
- Care Coordination
- Prior Authorization
- Patient Admissions
- Patient Scheduling
- Collections
- Eligibility and Coverage
- Bed Management
- Procure to Pay
- Employee Hiring and Onboarding
- Customer Service
- Shipping
- Fraud Detection

Each of these processes consists of a sequence of steps. Some of these steps may be automated while some may be manual. If one thinks of a business as a sequence of steps, each step at its most basic level can be thought of as "proceed to next step", "do this", or "do that".

This implies that there can be hundreds, thousands, or millions of tiny decisions that can be made in a business each day. Each one of these decisions may be able to be augmented with data and analytics to make a smarter decision.

It is imperative that the project teams really understand the processes within their organization and how decisions get made. By some estimates, it has been estimated that "Managers at a typical Fortune 500 company may waste more than 500,000 days a year on ineffective decision making" (Smet et al., 2019).

> "Managers at a typical Fortune 500 company may waste more than 500,000 days a year on ineffective decision making". (Smet et al., 2019)

There are a myriad of reasons but if data and analytics can help improve and optimize even a small portion of the decisions within an organization, the benefits could be enormous.

What Is a Business Decision?

Now within an organization, there are different types of decisions that can be made which include strategic, tactical, and operational which will be discussed in the next section. When data and analytics are used to help make or inform decisions, we often refer to these as "digital decisions". To use data and analytics to make a decision, it is useful to think of this as a flow as illustrated in Figure 2.1

To expand on this a bit, we can look at Figure 2.2 (adapted from Siegel, 2013) that illustrates how predictive analytics can be used to make a decision.

In the example above, input data is accessed and aggregated from disparate data sources. After the data is aggregated and prepared for analytics, models are created; these can be statistical models, data science models, optimization models, forecasting models, machine learning models, or a combination of models, all created from the input data (please note, the training and testing phases of modeling are not illustrated above). Next, a predictive model (formula) is then applied to new data the model has never seen before. Subsequently, the output of this is oftentimes a score which is a probability that something will happen: The probability that someone will buy or click something on the website, that someone may become diseased, infected, or readmitted, or that a machine could break down or become defective. The output score is then generally embedded into a business process or application.

Now that we have a good understanding of how data and analytics work and how they can potentially be used to improve business decisions, it is

Digital Decisions

Figure 2.1   **Conceptual flow for business decision.**

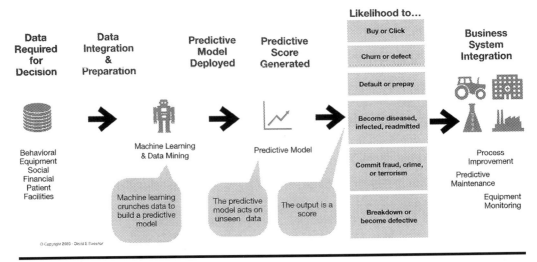

Figure 2.2   Example of predictive analytics in action.

important to have a basic understanding on the potential value of a business decision that is informed by a predictive analytic output.

The Value of a Decision Which Uses Data and Analytics?

Now that we have a sense for how analytics are used to make decisions, how can that impact the bottom line? Figure 2.3 below adapted from Siegel (2013) represents the flow for a direct mail campaign.

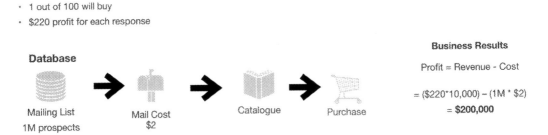

Figure 2.3   The value of a decision before analytics.

Direct Mail Campaign
The Value of a Prediction

Assumptions

Analytical Model output:
- 25% of the entire list are 3x more likely to respond

Database

Mailing List
1M prospects

Analytical
Model
(Decision Tree)

Mail Cost
$2

Catalogue

Purchase

Business Results

- Profit = Revenue - Cost
- = ($220 * 7,500) - (250K * $2)
- = **$1,150,000**
- **5.75x** improvement by mailing fewer people

Figure 2.4   The value of a decision after analytics, a 5.75× improvement!

Before Analytics

Assume that it takes $2 to mail a holiday catalog to each prospect on our mailing list and 1 out of every 100 responses will buy an item from the catalog. Further assume that we make $220 for each response. Now, if we mail the catalog to one million prospects, we will make $200,000 in profit. Not bad, huh?

After Analytics

Now, given the same assumptions as above, let's further assume that the output of our analytical model suggests that 25% of the entire database of 1 M potential customers are three times more likely to respond. This means that now, we only have to mail the catalog to 250K prospects. Given the same scenario, after some quick math, we see that our profit jumps from $200,000 to $1,150,000 which represents a 5.75× improvement. I'd take that prediction any day. This is illustrated in Figure 2.4.

Case Study: The Power of a Healthcare Prediction

Surgical site infections (SSIs) are the one of the leading and most costly types of hospital-acquired infections. In fact, it is estimated that 2 million patients have these infections and 90,000 are expected to die. It is estimated that costs associated with these infections range from $28 billion to $45 billion in the United States alone (Stone, 2009). For an individual patient, the cost of a hospital-acquired infection can increase the total hospital cost by over $20,000 (Surgical Site Infection, 2019), (Gbegnon et al., n.d.). This makes it extremely important for healthcare providers to do everything they can to reduce the risk of these infections. At the University of Iowa, they have taken a novel approach and used predictive analytics to reduce these risks.

The University of Iowa Hospitals and Clinics has created a predictive model to predict the likelihood of a surgical site infection (Gbegnon et al., n.d.). The model uses data from EPIC (the healthcare record), insurance data, and real-time data collected during the surgery.

Similar to our fictitious catalog mailing example above, the following assumptions were made (Gbegnon et al., n.d.):

Assumptions:

- Consider negative pressure wound therapy
- 60%–80% effective at reducing SSI in high-risk wounds
- Total cost approximately $1,500
- We can address 64% of SSI by using therapy in ⅓ of patients

For this specific scenario, the cost of an SSI was estimated to be $28,000 per patient and the cost of intervention was approximately $500. Financially speaking, this implies that they could financially afford 56 false positives for every false negative to break even. The model tested (SVM +ChiMerge) had only nine false positives for one false negative.

When a patient is undergoing surgery at the University of Iowa Hospitals and Clinics, a predictive model is run in real time. If the score is above a certain threshold (generally 0.12), the surgeon takes preventative measures (negative pressure wound therapy) immediately during the surgical procedure.

This has resulted in a 74% reduction in the occurrence of SSIs (DASH Analytics High Definition Care Platform Chosen for CDC Epicenter Trial in Surgical Site Infection, 2018). It is estimated that this has saved the hospital over $2.2 million dollars over a 3-year period (University of Iowa Hospitals and Clinics, n.d.) for one specific type of infection (CDiff) and one specific type of surgery.

Types of Decisions

As previously mentioned, within any business, there are thousands if not millions of decisions that are made in businesses every day. If one considers the various types of decisions that can be made within an organization, they can range from "should we offer a new product or service" to "whether a patient should be admitted to a hospital or not". Broadly speaking, decisions are often classified into three broad categories: strategic, tactical, and operational.

Strategic Decisions

Organizations generally make a few strategic decisions every year. They typically involve a board of directors as well as the Executive Leadership Team. Oftentimes, each of these strategic decisions are unique and will have a broad reaching impact on the organization. Strategic decisions may include:

- Should we build a new hospital?
- Should we enter or exit a specific market?
- Do we want to change our corporate brand?

These decisions are complex and are oftentimes not repeatable. Now, there are various decision-making frameworks (Khosrowshahi & Howes, 2005) that help people think through the critical issues in a systematic and structured way but in the end, ingenuity, creative problem-solving, and risk assessments are required to make effective decisions.

Tactical Decisions

Tactical decisions are generally decisions that define the methods, policies, product, and procedures that are used to support the strategic decisions that are made within the organization. They are more tactical decisions compared to strategic decisions. Examples of tactical decisions include:

- What is the loan approval process?
- How should we charge for a particular product or service?
- What features or services should we include in a new product or service?

Operational Decisions

Operational decisions are decisions that exist to support the tactical decisions and supporting processes within the organization. These are the most numerous types of decisions that exist within an organization. Examples of operational decisions include:

- Should we admit this specific patient to the hospital?
- Is this particular transaction fraudulent?
- What price or discount should we offer this specific customer?

One hallmark of operational decisions is that they support the various business processes that exist within your organization (See "Anatomy of a Business Decision"). These decisions are very structured and there may be thousands upon thousands of these decisions that occur in your business every second, minute, hour, or day. Since the decisions and processes are well known and structured, there is tremendous opportunity to use data and analytics to automate these decisions.

Human vs. Automated Decisions

Oftentimes, when one thinks of a decision, we think that a human is involved in making the decisions. But, when we use data and analytics to automate a decision, does a human still need to be involved? As with most things, there is a continuum (or spectrum) of involvement in these decisions. The industry analyst firm IDC has developed a five-level framework with the different options titled "IDC's AI-based automation evolution framework" (Introducing IDC's AI-Based Automation Evolution Framework | IDC Blog, 2019). IDC's framework includes:

- Human Led
- Human Led, Machine Supported
- Machine Lead, Human Supported
- Machine Lead, Human Governed
- Machine Controlled

Table 2.1 adapted from the IDC Blog (Introducing IDC's AI-Based Automation Evolution Framework | IDC Blog, 2019) further breaks down these categories in terms of who produces the insights, who decides and how, and who acts based on the decision.

In addition, IDC has defined a hierarchy to help organizations think through the various types of decisions. IDC's hierarchy includes tasks, activities, processes, and systems. Like the famous Russian Matryoshka dolls, a task is the smallest possible unit of work, activities are collections of tasks, processes are collections of activities, and systems are collections of processes.

Table 2.1 Human and Machines Led Decision Process

	Human Led	Human Led, Machine Supported	Machine Led, Human Supported	Machine Led, Human Governed	Machine Controlled
Who produces insights?	Human analyzes and produces insights using limited tools	Human analyzes and produces insights based on multiple tools	Machine analyzes and produces insights. Human reviews	Machine analyzes and produces insights without human review	Machine analyzes and controls
Who decides and how?	Human decides based on experience and heuristics	Human decides based on machine recommendations	Human decides based on recommendations and simulations	Machine decides based on heuristics and human governance framework	Machine decides
Who acts based on decisions?	Human acts or executes	Human acts or executes	Human acts or executes with machine oversight and automation	Machine acts or executes with machine automation and human oversight	Machine acts or executes

Lastly, to help evaluate the technical architecture that would be needed to make decisions, IDC has developed a framework and a set of decision-making characteristics (Vesset, 2020).

The decision-making characteristics are defined as follows:

- Scope: Does the scope of the decision impact a single person, activity, or process or does it impact many? How wide and extensive is the decision?
- Latency: How fast does the decision need to be made? Does the decision need to be made on a sub-second time frame, minutes, hours, or longer?
- Variability: How repeatable is the decision? Does it use the same input data and processes?
- Ambiguity: Is the decision well defined or open to interpretation?
- Risk: What is the impact of potentially making an incorrect or correct decision? Could it potentially expose our company, business, or patient to financial, safety, or health consequences?

IDC suggests that these questions can be used to capture decision requirements in a structured manner. Using this approach will allow the organization to understand commonalities across all of the use cases which can then be used to help inform and define an IT architecture and its required capabilities.

Speed Is Everything

All data begins as a business event. As soon as the business event is created, the information value within the data begins to decay. The faster one can ingest, process, and analyze the data contained in the event, the more value one will receive from it. In 2009, at an IEEE Conference proposing a new Event Query Language, Rozsnyai et al. (2009) illustrated this information decay overtime. The steps included,

Business Event → Data Stored → Information Delivered → Action Taken

and between each of these steps there were delays associated with data, analysis, and decision and response latency.

This is illustrated in Figure 2.5 which compares the value of a decision vs. time. In Figure 2.5, one can see that a business event is created, data is

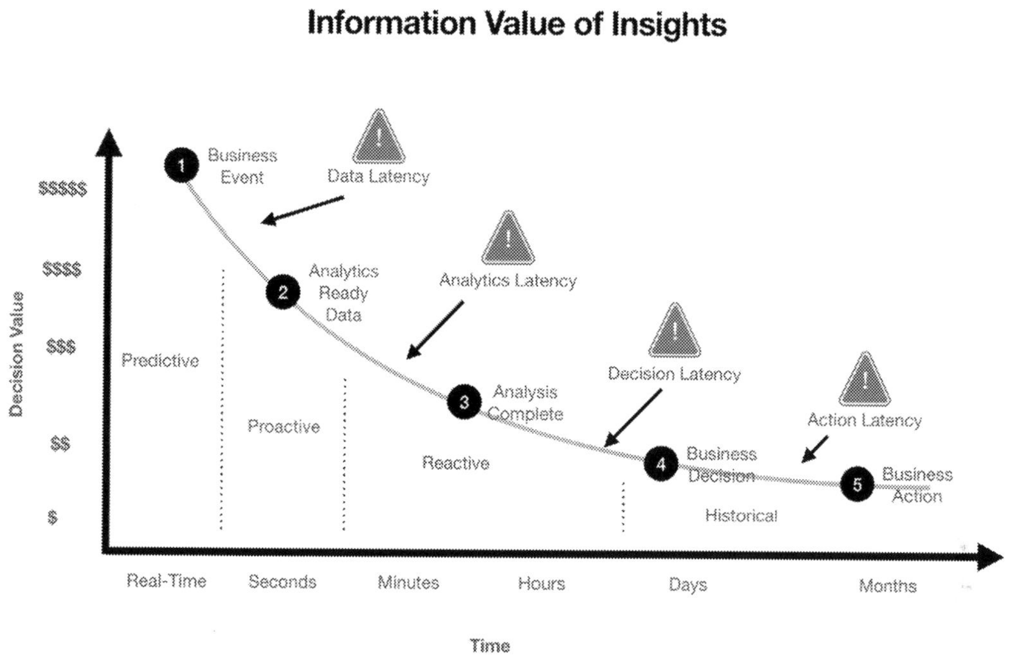

Information Value of Insights

Figure 2.5 Information value of insights decays over time.

stored, information is delivered, and then an action can be taken.

Building upon this notion that the value of data decays over time, Mike Gualtieri and Rowan Curran of Forrester Research continued this research and published "Perishable Insights — Stop Wasting Money On Unactionable Analytics" (Gualtieri & Curran, 2016). Gualtieri would suggest that it's not the data that diminishes in value over time but rather, the *insight* that is generated from the data.

"Data is inherently dumb. It doesn't do anything unless you know how to use it, how to act on it, because algorithms is where the real value lies. Algorithms define action".
–Peter Sondergaard, Gartner Research senior vice president.
(Chanthadavong, 2015)

If we can shorten the event to action cycle, we will receive more value as illustrated in Figure 2.6.

Well Why Does It Matter?

Now that we understand the different types of decisions within an organization, why does it matter? Simply put, companies who use data and analytics to automate decisions within their organization outperform those that

Information Value of Insights

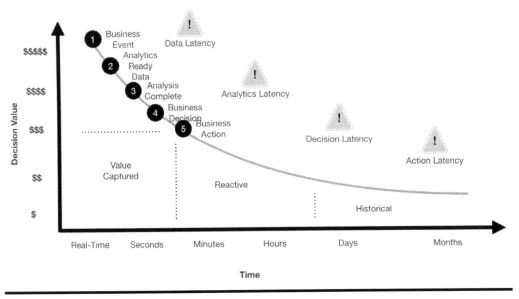

Figure 2.6   Value captured by reducing business event to action cycle.

do not. Research conducted by the International Institute for Analytics has collected some interesting data on the subject (Phillips & Alles, 2020). Those companies that are more analytically mature outperform companies who are less mature in several dimensions. For example, when they examined companies who were at analytically mature Level 2 companies with those at Level 4, they found the following:

- 5-year revenue: 1.7% vs. 15.3%
- 5-year operating income: 7.0% vs. 26.3%
- 5-year return on investment (ROI): 0.2% vs. 21.2%

A recent McKinsey survey (Cam et al., 2019) found that every business function can benefit from data and analytics technology. By applying technology to these functional areas albeit HR, sales and marketing, business operations, or finance, they can realize both revenue increases and cost reductions. Revenue increases occurred most often in marketing and sales, with 40% of respondents reporting 5% gains and 30% of respondents 6%–10% gains. Cost decreases occurred most often in manufacturing, with 37% of respondents reporting decreases of over 10%.

Within the healthcare space, there are a number of areas where data and analytics are being used. These include (Pastorino et al., 2019):

- Being able to diagnose diseases earlier
- Being able to evaluate quality and efficacy of treatments earlier
- Prevent diseases by understanding risk factors
- Better decision-making of pharmacovigilance
- Prediction of outcomes

There are also several other quantifiable metrics including innovation, value creation, and cost reductions. Nevertheless, it is safe to say that organizations who use data and analytics will have a sustainable competitive advantage compared to those who do not.

Summary

Success breeds success, so start small and pick tangible use cases (in tight alignment with your company's strategic goals) that can be accomplished within a realistic timeline (6–9 months). After this, you can continue to evolve and build your organization.

In this chapter, we discussed the importance of starting with the end in mind before embarking on any data or analytic initiative. We then discussed understanding the decision to be made within the organization and working backward from there. Next, we discussed the different types of decisions, the value of a decision, and human vs. automated decisions. Lastly, we discussed the financial impact of such decisions.

References

Cam, A., Chui, M., & Hall, B. (2019, November 22). *Survey: AI adoption proves its worth, but few scale impact | McKinsey.* Www.mckinsey. com. https://www.mckinsey.com/featured-insights/artificial-intelligence/global-ai-survey-ai-proves-its-worth-but-few-scale-impact.

Chanthadavong, A. (2015, October 27). *Big data is useless without algorithms, Gartner says.* ZDNet. https://www.zdnet.com/article/big-data-is-useless-without-algorithms-gartner-says/.

DASH Analytics High Definition Care Platform Chosen for CDC Epicenter Trial in Surgical Site Infection. (2018, August 14). Www.businesswire.com. https://

www.businesswire.com/news/home/20180814005047/en/DASH-Analytics-High-Definition-Care-Platform-Chosen-for-CDC-Epicenter-Trial-in-Surgical-Site-Infection.

Gbegnon, A., Street, W., Monestina, J., & Cromwell, J. (n.d.). *Predicting Surgical Site Infections in Real-Time*. Retrieved December 1, 2020, from https://dollar.biz.uiowa.edu/~street/research/hikdd14.pdf.

Gualtieri, M., & Curran, R. (2016). *Perishable Insights -Stop Wasting Money On Unactionable Analytics Use Forrester's Perishable Insights Framework To Prevent Fresh Data From Going Stale Key Takeaways*. Forrester Research, Inc. https://advance.biz-tech-insights.com/whitepaper/Perishable-Insights-Stop-Wasting-Money-On-Unactionable-Analytics.pdf.

Introducing IDC's AI-Based Automation Evolution Framework | IDC Blog. (2019, January 9). Blogs.idc.com. https://blogs.idc.com/2019/01/09/idcs-ai-based-automation-evolution-framework-a-new-way-to-think-about-ai-automation/.

Khosrowshahi, F., & Howes, R. (2005). *A Framework for Strategic Decision-Making Based on a Hybrid Decision Support Tools*. http://vuir.vu.edu.au/35989/1/A_Framework_For_Strategic_Decision_Making.pdf.

Pastorino, R., De Vito, C., Migliara, G., Glocker, K., Binenbaum, I., Ricciardi, W., & Boccia, S. (2019). Benefits and challenges of big data in healthcare: An overview of the European initiatives. *European Journal of Public Health*, 29(Supplement_3), 23–27. https://doi.org/10.1093/eurpub/ckz168.

Phillips, J., & Alles, D. (2020, July 14). *Analytics Maturity & Company Performance/ROI*. International Institute for Analytics. https://www.iianalytics.com/analytics-maturity-company-performanceroi.

Rozsnyai, S., Schiefer, J., & Roth, H. (2009). SARI-SQL: Event query language for event analysis. *2009 IEEE Conference on Commerce and Enterprise Computing, CEC 2009*, 24–32. https://doi.org/10.1109/cec.2009.14.

Siegel, E. (2013). *Predictive Analytics: The Power to Predict Who Will Click, Buy, Lie, or Die*. Wiley, Hoboken, NJ.

Smet, A. D., Jost, G., & Weiss, L. (2019, May 1). *Three keys to faster, better decisions | McKinsey*. Www.mckinsey.com. https://www.mckinsey.com/business-functions/organization/our-insights/three-keys-to-faster-better-decisions.

Stone, P. W. (2009). Economic burden of healthcare-associated infections: An American perspective. *Expert Review of Pharmacoeconomics & Outcomes Research*, 9(5), 417–422. https://doi.org/10.1586/erp.09.53.

Surgical Site Infection. (2019). Dashpredict. https://www.dashpredict.com/surgical-site-infection.

University of Iowa Hospitals and Clinics. (n.d.). TIBCO Software Inc. Retrieved December 1, 2020, from https://www.tibco.com/customers/university-iowa-hospitals-and-clinics.

Vesset, D. (2020). *Predictive Analytics at Scale An IDC White Paper, Sponsored by Micro Focus/Vertica and HPE*. https://www.vertica.com/wp-content/uploads/2020/05/Microfocus-Vertical-HPE-Partnership-White-Paper_US46394220TM-June112020pdf.pdf.

Chapter 3

Trustworthy AI

Dave Bowman: Open the pod bay doors, HAL.

HAL: I'm sorry, Dave. I'm afraid I can't do that.

Dave Bowman: What's the problem?

HAL: I think you know what the problem is just as well as I do.

Dave Bowman: What are you talking about, HAL?

HAL: This mission is too important for me to allow you to jeopardize it.

Dave Bowman: I don't know what you're talking about, HAL.

HAL: I know that you and Frank were planning to disconnect me, and I'm afraid that's something I cannot allow to happen.

2001: A Space Odyssey

Introduction

As companies continue to develop artificial intelligence (AI) systems that are powered by data science and machine learning (ML) algorithms, organizations need to understand whether customers will trust the AI recommendations before any significant investments are made. In fact, evidence suggests that if AI recommendations are utilitarian or functional in nature (think dishwashers and washing machines), humans trust these more compared with recommendations that include experiential or sensory-type qualities (like foods, wines,

DOI: 10.4324/9780429343957-4

and health spa experiences) (Longoni & Cian, 2020). In other words, you may trust an algorithm to recommend the next movie to watch or product to buy (based on historical purchases) but you may not feel comfortable relying solely on AI to plan your next dream vacation.

In addition to having a solid understanding of consumer sentiment and preferences as they relate to AI, there is also an obligation for organizations and governments to create AI systems that are unbiased, fair, and trustworthy. There have been many reports of AI systems that were producing biased recidivism results in the criminal justice system against minorities, unfair hiring practices against women, and even in language translation services (Mcgregor, 2020).

This begs the question, as more and more decisions are being made by AI, how can we ensure that the analytics system is fair and trustworthy?

Don't Be Creepy – Be Fair, Unbiased, Explainable, and Transparent

Now that we understand some of the criteria required for model ops, organizations need to consider fairness, bias, and transparency. In the previous section, we discussed some of the technical capabilities required for governance like lineage and dependency tracking, explainability, and transparency and will expand on some of those concepts here.

Creepiness

First and foremost, don't be creepy. Just because you can do something, doesn't mean you should do something. In 2012, the *New York Times* shared the story of the retail giant Target's "pregnancy prediction model" (Duhigg, 2012). Essentially, Target was able to predict with high likelihood if a female was pregnant based on her purchases. It turns out, one of the predominant factors in the model was the purchase of unscented lotion and specific vitamin supplements depending on the trimester. With this foresight, Target started to send pregnancy-related coupons to the women who had high propensity scores.

About a year after Target had implemented the program, an angry father walked into a Target store in Minneapolis demanding that the manager explain why his daughter was receiving baby coupons. The father wanted to know if Target was encouraging his daughter to get pregnant. The manager apologized to the upset father and a few days later, decided to call the father to apologize again. However, this time, the father was pretty embarrassed and relayed to the store manager that certain activities were transpiring in his house that he was unaware of and his daughter was in fact, pregnant. Needless to say, this became a public relations nightmare for Target. However, they did not really discontinue the practice. It turns out that there were some women who did not like receiving specific baby coupons from Target (if they hadn't registered for a baby registry). Ultimately, what Target ended up doing was to send a coupon flyer with both baby-related coupons and coupons for things that the woman would never buy. This had the appearance of randomness to the consumer and largely went unnoticed.

Now, many companies (especially in a digital world) track consumer habits and serve up coupons all of the time. Why had this struck a nerve? Was it too overt and direct? Is it any better to camouflage the coupons in a larger mailer?

I will not try to analyze the "creepiness factor", but it is important for organizations to understand what they are predicting and ask themselves, is this considered sensitive or private information? Should we have access to this information? Will the analytic output make the consumer or citizen feel uneasy or uncomfortable? It's a delicate balance in understanding consumer behavior but in the end, don't be creepy or you could put your organization at risk!

Fairness and Bias

When designing a data science and ML model, one must ensure that they are fair and unbiased. But, what does that exactly mean? Google defines model fairness as, "Fairness is the process of understanding bias introduced by your data, and ensuring your model provides equitable predictions across all demographic groups" (Robinson, 2019). Bias can be introduced at many stages in the data science and ML process and can stem from (Hao, 2019):

1. **Framing the problem** – going back to our loan example, if you were to define "creditworthiness" as the ability to maximize profitability, an algorithm could simply do this by giving out more subprime loans. Is this what the organization wants?
2. **Data collection** – when creating data science and ML pipelines, one needs to try to make sure that you have equal representation in the training data as you do in the overall population. As an example, many

popular facial recognition algorithms falsely identify African-American and Asian faces 10–100 times more than Caucasian faces (Singer & Metz, 2019).

3. **Data prep and proxies** – when you select variables or new features for your data science or ML models, the attributes that are selected could have a significant impact on the biases of a model: variables such as age, gender, education level, or years of experience. Some of these may even be against certain regulations! Oftentimes, some of these variables are recoded to numbers (e.g., male and female may become a 1 or 0) in the data set which makes it harder to recognize.

Explainable and Transparent

When an organization makes a digital decision, they are responsible for ensuring that the decision is fair, unbiased, and transparent. Digital decisions are everywhere and we need to be able provide responses to some of these questions:

- Why did you reject my credit or loan application?
- Why did you reject my insurance claim?
- Can you explain how you arrived at this specific healthcare treatment recommendation?

If you are using an algorithm to inform or make the above decision, a business cannot simply say that a specific decision or course of action was made because the "algorithm told me to do so." Whether you operate in a regulated environment or not, it is YOUR responsibility to ensure that the decisions being made are fair. It is YOUR responsibility to ensure that the decisions are made in an unbiased way, and it is YOUR responsibility to be transparent and be able to explain how you arrived at the decision.

Ethics

As AI continues to evolve, there are several ethical frameworks that are emerging as a result. In fact, by some estimates, there may be between 60 and 80 different sets of ethical guidelines in the literature (Rakova et al., 2020). A few of the best practice guidelines include:

1. **Partnership on AI** – this organization has over 100 partners who are working together to share best practices, educate the public, facilitate public dialogue, and research on artificial intelligence (*The Partnership on AI*, 2018).

2. **Responsible AI practices from Google** – Google has put together a set of responsible AI practices which include a human-centered design approach, identifying metrics for training and testing, examining the raw data, understanding the limitations of data, testing, and monitoring (*Responsible AI Practices – Google AI*, 2019).

3. **Responsible AI practices from Microsoft** – Microsoft's AI practices include topics such as fairness, inclusiveness, reliability and safety, transparency, privacy and security, and accountability (*Responsible AI principles from Microsoft*, n.d.)

4. **Ethics guidelines for trustworthy artificial intelligence** – the European Commission defined seven principles for trustworthy AI. The commission stated that for AI to be trustworthy, it needs to be lawful, ethical, and robust. The seven principles include (*Ethics guidelines for trustworthy AI*, 2019):
    – Human agency and oversight
    – Technical robustness and safety
    – Privacy and data governance
    – Transparency
    – Diversity, nondiscrimination, and fairness
    – Societal and environmental well-being
    – Accountability

5. **OCED principles on AI** – adopted by 42 countries, the Organisation for Economic Co-operation and Development (OCED) stated that responsible AI should include (OCED, 2019) the following:
    – AI should benefit people and the planet.
    – AI systems should respect the law, human rights, democratic values, and diversity and enable human intervention if necessary.
    – Responsible disclosure and transparency so people can challenge AI recommendations.
    – AI system should be robust, secure, and safe.
    – Accountability – organizations that define and create AI systems should be accountable for their output and impact on individuals and society.

Framework for Trustworthy Analytics

Jobin's analysis of the frameworks (Jobin et al., 2019) found that there are five ethical principles that are common across the various frameworks. The five core ethical principles included:

- Transparency
- Justice and fairness
- Non-maleficence
- Responsibility
- Privacy

Based on these findings, we will use the European Commission's report to outline considerations for AI system designers.

The European Commissions' Independent High-Level Expert Group on Artificial Intelligence published a report titled "Ethics guidelines for Trustworthy AI" in April 2019. The report defined three guiding principles for building trustworthy AI (Ethics guidelines for trustworthy AI, 2019):

1. **Lawful** – the AI system should be respectful of the law and local regulations.
2. **Ethical** – the AI system should be ethical and adhere to ethical principles and values.
3. **Robust** – since AI could do significant harm, the AI system should be robust from a technical and social perspective.

Of course, this does raise the question, what is lawful and ethical in one region of the world may or may not be in another part of the world. In the end, it's really a question of society.

For example, it has been widely documented that China has a facial recognition system in place designed for social engineering and targets minority groups (Ng, 2020). The system is constantly monitoring people and putting their names on public billboard displays and charging fines for seemingly minor or innocuous "crimes" like jaywalking or wearing pajamas in daylight that the state considers unacceptable.

My goal in providing the above example is not to pass judgment per se but rather, to provide some context to what multinational organizations need to consider when they are designing AI systems. In the end, for AI, "one size may not fit all!"

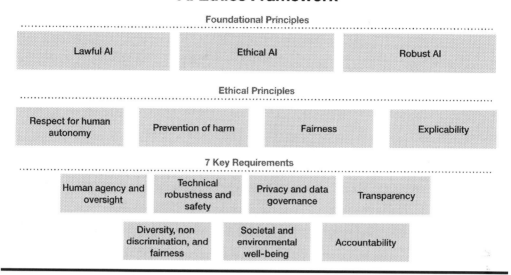

Figure 3.1 Framework for trustworthy AI.

Figure 3.1 provides an overview for the trustworthy AI framework. Based on Figure 3.1, we can see that trustworthy AI is based on three fundamental principles: lawful, ethical, and robust.

Ethical Foundations for Trustworthy AI

Building upon the foundational principles that trustworthy AI should be lawful, ethical, and robust, there are four ethical principles in the framework that companies need to consider when designing an analytics system. The EU and many other governments and entities adhere to a set of "indivisible rights" that are set forth in international human rights law. Designers of AI systems should strive to adhere to a set of "ethical imperatives" that have been contextualized for AI systems (Ethics guidelines for trustworthy AI, 2019):

▪ **Respect for human autonomy** – this principle establishes the premise that humans should have freedom and be self-sufficient. More specifically, "Humans interacting with AI systems must be able to keep full and effective self-determination over themselves, and be able to partake in the democratic process. AI systems should not unjustifiably subordinate, coerce, deceive, manipulate, condition or herd humans" (Ethics guidelines for trustworthy AI, 2019).

- **Prevention of harm** – seemingly straightforward, this assertion establishes the notion that AI systems should not cause physical, mental, or emotional harm. "Particular attention must also be paid to situations where AI systems can cause or exacerbate adverse impacts due to asymmetries of power or information, such as between employers and employees, businesses and consumers or governments and citizens" (Ethics guidelines for trustworthy AI, 2019).
- **Fairness** – this idea surmises that AI systems should provide equal and unbiased distribution of "benefits and costs" and that the system should not be biased or discriminatory. "Moreover, the use of AI systems should never lead to people being deceived or unjustifiably impaired in their freedom of choice. Additionally, fairness implies that AI practitioners should respect the principle of proportionality between means and ends, and consider carefully how to balance competing interests and objectives" (Ethics guidelines for trustworthy AI, 2019).
- **Explicability** – the right to an explanation is increasingly at the forefront of any discussions on analytics and AI. AI processes and workflows need to be transparent and individuals and groups have the right to an explanation as to why specific decisions have been made. "An explanation as to why a model has generated a particular output or decision (and what combination of input factors contributed to that) is not always possible. These cases are referred to as 'black box' algorithms and require special attention. In those circumstances, other explicability measures (e.g., traceability, auditability and transparent communication on system capabilities) may be required, provided that the system as a whole respects fundamental rights" (Ethics guidelines for trustworthy AI, 2019).

The EU framework goes on to mention that there can be conflict between the different principles. For example, predictive policing provides an interesting dilemma. Do societal benefits outweigh individual liberties and freedoms? Is predictive policing fair and unbiased? If the algorithm "decides" that a person is likely to commit a crime or is likely to reoffend, should society take preventative action?

Similar to the popular 2002 movie *Minority Report*, if a "recog" says you will commit a crime sometime in the future, should you be arrested? Does one have free will or is the fate of the universe determined? Food for thought for sure. As the statistician George Box stated, "all models are wrong, but some are useful".

OF SYSTEM DESIGN AND MIXED MOTIVES

Architects of AI systems need to think very carefully on how the systems behave and should be vigilant to unexpected consequences of such systems. In an essay that was posted on the Rockefeller Foundation's website, Tim O'Reilly, founder of O'Reilly Media, describes two principles of AI governance that practitioners need to consider (O'Reilly, 2020):

1. The micro-governance of constant updates in response to new information, expressed by building better algorithms and models.
2. The macro-governance of the choice of outcome for which algorithms and models are optimized.

O'Reilly believes that organizations are doing fairly well with principle #1 above but suggests that significant work needs to be done for principle #2.

Google's corporate mission is "to organize the world's information and make it universally accessible and useful". Facebook's is "to give people the power to build community and bring the world closer together." Both are noble pursuits but how do you design such a system to achieve the vision?

For Facebook, they designed their system to optimize engagement for its user population. Their original premise was that more engagement would bring people closer together. But, in recent years, we have seen an increase in hate speech, fake news, misinformation, election influence, and an extreme polarization across society. Facebook certainly maximized engagement, but it also created Facebook addicts and trolls whose sole desire is to cause societal disruption. Now, Facebook has taken steps to address some of these issues but how does one express engagement mathematically? Also, O'Reilly notes:

> Most troubling is the question, "What are Facebook's alternatives if greater engagement with its services is not actually good for Facebook users?" The value of the company depends on growth in users and usage. Its advertising premium is based on microtargeting, wherein data about users' interests and activities can be used for their benefit but can also be used against them. In far too many cases, when the interests of its

users and the interests of its advertisers diverge, Facebook seems to take the side of the advertisers—even to the point of knowingly accepting false advertising over the protests of its own employees.

Google has suffered similar problems as Facebook. For their YouTube (video service) business unit, their algorithms tried to maximize time on the website which has led to misinformation problems. Larry Page and Sergey Brin, Google cofounders, understood the notion of mixed motives in their original 1998 research paper. They wrote, "We expect that advertising-funded search engines will be inherently biased towards the advertisers and away from the needs of the consumers."

To address AI system design failures and mixed motives, O'Reilly suggests the following:

We need to tear down and rebuild that machine, reprogramming it so that human flourishing, not corporate profit, becomes its goal. We need to understand that we can't just state our values. We must implement them in a way that our machines can understand and execute.

Easier said than done.

Key Requirements for Trustworthy AI

Now that we have examined the guiding principles and ethical foundations for AI, what can AI system designers do to adhere to the guidelines? The EU framework outlines the following seven requirements (Ethics guidelines for trustworthy AI, 2019):

1. **Human agency and oversight** – "Including fundamental rights, human agency and human oversight".
   a. Given the scope and span in which AI systems can be deployed, this requirement implies that AI should augment human decision-making and not replace it. Additionally, there should be mechanisms for those impacted to challenge the AI system. This would require a human to have oversight over the system and can override the decision if appropriate.

2. **Technical robustness and safety** – "Including resilience to attack and security, fall back plan and general safety, accuracy, reliability and reproducibility".
   a. Seemingly obvious, the AI system needs to be secure, robust, and not vulnerable to cyberattacks. However, in addition to traditional IT security requirements, cyberattacks on data science and ML systems may take different forms. For example, some could come in the form of "data poisoning" or bad actors could directly attack and adjust the models making the predictions. Data poisoning is an attack where a malicious actor tries to alter the data used to train models which would in turn cause the algorithm to misclassify new input data. For example, data poisoning could cause email spam-detection algorithms to label emails as safe or could cause your self-driving car to misidentify stop and speed limit signs (Dickson, 2020). Additionally, there should be backup plans in place in case the system fails. There are also provisions to ensure that the predictions are accurate and that the systems are reliable (e.g., can accept a wide variety of inputs) and reproducible.
3. **Privacy and governance** – "Including respect for privacy, quality and integrity of data, and access to data".
   a. AI system designers need to make sure that the data used is fair, unbiased, and adhere to all applicable data privacy regulations for the entire lifecycle of the application. Related to principle #2 (Technical robustness and safety), system designers need to have mechanisms in place to make sure that malicious data is not fed into the system (i.e., data poisoning). Additionally, only appropriate users should be able to access individual data.
4. **Transparency** – "Including traceability, explainability, and communication".
   a. Data used to build AI systems need auditable and traceable. That is, one should be able to trace the lineage of how the data was collected, transformed, and used in the AI system. Additionally, model outputs need to be explainable and when users are interacting with an AI system, they should be aware of that fact. In other words, the AI system should not pretend to be a human.
5. **Diversity, nondiscrimination, and fairness** – "Including the avoidance of unfair bias, accessibility and universal design, and stakeholder participation".
   a. AI systems need to be unbiased and fair. That is, the system behavior should treat all groups equally. To help achieve this, the

guidelines suggest that system designers should include people from diverse culture, experiences, and backgrounds. Furthermore, the system should be accessible to everyone regardless of any disabilities that they may have.

6. **Societal and environmental well-being** – "Including sustainability and environmental friendliness, social impact, society and democracy".
   a. The systems being developed should be environmentally friendly to the extent possible and sustainable. AI systems may positively or negatively impact society and the democratic process so organizations should think through these considerations very carefully.

7. **Accountability** – "Including auditability, minimisation and reporting of negative impact, trade-offs and redress".
   a. Designers of AI systems should be accountable for the decisions of the systems that they design. The system needs to be auditable and the designers need to work diligently to reduce any negative impact on the users. Those impacted by decisions should have a mechanism to rectify and correct any unfair decisions. Furthermore, the designers may be held liable for any harm done to individuals or groups.

The EU framework also provides technical guidance on how to implement the suggested ethical AI requirements. We encourage readers to read the document for more details on how to implement some of the requirements.

Although these principles make intuitive sense, Jobin points out that there is "substantive divergence in relation to how these principles are interpreted, why they are deemed important, what issue, domain or actors they pertain to, and how they should be implemented" (Jobin et al., 2019).

Other AI Ethical Frameworks

As previously mentioned, there are many other ethical frameworks that have been developed but they all are in general agreement with the aforementioned principles.

As an example, the "Executive Order on Promoting the Use of Trustworthy Artificial Intelligence in the Federal Government" in the United States outlined the following principles for the use of AI. AI system systems should be (Executive Order on Promoting the Use of Trustworthy Artificial Intelligence in the Federal Government, 2020):

- Lawful and respectful of our Nation's values
- Purposeful and performance driven
- Accurate, reliable, and effective
- Safe, secure, and resilient
- Understandable
- Responsible and traceable
- Regularly monitored
- Transparent
- Accountable

Summary

In this chapter, we examined AI ethics frameworks and noted that many of the frameworks have common core principles that system designers need to consider. We also discussed the notion that there may be friction or tension between the components and implementing specific human-type goals may be difficult to express mathematically. Organizations need to consider the ramifications of AI output and should strive to make their algorithms are fair, unbiased, and transparent.

References

Dickson, B. (2020, October 7). *What is Machine Learning Data Poisoning?* TechTalks. https://bdtechtalks.com/2020/10/07/machine-learning-data-poisoning/.

Duhigg, C. (2012, February 16). *How Companies Learn Your Secrets.* The New York Times. https://www.nytimes.com/2012/02/19/magazine/shopping-habits.html.

Ethics guidelines for trustworthy AI. (2019, April 7). European Commission. https://ec.europa.eu/digital-single-market/en/news/ethics-guidelines-trustworthy-ai.

Executive Order on Promoting the Use of Trustworthy Artificial Intelligence in the Federal Government. (2020, December 3). The White House. https://www.whitehouse.gov/presidential-actions/executive-order-promoting-use-trustworthy-artificial-intelligence-federal-government/.

Hao, K. (2019, February 4). *This is How AI Bias Really Happens—and Why It's so Hard to Fix.* MIT Technology Review. https://www.technologyreview.com/2019/02/04/137602/this-is-how-ai-bias-really-happensand-why-its-so-hard-to-fix/.

Jobin, A., Ienca, M., & Vayena, E. (2019). The global landscape of AI ethics guidelines. *Nature Machine Intelligence, 1*(9), 389–399. https://doi.org/10.1038/s42256-019-0088-2.

Longoni, C., & Cian, L. (2020, October 14). *When Do We Trust AI's Recommendations More Than People's?* Harvard Business Review. https://hbr.org/2020/10/when-do-we-trust-ais-recommendations-more-than-peoples.

Mcgregor, S. (2020, November 18). *When AI Systems Fail: Introducing the AI Incident Database.* The Partnership on AI. https://www.partnershiponai.org/aiincidentdatabase/.

Ng, A. (2020, August 11). *China Tightens Control with Facial Recognition, Public Shaming.* CNET. https://www.cnet.com/news/in-china-facial-recognition-public-shaming-and-control-go-hand-in-hand/.

O'Reilly, T. (2020, July 8). *We Have Already Let The Genie Out of The Bottle.* The Rockefeller Foundation. https://www.rockefellerfoundation.org/blog/we-have-already-let-the-genie-out-of-the-bottle/.

OCED. (2019). *Recommendation of the Council on Artificial Intelligence.* In *OCED. org.* https://www.oecd.org/going-digital/ai/principles/

Rakova, B., Yang, J., Cramer, H., & Chowdhury, R. (2020). Where responsible AI meets reality: Practitioner perspectives on enablers for shifting organizational practices. *23rd ACM Conference on Computer-Supported Cooperative Work and Social Computing, 1*(1). https://arxiv.org/pdf/2006.12358.pdf.

Responsible AI Practices – Google AI. (2019). Google AI. https://ai.google/responsibilities/responsible-ai-practices/.

Responsible AI principles from Microsoft. (n.d.). Microsoft. Retrieved December 18, 2020, from https://www.microsoft.com/en-us/ai/responsible-ai?activetab=pivot1%3aprimaryr6.

Robinson, S. (2019, September 15). *Building ML Models for Everyone: Understanding Fairness in Machine Learning.* Google Cloud Blog. https://cloud.google.com/blog/products/ai-machine-learning/building-ml-models-for-everyone-understanding-fairness-in-machine-learning.

Singer, N., & Metz, C. (2019, December 19). *Many Facial-Recognition Systems Are Biased, Says U.S. Study.* The New York Times. https://www.nytimes.com/2019/12/19/technology/facial-recognition-bias.html

The Partnership on AI. (2018). The Partnership on AI. https://www.partnershiponai.org/.

Additional Resources

O'Reilly, T. (2020, July 8). *We Have Already Let The Genie Out of The Bottle.* The Rockefeller Foundation. https://www.rockefellerfoundation.org/blog/we-have-already-let-the-genie-out-of-the-bottle/.

DESIGNING FOR
DATA SUCCESS

Chapter 4

Data Design for Success

The world is one big data problem.

Andrew McAfee, principal research scientist, MIT

Currently, seven out of the ten highest valued global brands are data companies. Data as the new oil? Clearly. When you invest in data, its storage, its management and its analysis, you're investing in innovation.

Thomas Harrer, CTO, IBM Systems

Introduction

We are now moving into the technology sections of the book. *Designing for People and Processes* is where most analytics programs fail; it is crucial to get this right. Nevertheless, getting this right assumes you have a firm technology foundation. You want to design your organization (people, process, culture, and knowledge) first and then align the technical architecture within the organization – we say for short – *design and align*.

> It's about the data…. Exactly! The world isn't run by weapons anymore, or energy, or money, it's run by little ones and zeroes, little bits of data. It's all just electrons.

> *Sneakers*

DOI: 10.4324/9780429343957-6

That line is one of Scott's (author) favorite quotes and it is from the movie *Sneakers* (see Lasker, et al., 1992) and it is Cosmo (Al Pacino) and Martin (Robert Redford) on a building roof top in a daring standoff when Cosmo says "It's about the data…. Exactly! The world isn't run by weapons anymore, or energy, or money, it's run by little ones and zeroes, little bits of data. It's all just electrons". But no, it is really more than just the data! **Data alone does nothing! Data by itself is just a cost!**

Data costs include the cost to acquire it, the cost to store it, the legal liability of keeping it, and the potential risk of a data breach. We normally think that data is cheap, but when you consider the total cost of ownership, it is really quite expensive. And maybe only 15%–30% of data collected is ever used (see Priceonomics, August, 2019; Barrett, 2018); it sits there and does nothing (it is called "Dark Data"). So, it is only when your action is based on data that you gain value from it; therefore – **It's about the analytics and** *It's All Analytics!*

> You can only offset the costs of all that data if you use it to the benefit of your organization.

As we are writing this, the country is in a crisis, a pandemic. For months, after the COVID pandemic started in early 2020, models were not the problem. Lack of visibility was definitely not an issue. Lack of attention from the public was not the issue. The media continually reporting on it was not the issue. **The Issue was Meaningful Data – The Issue was a Lack of Complete Data**. Some countries were not reporting the numbers they had available. Some countries lacked the numbers due to economic conditions and poor infrastructure. The biggest issues were the lack of meaningful data around testing – we didn't know the number of people being tested; all we knew were positive numbers of COVID. The key measures reported were total confirmed cases, total deaths, and total recovered. We did not have the number of people that were tested. We did not know the number of people that already had the virus and thus most likely had immunity. We had no controls – we needed widespread testing of the general population to know the true incidence rate. The testing being done was heavily biased by the sick, not the population as a whole.

In early 2021 economies are still being shut down. We have no idea when we will be completely open again, if ever. Will there be additional waves, will super COVID be an issue? We cannot make wise policy decisions without meaningful, quality data. We were crippled and still reeling:

We were crippled for lack of data, nothing else.

Until we have the right data, we cannot make the right decisions. This is fundamental. In a world that is swimming in data, we must have the right data to make effective decisions. The media, politicians, social media warriors, and others including respected epidemiologists, were all saying the models are wrong! Yes, but not because of the lack of science and modeling expertise – it is not "modeling" that is wrong – it is **Lack of the Right Data**!

Science, business, and virtually every intelligent human endeavor today requires good data. **You cannot make good decisions without the right data**.

COVID and the Need for the Right Data

COVID has proven that regardless of how many smart people are involved and how hard they work, you cannot overcome bad data!

Given the time and energy, I (Scott) would have loved to have kept a journal, write, and blog about the gaps I saw with reporting and "experts and news" commentary. But, I had other commitments and did not write about it with one exception, I did write a LinkedIn article very early in the process (https://www.linkedin.com/pulse/covid-19-issue-modeling-scott-burk/, 4/10/20). It was early in the pandemic. It was the frustration with the reporting and commentary about all the models being wrong. It was insinuating that the scientists involved in presenting to the public didn't know what they were doing; that "the models are wrong", that "the analysis is wrong", and that "the epidemiologists are wrong". However, it was not the math or the underlying theory that was the problem. It was not the statistical models that were as much to blame as *bias and insufficiency of data*. No matter how great a scientist, epidemiologist, or statistician, you cannot provide good analytics or make good decisions with bad data.

The next six chapters, Part 2 (this Chapter, plus Chapters 5–9), are about **data strategy** and **data management**. There is no "one size fits all" solution and therefore we do not make specific recommendations. What we do is lay out fundamental pieces, Lego blocks if you will, to choose and build upon. We do want to impart the importance of data and getting that data strategy right and then governing and protecting all those potentially valuable assets.

Why Is Data So Important?

A process is a series of actions or steps taken to achieve a particular end goal. Life is all about processes. We have biological and chemical processes that govern our health and well-being. We have business processes that impact the success or failure of our business. We have government agencies that have processes to provide oversight and administrate. Anything that you desire to understand or improve involves a process. **Data is just the artifacts of a process**. Therefore, data are key to any consciously based improvement.

Billions and Data

Billions is an American television drama series that tells the story of hedge fund manager Bobby Axelrod (Damian Lewis) as he accumulates wealth and power in the world of high finance. Axelrod is very data driven (and for dramatic effect unscrupulous, no correlation implied). There is an interesting scene with Axelrod at a horse track where he says

> So I started watching that (pointing to the leader/information board) instead of watching that (pointing to the track).The numbers told the story, they always do.

Yes, Axel, numbers are data, and data tells the story.

Data Is the Cornerstone of Improvement

You cannot improve what you do not measure.

You cannot even determine how you are doing until you compare at least two data points. "Everything is relative" is attributed to Albert Einstein. This is true in physics and most everything. All quantitative and qualitative assessment is by comparison, relating two or more things. A comparison of two groups or two periods of time results in one of three outcomes – things are the same, they are improving, or they are getting worse.

Even if we do not tangibly collect the data and even if we do not record the data anywhere but instead only mentally note it, we still use the same process of comparison in trying to determine cause and effect. The data exists if nowhere but our minds. We are making thousands of comparisons each day to determine our relative progress toward our stated or unstated goals and intentions. That is human evolution. That is why data are so important.

Data is at the heart of

1. Maintaining status quo
2. Improving on the status quo
3. Determining how I am doing

In fact, the saying goes, data is the new oil! As we will see, you can even buy data (or at least rent it). Most data are NOT captured anywhere. Data are artifacts of process and observation. They may be recorded or unrecorded. Humans observe. Machines observe. Activity and process drive data, observation drives data.

In analytics we often[1] go beyond these subjective determinations and require stored data to perform the analysis. We focus on capturing and storing data in this chapter.

Processes Are Everywhere

We often do not think in these terms, but you participate in and observe thousands of processes and systems in a day. Virtually everything we do is a process. From our personal routines like getting ready for work, planning a vacation to a workout routine. Our work day is full of hundreds of processes, regardless of your work function. A *process* is just a series of steps to accomplish an objective.

A *system* is a set of interrelated processes. We often think in terms of computer or mechanical systems. These systems are composed of thousands of processes. Each and every one of these processes generates an observable result. Each observable result can be recorded. Recorded results are data.

The Problem – Issues with Data Continue to Persist

Sourcing, merging, cleansing, and making data ready for analytics development and analytics production are the real bottlenecks these days; but it has been that way for more than the last 30 years. Today, even with all the progress in technology, getting and cleaning data still

---

[1] Exceptions exist where the data are generated synthetically by an algorithm such as simulation, Bayesian Statistics, see Burk and Miner (2020).

consumes up to 80%–90% of an analyst or a data scientist's time, thus limiting productivity.

We always seem to be on the horizon of overcoming these challenges, but they don't materialize. One of the current promises is using AI methods themselves to help in feature extraction and data preparation for AI work. A prefilter, so to speak, to remediate data problems.

> By 2025, it's estimated that the amount of data will double every 12 hours. Thanks for sensors and wireless connectivity connected devices are generating oceans of data each day.

There are improvements in systems and processes that treat data. However, data is getting more complex, the growth of data is increasing, and interesting problems to solve with analytics are exploding. Our data management improvements are not keeping up with this pace.

Data Management Growth Doubles in the Next Few Years

The global enterprise data management market is expected to more than double from $61.95 billion in 2019 to $135.88 billion by 2027, according to U.S. consultant Grand View Research (Reuters, https://www.reuters.com/article/us-tibco-m-a-information-builders/vista-backed-tibco-agrees-deal-for-information-builders-sources-idUSKBN2771WP).

Firms Are Failing to Be Data Driven

Only 31% of businesses claim to have managed to evolve into "data-driven organizations", and only 28% say they have built "data cultures".

According to Laplate 2020:

On every metric except driving innovation with data, firms ranked themselves as failing to transform their businesses:

- 71.7% of firms report that they have yet to forge a data culture.
- 69.0% of firms report that they have not created a data-driven organization.
- 53.1% of firms state they are not yet treating data as a business asset.
- 52.4% of firms declare they are not competing on data and analytics.

Data and Analytics Explosion

The volume of data collected is growing exponentially with no end in sight. According to a study by IDC (International Data Corporation), an analyst reported (Reinsel et al., 2017):

1. IDC predicts that the Global Datasphere will grow from 33 zettabytes in 2018 to 175 zettabytes by 2025 (a zettabyte is 1,000,000,000,000,000,000,000 bytes, 1 billion terabytes). If one person downloaded this amount of data at 25 megabytes per second (average speed in the United States today), it would take 1.8 billion years to download it. If everyone on the planet joined in 24 hours a day it would still take 81 days. See Figure 4.1. (Adapted from Reinsel et al., *Data Age 2025; The Digitization of the World* (IDC Nov 2018).)
2. The compounded annual growth rate of 61%, and this estimate increased by 9% from 2017 to 2018.
3. In November 2018 there were 5 billion consumers that interacted with data, but by 2025 it will be 6 billion or 75% of the world's population.
4. In 2025 there will be 150 billion devices creating data in real time. Many will be edge devices on the manufacturing floor or sensors in smart cities.

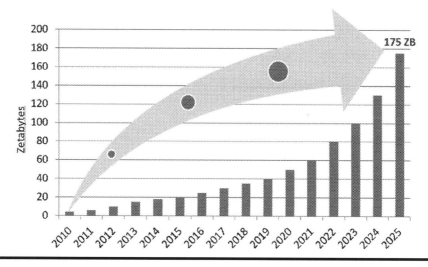

Figure 4.1 Annual size of global data. (Adapted from Reinsel et al., *Data Age* **2025; The Digitization of the World IDC Nov 2018.)**

Some statistics similar to the IDC report are presented by a product manager at a hardware company, Cisco (see Stack, Feb 2018) on data, titled "Who is Using Data and How":

Internet of things (IoT) and data statistics are staggering, to the point of appearing fantastical:

- *Five quintillion bytes of data* produced every day (that's 2.5 followed by 18 zeroes).
- By the year 2020, the IoT will comprise more than *30 billion connected devices.*
- These sensors, satellite data, and much more. And of course automated factories and warehouses are full of sensors and data. Devices include smart home and smart car devices, medical devices from routine patient monitoring like blood pressure and heart rate monitoring to implanted medical devices like pacemakers and defibrillators (see section on "Next Generation Medical Devices – Human Enhancement" for what may be coming). Even Agriculture 3.0 includes self-driving tractors.
- It would take a lifetime to manually analyze the data produced by a single sensor on a manufacturing assembly line.

No wonder studies reveal that:

- Only 26% of companies surveyed reported that their IoT initiatives have been successful.

No wonder the *Harvard Business Review* (Davenport, 2017) found that:

- *Less than half* of structured data is actively used in decision-making.
- *Less than 1%* of unstructured data is analyzed or used at all.

On a Personal Note

According to Bernard Marr and Forbes, last year (2020) it is estimated that 1.7 MB of information was generated per person per second for everyone on the planet!

Collecting data is a cost and a liability. First, it takes money to create the connectors into the source data. This could be creating pathways or pipes into databases or data lakes through extract, transform, and load processes. More common now is the creation of application programming interfaces (APIs) that bring data from the web (services), cloud, software as a service (SaaS), and other data connections – more about this in Chapter 5.

Second, in addition to the cost of creating and supporting the connections, there is the cost of the pipes themselves, fiber, networks, and wireless devices. There is the cost of storage. These costs are not just buying or renting the infrastructure, but the labor associated with keeping everything running – fail-over redundancy and back-up recovery plans. This runs into $-billions in the United States. You could say that this is the cost of running business. *But not really, as most of this data sit idle.* We collect far more than we ever analyze. It is like all the boxes of memorabilia, clothes, and knick-knacks in your attic that you keep because you might want it or need it someday. But you never take it out, and as it ages, it loses value.

More importantly, all this excess data is a *liability*. Have you heard of any data breaches lately? Companies are often not aware of the information that sits in legacy databases. Moreover, there is legal liability from (former) employees on email systems and related databases that are never purged and thus discoverable in lawsuits and other legal proceedings.

According to *Forbes* (Meehan, 2016) it is estimated that as much as 90% of big data is never analyzed. In fact, the amount of data never analyzed is so large that Gartner has coined a term called "Dark Data". Dark Data describe the information assets organizations collect, process, and store, during regular business activities, but generally fail to use for other purposes like for example, analytics, business relationships, and direct monetizing. Most organizations fail to use this data, but it could and should be used. **Data is a strategic asset.**

We have a problem:

We have all this data being collected at a great expense, but we are not gaining value from it. The objective should be taking data that took money to collect, provision, and store and turning into actionable insights that drive value by decreasing costs, driving revenue, and improving quality. In addition, the value of data decreases with time, so data sitting in silos decrease in value every day.

The Potential of Data = Analytics

Now we look at the potential in collecting all that data. Estimates differ, but according to Forbes (Press, 2017) the market for business analytics will be $203 Billion in 2020 and is growing at a 12% compound annual growth rate. Contrast this with the Computing Technology Industry Association (CompTIA) estimated the global information technology industry would grow at a rate of 4% in 2019 (CompTIA, 2019), much slower than the analytics market. "Data monetization", which is the process of using data to generate revenue, will become a major source of income for this 17× increase in data being collected from 2015 to 2025, and these estimates are constantly being raised so the growth is a rising exponential function.

In summary, there will be increasing demand for people that know how to turn data into insights or how data can impact their enterprise or community.

We estimate that virtually every worker in the United States will be impacted by these developments in the next 5–10 years. These impacts may be direct, meaning you will be responsible to employ one or more of these methods into your work function.

Framework for Data and Analytics – Some Fundamentals

The Typical Story of Data Growth, Data Complexity, and Data Needs

As we enter this section on creating a successful analytics data architecture, we should highlight the natural progression many organizations move through. Not every one of these applies to every business, some are not applicable, some are skipped. It is not meant to a strict chronological flow, as many of these overlap. But it does provide a general time lapsed progression. Following is a general theme for data in digital systems:

1. **Operational systems and online transaction processing (OLTP)** – OLTP systems support the everyday business needs of the organizations. Examples are electronic medical record systems (EMRs), order entry and point of sale systems, enterprise resource planning systems, accounting, HR, and systems that support virtually any department. These systems are used by frontline workers or for customer self-service applications. They are optimized to be very fast and highly reliable. OLTP captures, stores, and processes data from transactions in real time.
2. **Operational data stores (ODS)** – An ODS is a database designed to separate data from OLTP systems so it can be used in reporting and non-production operations. It is best practice to minimize the number of queries against the OLTP systems; otherwise users would slow them down. As businesses needed access to this data to support knowledge workers and management the ODS was created for reporting, control, and operational decision support.

3. **Arrival of the data warehouse** – Over the years, information systems grew in number and data complexity, the ODS multiple and lacked a holistic (360°) view of the business. Data marts and data warehouses were created to support these views. We will explore these as well as ODS in Chapter 6.

4. **Arrival of business intelligence (BI)** – This data warehouse supported BI needs and so the corporate IT group configured it and created corporate reports and user reporting capabilities (we dedicated a chapter to BI in our first book).

5. **New on-premise systems** – Data requests for new data sources came into IT from the business. New on-premise systems came online and IT added them to the data warehouse.

6. **Special projects require special data sources** – Special projects came on and new data marts were generated to support them. Service requests came into IT to join data from multiple new marts to the DW.

7. **REST and web APIs** – In addition to the special connections that were made from system to system or from source system data into the data warehouse RESTful and web APIs became popular and remain very popular today.

8. **Self-service visual BI** – There is a new self-service analytics initiative for visual BI. The primary data source is the data warehouse, but a deluge of service requests are coming into IT for additional data sources.

9. **Message-oriented middleware and enterprise service bus (as software, ESB)** – ESB allows the tracking of events and services at different points in time and location and generates associated data to create an important data trail for understanding process flows and triggers.

10. **Software as a service (SaaS)** – The company signed several SaaS contracts with different providers for various operational and support systems. IT is getting service requests for some of this data for analytics use. However, these systems are interactive and the databases within them are not accessible so IT cannot fulfill the requests. As a workaround, people are querying the systems and results are added to local, ad-hoc spreadsheets since there is no way to get this data from the data warehouse.

11. **Big data time, the data lake** – Executive and IT leaders receive a lot of pressure to join the big data wave and create Hadoop and Spark Clusters.

12. **Data virtualization (DV)** – DV creates new ways to bring together data stored in traditional sources like the Data Warehouse and disk storage along with data aggregated from SaaS and APIs.

13. **Streaming operational data** – Streaming data becomes important as businesses want to gain access to data from sensors in hospitals, manufacturing, and CCTV (closed-circuit television) cameras in smart cities. This forces data volumes to continue to explode.

14. **Moving systems to the cloud** – IT is now moving some legacy systems to the cloud. This is causing a moratorium of service requests for the data warehouse. The rest of the business is getting frustrated. Executives cannot get the answers they need to make critical decisions. There is no clear plan on how the business will extract the data collected in these systems.

15. **Third-party purchased data** – This is data purchased to extend the in-house data an organization collected on its own. It could be available via an API, but unlike many publicly available ones that are free. This data is being monetized by a company due to its value. As an example a marketing company may sell "secret sauce data" that purchases estimates of demographic and discretionary spending by geographic location.

Data Architecture

Data architecture is a framework of rules, policies, procedures, standards and systems that govern data in the organization. Today, **data and people are the two most valuable and strategic assets in the enterprise**. Data architecture **links collected data to the business rules that translate it into meaningful contexts**. Data architecture specifies what data is accessible, whether it is stored, and how it is used. It provides data governance which covers access, security, change management, scale, reliability, and sustainability (mentioned in Chapter 2).

Processes -> Data -> Analytics -> Improvements -> Processes -> Data

At the heart of data is a process, at the heart of improvement is analytics. Here is a short story of improvement.

1. Processes and systems are everywhere
2. Data are generated by a process
3. We collect some of this data
4. We analyze data and create models
5. Analytics and models provide insight
6. Insights inform action
7. Action improves life

PROCESSES, SYSTEMS, AND DATA

Analytic models are trained and made operational with data via algorithms. For algorithms to generate models, or execute models, we must feed them data. We collect data at a dizzying rate these days. We collect data in a variety of ways – manual entry into smartphones, computers, and notepads. Operational systems that run organizations are generating data. Devices collect most of the data without us even knowing – cameras, sensors, voice, electronic controls, machines, devices, and telemetry. At the heart of this collection are again systems and processes. We do not think about it most of the time, but when we do, we realize life consists of processes. Therefore, we have a great opportunity to improve life by understanding these processes via analytics.

Following are some examples of processes and systems and the data they generate.

Examples of Processes and Systems	*Data Generated*
Human/biological systems	EKGs, ECGs, and Smart Watch Data
Smart phone video recording	Video (MOV and MP4 data)
Book, Blog writing	Handwritten pages or word processing files
Delivery, postal, and transportation	Telematics, GPS, and logistics data
Smart cities	Data from sensors, cameras (CCTV), and traffic impedance detectors
Doctor's visit	Data in an electronic medical or health record (EMR/EHR) system or computerized physician order entry (CPOE)
Exercising, gym routines, and workouts	Log book and smart phone app
NFL games	Video, sport statistics, and play movement
Medical bill payment	Billing codes, patient info, claim adjudication, payment splits, and payment processing
Customer survey process	Customer ratings and comments

There are millions of things that could be collected as data. However, we only collect a small fraction. The amount is increasing, think about video. The streets of most cities a few years ago were just as full with the bustle of activity as they are today. However, today, that bustle is captured on video, being recorded, and generating data that can be analyzed.

As said by a famous statistician (W. Edwards Deming) a long time ago "In God we trust, all others bring data". We can do that more than ever today. Data has the ability if used correctly to separate anecdote and hyperbole from facts. For more on using how to use data intelligently to build analytical models we recommend the first book in the series. We cover steps 4 to 7 in detail there. In this book we want to focus on the design of people, procedure, and technology to help you in your journey toward success by applying data and analytics.

Today's biggest data challenges are due to one or more of the "Data V's". Initially there were three:

1. Data volume
2. Data variety
3. Data velocity

Then two more qualities were later added to make it the 5V's of Data:

4. Data value
5. Data veracity

Data Volume

Data volume is the sheer amount of data. The authors estimate that more data was generated per day in 2020 than was produced in the entire year of 2005 (Marr, 2018). The volume is daunting, overwhelming, and most of it goes unused. It should be of great value. Why collect if you are not going to use it? Yet, according to *Harvard Business Review* (Davenport, 2017):

- Less than half of structured data is actively used in decision-making.
- Less than 1% of unstructured data is analyzed or used at all.

Data Variety

Data variety describes the disparate data sources, data types, different structures, and formats of data. We source data for analytics via traditional database connections, web data, SaaS, and data lakes. We source data in a wide variety of formats and data structures. Enterprises must have access to both on-premises and cloud data. We explore technology that helps tremendously with these problems, see Chapter 7.

Data Velocity

Data velocity describes how fast data is being added to systems and how often it is refreshed. Many forms of data today are streaming or event-based information. We provide valuable information on these technologies in Chapter 5.

Data Value

Data value is the return on investment (ROI) for sourcing, transforming, securing, and protecting data. Collecting and storing data is a huge cost. Therefore, the only way to get a positive return on data is to offset this cost is by applying and operationalizing analytics.

Data Veracity

Data veracity is the quality, reliability, and trustworthiness of the data. Data quality is one of the biggest limiting factors in business today. You will need technology to help remediate the data in virtually every link in the data chain and your analytics tools. We cover this in Chapter 8.

The Pieces Are Interdependent and Circular – Keep Looking Forward for Next Generation Data

Data design is dependent on the analytics program's mission, goals, and project list. And likewise, you cannot support projects where you do not have data. Therefore the organization must constantly be forward thinking about what kind of data should be collected to support future projects. Do you need new sensors or cameras to collect new data? Do you need to manually collect data on processes? Should you buy external data? Do you need to create new ways to survey your customers?

> Trying to solve problems with the wrong data is like the drunk searching for their keys by the light post.

Leaders often have lofty goals without the data collected to address them. If taken at face value this can turn leadership off data-driven initiatives. Trying to solve problems with the wrong data is like a drunk searching for their keys by the light post. Not because that is where they lost them, but because the light is better.

Analytics are performed with data collected over a long period of time, often months and years. You must get ahead of your business direction and analytics project by collecting data months and years before you need it. Businesses must be proactive. They must constantly be looking down the road toward the next generation of projects and start collecting the data to support these projects. We suggest some sort of system to catalog your future aspirations. With the advent of so many team collaboration software tools and communication tools, it should be easy to set up channels with ideas, to bring plans into the fold, and capture data on the initiatives you seek to improve. Data collection is always a leading requirement for project success.

The Value of Data and Analytics

There is little doubt there is a very positive return on your data investment if it is planned carefully and executed proficiently. Specific analytics project ROI will swing widely, but overall we have seen significant improvements to the bottom line – direct monetary impact. Possibly more important, analytics projects will also contribute to the efficiency, effectiveness, and knowledge of the organization for future projects. One can use whatever metaphor you wish, like gaining traction or building muscle, but the bottom line is that data-driven efforts yield compounding gains. Therefore, it is important to keep the long game in mind. A few brief pointers:

- Develop a robust data strategy that not only supports operations but will support current and *future* business initiatives
- *Design and align* your data strategy to your analytics strategy
- Measure impacts (hard/direct ROI and soft ROI)
- Plan for the long game
- Support a culture of analytics from top to bottom
- Support data literacy and analytics literacy programs

Measuring analytics ROI requires good data as a baseline. It is important for business programs to have good financial metrics they can use to support or challenge the results of analytics and AI efforts. Most organizations support these metrics with a BI platform. *It is ill-advised for any organization to jump into an advanced analytics or AI program until they have the ability to consistently and accurately report business metrics.* That is the reason most organizations start with BI and then jump into more advanced data-driven techniques and technologies.

Once these metrics are in place there are standard (hard) ROI methods that can be deployed. However, organizations should compare all potential impacts of projects. To borrow from the balloon metaphor, you don't want to squeeze/reduce costs in one department only to have added costs inflated in another. It is important that you consider all relevant metrics. A few variables that might be used in the (hard/direct) ROI calculation might be:

- Reduction in direct costs or future expenses
- Revenue enhancements

NOTE: Many of the possible impacts of the AI and analytics program are not directly numeric. Organizations can estimate/convert these impacts to numeric measures for standard ROI calculation or they can use soft ROI measurements. Some example of soft ROI metrics are:

- Revenue growth
- Customer loyalty/lifetime value and retention
- Risk mitigation
- Stability of business operations and financial returns

In many situations these are **more important than short-term ROI calculations**. Hard ROI will appear, but it could take a long time. Remember, **Amazon** did not show a profit for almost 10 years. They were heavily investing in their growth strategy. Those investments included large IT, analytics, and AI investments. If they had focused on short-term results they would not be the success story they are today.

The authors have heard that some results are not measurable. We do not agree. First, we suggest an interesting read by Douglas Hubbard, *How to Measure Anything: Finding the Value of Intangibles in Business* (see Hubbard, 2014). This book demonstrates how to measure intangibles, quantify risk as well as the value of information and more.

AI Data Strategy Questions Organizations Need to Ask

Mark Minevich writing for Forbes (March 2020) suggests four key questions that organizations must ask to improve their odds of creating a successful AI program:

1. What are your specific business goals or challenges that you're looking to address with AI solutions?
2. Is this the right technology to solve your business problem?
3. Do you have internal expertise to maintain AI integration and a team committed to training and improving the technology across your organization?
4. How will you measure the success of an AI deployment?

We believe there are an additional two critical question missing or the answer is assumed to be yes:

1. Do you have the right data to support the AI program goals?
2. Do you have the data infrastructure to operationalize your AI pipeline and platform?

Minevich also states that:

> According to Venturebeat, an estimated 87% of data science projects never make it to the production stage, and TechRepublic claims that 56% of global CEOs expect it to take 3–5 years to see any real ROI on their AI investment.

We firmly believe that any mid to large business will not survive if they are not making a significant investment in

- Data infrastructure specifically support analytics (beyond operations)
- Analytics architecture
- People and process to specifically support analytics programs

Government and public agencies are also investing heavily in data and analytics. We will cover these domains and specific use cases in our upcoming book, *The Applications of AI, Analytics, and Data Science: An Overview for Professionals in Healthcare, Business, and Government.*

Data and Analytics Literacy Are Requirements to Successful Programs

You cannot create value from data and analytics without specialized knowledge. Our first book covered the foundations of AI, analytics, and data science for professionals. It also included fundamentals of BI, machine learning, data mining, and statistics. We covered data uses and types of data for developing analytics. Analytics literacy and data literacy are cornerstones of a data-driven organization.

Kasey Panetta (Panetta, 2019) stated this clearly: "...[Our Need is to]... Champion data literacy and teach data as a second language to enable data-driven business"; she continued by stating:

> Imagine an organization where the marketing department speaks French, the product designers speak German, the analytics team speaks Spanish and no one speaks a second language...... That's essentially how a data-driven business functions when there is no data literacy.

She points out that this year (2020) half of all organizations will lack data literacy skills that are needed to achieve business value.

Valerie Logan, Senior Director Analyst, Gartner, points out another important fact (see Panetta, 2019), that the:

> prevalence of data and analytics capabilities, including artificial intelligence, requires creators and consumers to "speak data" as a common language, ... Data and analytics leaders must champion workforce data literacy as an enabler of digital business and treat information as a second language.

You will learn much about data technologies in this Part 2, Designing Data for Success. It will provide you the basis and foundation for you to build upon. Finally, we provide several useful references and educational recommendations in the "Additional References" section at the end of this chapter.

Summary

Data strategy is crucial to your analytics program. It forms one of our three pillars:

- ■ Strategy and architecture for analytics in the organization
- ■ Strategy and architecture for data technology
- ■ Strategy and architecture for analytics technology

Organizations must design and align these three pillars to increase the viability and return of their AI and analytics program.

How This Part Is Organized

Chapter 4 – Section Overview, Data Design for Success
 Chapter 5 – Data Pipes, APIs, Streaming, and Events
 This chapter covers data movement. It sets the stage for understanding and planning data strategy around modern data architectures including messaging, APIs (application programming interfaces), microservices, and events (webhook and streaming). It also includes containers and IoT applications.
 Chapter 6 – Data Stores, Warehouses, Big Data, Lakes, and Cloud Data
 This chapter covers on-premise and cloud data architecture options for data storage. It includes traditional data warehouses/marts, ODS, memory types, big data concepts and technology (clusters and data lakes) and more.
 Chapter 7 – Data Virtualization
 Data virtualization is an extremely promising technology that provides an extension to traditional data stores. There are a wealth of benefits with data virtualization allowing users to access "data from anywhere" in a collaborative environment endorsed by IT while supporting corporate standards.
 Chapter 8 – Data Governance and Data Management
 Data governance involves people, processes, and information technology required to create consistent and proper handling of an organization's data across the enterprise. Data management and data governance work hand-in-hand and both are critical to an organization's data design and strategy.
 Chapter 9 – Data Miscellanea – Curated, Purchased Data and Data for Tomorrow
 We end Part 2 with a few miscellaneous topics that include nascent and emerging data, data for purchase, and data monetization. We always speak of preparing for tomorrow and keeping an eye toward data that will keep you competitive or as operationally efficient as possible, and we speak of data taxonomies and categorization of the IT infrastructure to support data.

References

Barrett, J. (2018). Up to 73 Percent of Company Data Goes Unused for Analytics. Here's How to Put It to Work. https://www.inc.com/jeff-barrett/misusing-data-could-be-costing-your-business-heres-how.html.

Burk, S., & Miner, G. (2020, June). *It's All Analytics; Designing an Integrated AI, Analytics, and Data Science Architecture for Your Organization.* CRC Press, Boca Raton, FL.

CompTIA (2019). IT Industry outlook for 2019. (January, 2019 – as seen on August 12, 2019). https://www.comptia.org/resources/it-industry-trends-analysis.

Davenport, T. H. (2017, April). What's Your Data Strategy? *Harvard Business Review*, https://hbr.org/webinar/2017/04/whats-your-data-strategy.

Guo, H., Wang, L., Chen, F., & Liang, D. (2014). Scientific big data and digital earth. *Chinese Science Bulletin (Chinese Version)*, *59*, 1047. doi:10.1360/972013-1054.

Hubbard, D. W. (2014). *How to Measure Anything: Finding the Value of Intangibles in Business*. John Wiley & Sons, Inc., Hoboken, NJ.

Lasker, L., & Parkes, W., (Producers) & Robinson, P. A., (Director), (1992) Sneakers, United States, Universal Studios.

Marr, B. (2018, May). How Much Data Do We Create Every Day? The Mind-Blowing Stats Everyone Should Read. *Forbes*.

Meehan, M. (2016, December 8). "Where data goes to die", *Forbes*. https://www.forbes.com/sites/marymeehan/2016/12/08/where-data-goes-to-die-big-data-still-holds-answers-but-theyre-not-where-your-looking-for-them/#5624533a5896.

Panetta, K. (2019, February 6) A Data and Analytics Leader's Guide to Data Literacy; Gartner. https://www.gartner.com/smarterwithgartner/a-data-and-analytics-leaders-guide-to-data-literacy/.

Press, G. F. J. (2017). 6 Predictions For The $203 Billion Big Data Analytics Market https://www.forbes.com/sites/gilpress/2017/01/20/6-predictions-for-the-203-billion-big-data-analytics-market/#6f9abcc12083 (extracted 6/9/19).

Priceonomics (2019, August). Companies collect a lot of data but how much do they actually use? https://priceonomics.com/companies-collect-a-lot-of-data-but-how-much-do/.

Reinsel, D., Gantz, J., & Rydning, J. (2017). Data Age 2025: The Evolution of Data to Life-Critical Don't Focus on Big Data; Focus on the Data That's Big. IDC (International Data Corporation) White Paper © 2017 IDC. www.idc.com; found in: https://assets.ey.com/content/dam/ey-sites/ey-com/en_gl/topics/workforce/Seagate-WP-DataAge2025-March-2017.pdf.

Stack, T. (2018, February 5). Internet of Things (IoT) Data Continues to Explode Exponentially. Who Is Using That Data and How? https://blogs.cisco.com/datacenter/internet-of-things-iot-data-continues-to-explode-exponentially-who-is-using-that-data-and-how.

Additional Resources

Data and Analytics Literacy References

Gartner is championing data literacy. There are several good articles on their site, here is a good start:

"Champion data literacy and teach data as a second language to enable data-driven business", Kasey Panetta, February 2019. https://www.gartner.com/smarterwithgartner/a-data-and-analytics-leaders-guide-to-data-literacy/.

The IIA (International Institute for Analytics, https://www.iianalytics.com/) is championing data literacy and has a dedicated page, https://www.iianalytics.com/blog/2020/12/8/struggling-with-data-literacy-thats-great-news.

Additional Terms Related to This Chapter

Quantitative Data, Qualitative Data, Machine Data, Systems, Processes, Data Literacy, Analytics Literacy, Data Strategy, Data Architecture, Data Management.

Process and Data Quality References

Deming, W.E. (2018). *The New Economics for Industry, Government, Education.* 3rd Edition. Cambridge: MIT Press. Deming is a master for understanding process and systems are essential to any enterprise.

Hunter, J. (2014, March 10). Lessons from the red bead experiment with Dr. Deming. The W. Edwards Deming Institute Blog. https://blog.deming.org/2014/03/lessons-from-the-red-bead-experiment-with-dr-deming/.

Wheeler, D. J. (1998, January). *Building Continual Improvement: A Service Industry Guide.* SPC PRESS (Statistical Process Control).

Wheeler, D. J. (2010, June). *Understanding Statistical Process Control.* Third Edition, SPC PRESS (Statistical Process Control)

Chapter 5

Data in Motion, Data Pipes, APIs, Microservices, Streaming, Events, and More

It is a capital mistake to theorize before one has data. Insensibly one begins to twist facts to suit theories, instead of theories to suit facts.

Sir Arthur Conan Doyle, Sherlock Holmes

Introduction

As we said in the introductory chapter of Part 2 (Chapter 4, "Overview"), there are many ways to categorize and organize the subject of data topics. Regardless of how organized, one element that is important to any data architecture is the different ways to connect and move data within and between what we generically call "data stores"; this could be anything that stores data from enterprise databases to local files to data stored in the cloud.

Understanding the piping, the way that data flows (moves), is important to your data architecture plan. We will not present this information at a detailed or technical level. However, everyone, as part of their analytics education, should have a basic understanding of some of the technologies that support the operational and decision-making capabilities of the organization.

As we move through this chapter we will continue to return the "The Typical Story of Data Growth, Data Complexity and Data Needs" that we

DOI: 10.4324/9780429343957-7

introduced in Part 1, Data Design for Success, to provide perspective for each chapter and where it fits in this continuum.

Much of this *Data Design for Success* involves where you "park" or store the information; these "parking" or "storage" areas are the focus of the next chapter.

This chapter is about the highways: when and how you move the vehicles along and where they are allowed to go. Technologies are developed all the time for new platforms like smartphone and tablets, quicker application development, innovations in process tracking, and speed. All of this becomes part of the "pipeline" and "storage" of data and has to be modified as new technologies come into use.

We will focus on the following bolded technologies, along with ETL (extract, transform, and load) and ELT (extract, load, and transform), which are important to our next chapter on data stores:

- Operational systems and online transaction processing (OLTP)
- Operational data stores (ODS)
- Enterprise data warehouse
- Business intelligence (BI)
- New on-premise systems
- Special projects requiring special data sources
- **RESTful and Web APIs (application programming interfaces)**
- Self-service and visual BI
- **Message-oriented middleware (MOM) and enterprise service bus (ESB)**
- Software as a service (SaaS)
- Big data time and data lakes
- Data virtualization
- **Streaming operational data**
- Cloud-based infrastructures
- Third-party purchased data

REST and Web APIs (application programming interfaces) are about making new pathways available to new devices and platforms as web interfaces, such as SaaS, cloud, and more. REST APIs are a key part in modern web applications; some of these applications include Netflix, Facebook, and many others. Consider the explosion of smartphones, web apps, SaaS, and cloud over the last several years. APIs allow for all of these applications as well as much more rapid app development.

At one time it was difficult to know when an event occurred. Organizations literally did not know if and when things happened in a timely manner. An analyst would have to take large tables of data and manually calculate date and outcome differences to know the time gaps between events. With the advent of the Message Oriented Middleware (MOM) and ESB (Enterprise Service Bus) technologies, businesses can track what events happened, when these events happened, and correlate these events to other data sources. If they did not happen, they can interpret exactly why they did not happen. They can even embed AI, machine learning, and business rules within these systems for automated action or intelligent/augmented human decision-making.

Digital Messaging

Digital messaging has been around for a long time. The first digital, computer-to-computer messaging was performed in October 1969 on Arpanet. Today commercial enterprises of any size have commercial message systems.

In our hyperkinetic world we want to know what is happening in real time from a multitude of data sources. We should as the value of data degrades very rapidly (Arbesman, 2013). Operational streaming data and complex event processing (CEP) technologies were created to capture and make sense of all of this data. We will see in a following section that these technologies are having explosive growth in fields from Smart Cities to Industry 4.0.

We will explore each of these technologies from a data perspective in this chapter; specifically, we talk about several technologies that apply to movement and intelligence inside an organization. But we should note that AI, machine learning models, and embedded visual analytics are really just data also, so these technologies are very important to Part 3, Designing for Analytics Success. This involves how and what raw information we gather using these methods, how we analyze and create analytic models, and then how we use the same methods to operationalize and embed them into business processes. Organizations need to be:

1. API and event driven to optimize their businesses in near real time.
2. Storing this data for operational use and future revenue generation (data monetization).
3. Building and supporting analytics and AI everywhere.
4. Augmenting decisions and automating actions by deploying models and analytics into operational pathways and decision processes.

Event Analytics – Event-Driven Architectures and Package Delivery

In 2020 package delivery was at an all-time high and competition among package carriers was fierce. There were billions of order transactions that the major package delivery carriers had to deal with, resulting in tens of billions of events. Analyzing all these events across time and thousands of locations is a daunting task.

How do you keep up with all these events? An event-driven architecture (EDA) is needed. An EDA is a software architecture paradigm promoting the production, detection, consumption of, and reaction to events.

What are the goals for these package carriers?

First, they want to keep their customers continually informed where the packages are via web and phone apps. They want the customers to easily track when the order was sent to them, when the packages were picked up in a warehouse, when it was put on a plane and/or a truck, and when it was delivered to the final destination.

Second, they are constantly looking to improve operational efficiencies. By geolocation of trucks, packages, and other parameters they can optimally route deliveries more up the minute and even seconds. This is especially important during unforeseen events such as third-party delays, accidents, and weather-related events.

APIs and Microservices

A basic definition of an API (short for application programming interface) is a computing interface that defines interactions between multiple software intermediaries, thus allowing them to "speak" to one another. APIs offer a mechanism that allows the interaction between two applications by using a set of rules.

An API defines the kinds of calls or requests that can be made, how to make them, the data formats that should be used, the conventions to follow, etc. It can also provide a framework for developers to extend existing functionality in various ways and to varying degrees. An API can be entirely custom, specific to a component, or designed based on an industry-standard to ensure interoperability. Through information hiding, APIs enable modular programming, thus allowing users to use the interface independently of the implementation.

Everyday APIs

You would simply be amazed at the hundreds or thousands of times an API is working for you every day. Here is a relatable example for many:

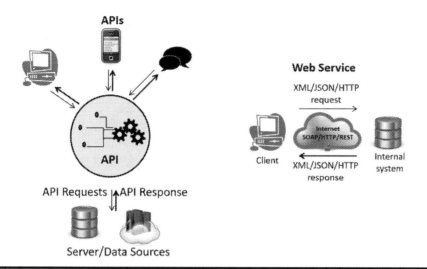

Figure 5.1   Some API and web service basics.

Every time you open up an app, like Instagram or Facebook Messenger, to direct message someone or view a profile, you're using an API. Each time you do something on one of these apps your phone will send data to a server over the Internet. A request is made based on the data received by the server.

> We have added some basic definitions on the acronyms used in this section in the "Additional Resources" section found at the end of the chapter.

The server will then read your request and respond back to your phone with the data or information it needs to carry out your task. The process managing the communication is the API.

A commonly used example is to consider yourself a customer (the app) in a restaurant. Your waiter acts like an API: they would take your order request (input data) to the kitchen (i.e., server in the app example), the kitchen (server) will process the order, and then provide your completed order (output data) it to the waiter (API) to take your back to you (the app) (Figure 5.1).

APIs have existed since the beginning of computers, but as the web became ubiquitous APIs have been repurposed to refer to HTTP REST-based services. REST (representational state transfer) is a commonly used concept that provides access to resources using standard HTTP operations.

A web service and an API are two very similar concepts, so it can be difficult to understand the similarities and differences. A web service is a way for two machines to communicate with each other over a network.

A web server running on a computer listens for requests from other computers. When a request from another computer is received, over a network, the web service returns the requested resources. This resource could be JSON, XML, an HTML file, images, audio files, and other types of data (or files).

An **API** is a set of definitions and protocols that allow one application to communicate with another application.

While APIs and web services are ways for two computers to communicate with each other over the Internet, they may sound like the same thing. Yet, there is one key difference: not all APIs are accessible over the Internet (a network), while web services must always be accessed through a network. That is the key difference.

REST vs Restful

You will likely hear both terms at some point, REST and RESTful. In a technical planning session it may matter, but for most analytics professionals it does not. REST is an architectural pattern in software architecture used for creating web services. A RESTful service is one that implements that pattern.

The Five Architectural Constraints of REST APIs

For an API to comply with REST (i.e., be *RESTful*), it must follow the following five architectural constraints:

1. **Stateless** – REST APIs do not allow the server (or receiving end) to retain the information they receive from the client/sender. The client sends information to the server in packets that the server can understand in isolation (i.e., without context from past packets). When the client makes an HTTP request, it includes all information necessary for the server to fulfill that request. The server never relies on information from previous requests.
2. **Client-server architecture** – REST applications have a server that manages application data and state. The server communicates with a client that handles the user interactions. A clear separation of concerns divides the two components. This means you can update and improve them on independent tracks. This is called the "separation of concerns" and it enables each side to grow and scale on its own without needing (or affecting) the other.
3. **Cache** – The client side of a REST API should have the ability to cache or store information for a certain period of time. This reduces the number of times the application needs to call on the API and, in

turn, reduces server usage and saves resources. Caching also enables developers to improve the user experience of their applications by making them faster and more efficient.

4. **Uniform interface** – The client and server should communicate with one another via HTTP (HyperText Transfer Protocol) using URIs (Unique Resource Identifiers), CRUD (Create, Read, Update, Delete) and JSON (JavaScript Object Notation) conventions.

5. **Layered system** – The REST API should use different architecture layers, each contributing toward a clear hierarchy. Each layer is loosely coupled, which lets you encapsulate legacy code in one part of the API while changing another part of the API to a new technology.

Those are the five requirements set out by the creator of REST, Roy Fielding.

Other APIs – RPC and SOAP

There are many other types of APIs. The other two you will most likely come across are remote procedure call (RPC) and simple object access protocol (SOAP).

RPC – APIs are the oldest and simplest types of API. The goal of an RPC is for the client to execute code on a server. The main benefit of RPC APIs is they make it easier for developers to create applications involving multiple programs or services. There are XML and JSON versions of RPC.

SOAP – API is similar to REST in that it's a type of Web API. SOAP entered the web development scene in the late 1990s, around the time service-oriented architecture (SOA) took-off. SOAP was the first to standardize the way applications should use network connections to manage services. The authors primarily run across REST and SOAP architecture, more than RPC, in analytics projects.

SOAP is an official protocol defined by the World Wide Web Consortium (W3C, www.w3.org/TR/soap/) and it comes with strict rules, especially in terms of security. As an example, you must integrate ACID (atomicity, consistency, isolation, and durability, it ensures that a database transaction is completed in a timely manner) and other compliance measures into SOAP APIs.

However, these added security requirements make SOAP complex and, in some situations, very resource intensive. With the exception of niche use cases, most developers prefer using REST (thanks to its lightweight architecture and emphasis on speed and efficiency) over SOAP.

API Benefits and Drawbacks

Some of the benefits of microservices may appear obvious as they add structure to the design process. However, structure is a benefit as well as a drawback (Indrasiri & Siriwardena, 2018). We list a few of the benefits and drawbacks:

Benefits (Primarily to Developers)

- **Automation** – APIs allow computers to do the work rather than people, thus increasing productivity.
- **Flexibility** – APIs can access the app components, the delivery of services, and information is more flexible,
- **Personalized experience** – An API application layer can be personalized to create custom user experiences.
- **Accessibility** – APIs allows access of information generated at the organizational level be made available to everyone.
- **Efficiency** – content can be shared and distributed more easily.
- **Integration** – APIs allow content to be embedded from any site or application and this guarantees more fluid information delivery and an integrated user experience.
- **Adaptation** – needs change over time and APIs help to anticipate changes. When working with this technology, data migration is supported better, and the information is reviewed more closely. In short, APIs make service provision more flexible.

Drawbacks

- **Development expense** – Implementing and providing API capabilities can be costly in terms of development times and staff resources.
- **Maintenance and support resources** – Add more time and expense for staff.
- **Security** – It can be a concern as APIs add another potential attack layer to programs/websites.

Today, APIs play a key role in the development of **microservices** applications (Petracek, 2020). But to effectively use APIs in cloud applications, you also need to deploy many powerful – and complex – tools, such as containers, container orchestration systems, service meshes, and more.

This is a challenge for every IT team, big or small, when they lack experience and expertise in cloud development or cloud services. Building that knowledge base alone could eat away at precious time, which your competitors can use to not just take the lead but take over the market. More on cloud in Chapter 7.

Microservices

An *API* is a contract that provides guidance for a consumer in using the underlying service. A *microservice* is an architectural design that separates portions of an (usually monolithic) application into small, self-containing services. Each service runs a unique process and usually manages its own database. A service can generate alerts, log data, support user interfaces, handle user identification or authentication, and perform various other tasks. Characteristics of this architecture are

- Highly maintainable and testable
- Loosely coupled
- Independently deployable
- Organized around business capabilities
- Owned by a small team

The microservice architecture enables the rapid, frequent, and reliable delivery of large, complex applications. It also enables an organization to evolve its technology stack. Traditional applications have monolithic architectures where all your application's components and functions are in a single instance; microservices break apart monolithic applications into smaller parts. The following diagram compares monolithic and microservices architectures (Figure 5.2).

Are Microservices and Containers the Same Thing?

No, they are not. A container is not a "must have" in microservices architecture, but it helps you to save a lot of time to build your own desired level of scalability.

A microservice is a piece of software (small services running on independent processes) that can be executed on its own and has a generic interface for being accessed (HTTP being the most commonly used).

A container is a standard unit of software that packages up code and all its dependencies so the application runs quickly and reliably from one

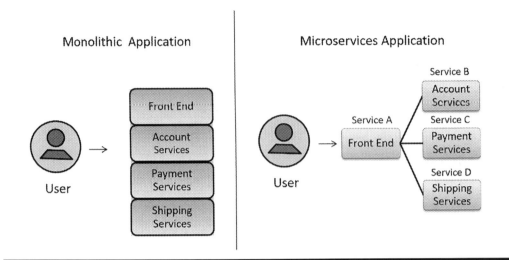

Figure 5.2   Advantage of a microservice application.

computing environment to another. Docker [an open source containerization (software in packages) platform] is the most prominent example of container technology.

Microservices and containers go together well, as you can use or build a container that contains all the required dependencies of a microservice. You can then deploy this container anywhere you want without needing to install any dependencies, besides the Docker runtime.

Microservice Benefits and Drawbacks

Some of the benefits of microservices may appear obvious as they add structure. However, structure is a benefit as well as a drawback. We list a few of the benefits and drawbacks of microservices:

Benefits

- They are easily deployed
- They require less development time
- They scale quickly
- They are reusable
- They contain fault isolation
- They can be deployed by small teams
- They work well with containers

Drawbacks

- They can add too much granularity
- They add extra effort designing communication between services
- They can cause latency during heavy use
- They typically require complex testing

What Is DevOps? How Do Microservices Enable DevOps?

DevOps is a set of practices that combines software development (Dev) and IT operations (Ops).

DevOps combines tasks between application and system operations teams. With increased communications between developers and operations staff it (DevOps) aims to shorten the systems development life cycle and provide continuous delivery with high software quality. DevOps is complementary with other software development practices (e.g., Agile).

DevOps combines tasks between application and system operations teams. With increased communications between developers and operations staff, an IT team is able to better create and manage infrastructure. IT operations ensure budgeting for capacities, operational tasks, upgrades and more. Developers and application teams can manage databases, servers, software, and hardware used in production.

Teamwork and collaboration between development and operations teams are needed to support the lifecycle of microservices, lending itself to DevOps teams. It's also why experienced DevOps teams are well-equipped for employing microservice-type architectures in software development projects.

We next dive deeper into event architectures. How do they differ from REST and other APIs? How are they important to automated actions and human decision-making?

We also cover the next generation of event and event-driven analytics – streaming and CEP. We will see how these are enabling the Internet of Things (IoT).

Events, Event-Driven Architectures and Streaming

The world is full of events – website clicks, credit card swipes, a patient receiving a lab result, or an operating room becoming available. Events are essentially "a change in status" or a "change in state". They apply in healthcare, government, and business but are generically called "business events".

We can determine a change in status from the data collected in our systems by querying one point in time and then a later point in time, then comparing to see if there has been a change in state, i.e., an event has occurred. However, this is a difficult and cumbersome process. "Event-based architectures" were created to overcome this difficulty.

An EDA is a software architecture paradigm promoting the production, detection, consumption of, and reaction to events.

The easiest way to explain an event is to start with contrasting a REST API to an event-based API. In the gray box near the beginning of this chapter, "Everyday APIs", we described an app as a waiter in a restaurant that took an order of a customer and delivered it to the chef (server) in the kitchen. In this example of a REST API architecture, the waiter would be constantly going back to the chef and asking, "Is the order ready?", the chef would answer "No". The waiter might wait a couple of minutes and then ask the same thing "Is the order ready?", the chef would answer "No". This cycle would repeat until the chef said, "Yes" and then the waiter would take the order to the customer.

Event-driven API interaction patterns differ from REST API. In an EDA, the waiter would not have to keep going back to the kitchen and repeatedly ask if the order was ready. There are multiple forms of this architecture, but we will focus on two popular items: *Webhook* and *streaming*.

We illustrate the Webhook method in Figure 5.3. Look at the contrast of methods. The first is the REST API version where we are repeatedly asking whether the order is ready – request/response. In the Webhook version (lower) the waiter subscribes to an event notification. When the order is ready the chef in the kitchen provides notification to the waiter that the order is ready.

Event-Driven APIs

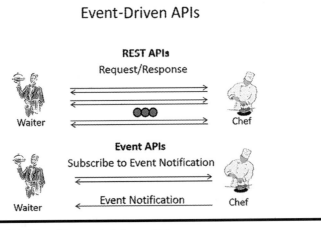

Figure 5.3   REST vs (Webhook) event-driven APIs.

BAM – an Alert-Based BI, BI Version 4.0

In our first *It's All Analytics* book (Burk & Miner, 2020) we described the various versions of BI with business activity monitoring (BAM). We called alert-based BI, BI Version 4.0. BAM has been around a long time, but in our estimation still has a long life ahead.

Business activity monitoring (BAM) describes the processes and technologies that enhance situation awareness and enable analysis of critical business performance indicators based on real-time data. BAM is used to improve the speed and effectiveness of business operations by keeping track of what is happening and making issues visible quickly. The BAM concept can be implemented through many different kinds of software tools; those aimed solely at BAM are called "BAM platform products".

Alert-based BAM is the addition of real-time messaging and events to monitor business processes.

Taking this example one step further we can contrast it to streaming events. In a streaming example, the chef is constantly updating the waiter with a status of the order. It might look something closer to the following illustration (Figure 5.4). In this illustration, the upper REST API version is where we are repeatedly asking whether the order is ready – request/response.

In the lower, event-driven streaming case, the chef is providing a constant update of what is happening with the order (every event) – locating ingredients, processing ingredients, placing orders in the oven, preparing plates,

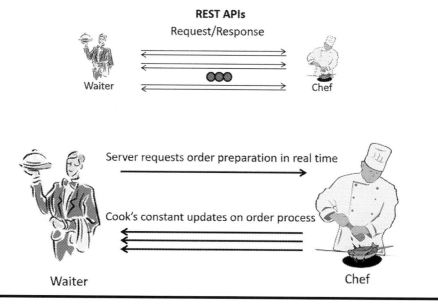

Figure 5.4   REST vs (streaming) event-driven APIs.

and notifying when the order is done. The waiter is in constant notification of the status of the order.

Once events are captured, they can be used in a variety of analytics, from simple dashboard displays to real-time streaming dashboard displays – these are *descriptive analytics*. Events can be used in understanding the relationship of causes and events, such as operating room or airline delays – *diagnostic analytics*. They can be used to glimpse into future events by predicting those events based on emergent data – *predictive analytics*. They can automatically trigger a system or inform a human on a preferred action to take – *prescriptive analytics*.

Some Drivers and Examples of Events, Streaming Events, and CEP (Complex Event Processing)

There are several forces that motivate the need for an event-based architecture. We presented an example near the beginning of this chapter in a gray box, "Event Analytics – Event-Driven Architectures and Package Delivery", that used the term events in a generic way. In reality, this is actually an example of an IoT application. It is sensor-based logistics that allows the major package carriers real-time visibility, not only truck and package location, but in-depth insights such as temperature, velocity, etc. for high-value or sensitive customer cargo. There are millions of sensors sending information to these companies. They are in warehouses, they are in the semi-tractor trailers that take the packages from the warehouses to the local distribution centers, sensors in the local distribution centers to the local delivery vehicles which are full of sensors from location to how the truck is performing mechanically. Sensors everywhere – IoT.

IoT Is a Big Driver of Real-Time Events

Technology is enabling a more widespread adoption of IoT, from pill-shaped microcameras that can pinpoint thousands of images within the body to smart sensors that can assess crop conditions on a farm and to the smart home devices that are becoming increasingly popular. Take, for example, **Smart Cities**, which use the concept of interconnecting cameras and sensors and sources of previously stored data that can be integrated and acted upon with a variety of analytics. We just mentioned streaming data which is an important technology that enables IoT, additionally event-driven messaging goes hand-in-hand with IoT. IoT has had a big impact on the way we live today, and similar impacts will be accelerated in the coming years. Please see gray box, "New Stanford IoT Hospital", for how Stanford University is using IoT-based technologies to create a hospital of the future.

(reference: https://online.stanford.edu/courses/xee100-introduction -internet-things).

New Stanford IoT Hospital

More than ten years in the making at a cost of $2.1 billion, Stanford opened the doors of a new 824,000-square-foot medical facility on October 23, 2019. The hospital includes a variety of new technologies from patient-centric controls in rooms to modular architecture, to a robotic pharmacy and IoT-based technology. According to the *Wall Street Journal* (see Rosenbush, Nov 2019):

> Sensors will track the location of staff and equipment in real time, improving efficiency and inventory control. The infrastructure can support 120,000 connected devices streaming 4K high-definition video. The infrastructure will be able to accommodate upgrades such as 5G wireless. Magnetic resonance imaging equipment and other systems will be integrated with one another in new ways.
>
> Doctors and nurses will be able to monitor multiple patients from a single remote location. Alerts and alarms will go directly to secure mobile devices carried by nurses and doctors instead of sounding at nursing stations – reducing noise levels. …*[What's Next]*…. Two patient rooms will test a bedside computer-vision system that uses depth and thermal sensors to improve patient safety.
>
> In our constant attempt to evolve things there is a new term that has been created, IIoT, the Industrial Internet of Things. The knowledge and technology to support IIoT is not new. It is another term that is catching hold and is just a subdivision of IoT.

IIoT (Industry 4.0) Market is Expected to Reach USD 156.6 Billion by 2024

The IIoT which is also designated as Industry 4.0 is set to explode due to the worldwide adoption of sensors and devices in manufacturing units, and growing focus on enhanced efficiency of machinery and systems. According to PR Newswire, December 18, 2019:

The Industry 4.0 market is estimated to be valued USD 71.7 billion in 2019 and is expected to reach USD 156.6 billion by 2024, at a CAGR of 16.9% from 2019 to 2024. Increasing adoption of the industrial internet worldwide in manufacturing units, growing focus on enhanced efficiency of machinery and systems, and reduced production costs play a significant role in the growth of the market worldwide. Also, the growing demand for industrial robotics is expected to fuel the growth of the Industry 4.0 market.

Event Processing Advantages

Event processing is the practice of taking events, or streams of events, and analyzing them in real time. The advantages are (1) enabling automated actions (those actions are embedded within systems) or (2) creating reports or dashboards or recommendations that assist humans in making better decisions. An event is anything that happens at a clearly defined time and that can be specifically recorded. Analysis can be based on predefined decision tables or more sophisticated machine learning algorithms, and there are a wide range of possible actions from generating a new event to changing a customer's experience to scaling cloud resources up or down.

With event processing you connect to all data sources, and then merge, transform, and filter data. You can then correlate events and add contextual data to ensure proper interpretation of events. You can apply business logic and rules or even allow machine learning to generate an automatic action. Event processing lets you act in real time to address threats or opportunities. It allows you to turn your data into action and empower business users to define the rules, which can be embedded in operational processes. It gives you a competitive advantage. This is illustrated in Figure 5.5:

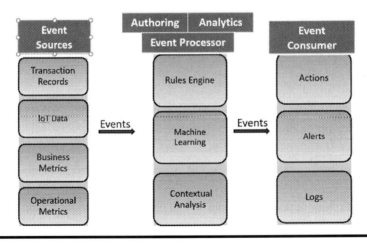

Figure 5.5 Event sources, event processing, and event actions.

What Is CEP (Complex Event Processing)?

Events are important to analytics, both in terms of data used to create predictive models and pushing the prediction back to the operational systems where the events occur. CEP allows companies to source hundreds or thousands of streams of data in real time. CEP consists of a set of concepts and techniques for extracting information from all these event streams as they arrive. The goal of CEP is to identify meaningful events, such as organizational opportunities or threats. These systems allow companies to cross correlate all the streams simultaneously.

CEP BUSINESS CASE EXAMPLE

The goals of becoming more efficient and customer-centric is requiring many businesses to transform digitally, as their existing systems can't meet expectations. A large national brand had two major goals – reduce costs and increase brand loyalty.

By interconnecting all data systems throughout the organization, leading with APIs and microservices, the company gained back control of their valuable business data. They then layered additional systems around real-time messaging and event management to extend the platform to a variety of new use cases, like enabling customer personalization across every touchpoint including web, in-store, guest services, mobile app, and more.

This data allows the business to train predictive and forecast models for more intelligent inventory and warehouse management, and new systems for more efficient and on-time order fulfillment.

The company is leveraging loyalty members and supply chain data to better understand the impact of geographic, and seasonal, and many other factors affecting supply and demand. In terms of strategic business decisions, they're able to create economic models to identify the best possible locations for new brick and mortar stores as well as make intelligent decisions using media mix modeling.

As a result, the company is more customer-centric than ever, with better control over their data and ability to adapt to the challenges presented by customers' demands, business growth, and frequent changes in product trends.

How Businesses Benefit from Event Processing

The ability to process events in real time and take automatic actions can provide competitive advantage to organizations. Some example business use cases include:

Improved Customer Service

- Enabling retailers to instantly suggest cross-selling and upselling offers based on customer status, location, inventory, and other factors.
- Supporting real-time visibility into order/consignment/package status.
- Proactively notifying customers of problems, changes, and delays in transportation.
- Service organizations to monitor service-level agreements and promptly take corrective actions to avoid unmet agreements.
- Banking and credit card companies are preventing and detecting fraud.

Reduction of Costs and More Efficient Use of Resources

- In retail, real-time inventory tracking and management with the ability to define and change product promotions dynamically based on trends and surplus.
- In government, cyber intrusion detection and prevention.
- In airlines, optimization of crew scheduling and efficient baggage tracking.
- Shipping – optimization of fleet routes based on weather, fuel consumption, and other resources.
- In manufacturing, proactive maintenance of key shop-floor equipment.
- In the energy sector, predictive outage and fault management of the grid.
- In hospitals, optimization of scheduling of expensive procedures such as MRIs in response to disruptions and no-shows.

Optimized Operations

- In telecommunications, identification of under-performing business systems to help ensure SLAs can be met.
- In hospitals, visibility into patient numbers and bed availability to ensure optimal decision-making.
- In financial services, visualization of market data, order executions, trades, deals, settlements, and pre-post trade exceptions.
- In retail and services industries, real-time visibility into order status.
- In insurance, real-time visibility into status of processing new customer applications.
- In factories, visibility into the status of machines and other shop-floor assets.
- In the logistics and transportation industries, visibility into the current location of trucks and packages.

ETL and ELT

When it comes to data movement it is important to briefly cover the way data moves from operational systems, the system that keeps organizations running, to the data stores. Data stores will be covered in the next chapter and are historically where data used for analytics is kept. Let us first define three fundamental steps that typically accompany movement of this data:

- **Extract** – Extract is the process of copying raw streams of data from virtual infrastructure, software, and applications.
- **Transform** – Data manipulation is performed on the copies of the data. This could be applying business rules, applying filters, mathematical and date manipulation, and "normalization" of data. Normalization is the process of breaking data tables down into fractional tables that speed query/application performance and reduces data redundancy.
- **Load** – Taking the data from the source and loading into the target system, such as a data warehouse or data lake.

Traditional data stores used for analytics, such as data marts and data warehouses, followed an **ETL** process, extract first by making a copy from the source, then transformations are made upon this copy, and then the data is loaded into the target system. ETL tools require processing engines for running transformations prior to loading data into a destination. Running these engines performing transformations before the load phase results in a more complex data replication process.

Because **ETL** transforms data prior to the loading stage, it is the ideal process when a destination requires a specific data format. This could include when there is a misalignment in supported data types between the source and destination, limited ability to quickly scale processing in a destination, or security restrictions make it impossible to store raw data in a destination

The shift from on-premises servers toward cloud data warehouses (and data lakes) is sparking a shift from **ETL** to **ELT**. The transformation of data, in an ELT process, happens within the target database. **ELT** asks less of remote sources, requiring only their raw and unprepared data.

Each method has its advantages. When planning data architecture, IT decision makers must consider internal capabilities and the growing impact of cloud technologies when choosing ETL or ELT. More about cloud data stores will be covered in the next chapter.

Textual Analytics and Textual ETL

W H (Bill) Inmon, known as the "father of the modern data warehouse", has created an interesting concept of textual analytics and textual ETL which is aimed specifically at unstructured information (see Chapter 6 for structured and unstructured data definitions and examples). It is estimated that 85%–95% of data is unstructured. Inmon has created a process that takes text and converts it into a form he calls textual ETL. As Inmon says the difference is the focus – text vs context:

"And then there came textual ETL (or 'textual disambiguation'). Textual ETL is built on the work that preceded it. There were many differences between textual ETL and NLP (natural language processing) and ML. But the primary difference between textual ETL and NLP was that NLP and ML focused on text and textual ETL focused on text and context, equally…".

He states the difference is the ability to tell the difference between "**what happened**" vs "**why it happened**". Understanding "why" is a much more difficult yet an insightful result in analytics.

Summary

We covered a lot of ground in this chapter. Our goal was to provide you some high-level detail. Here is a quick recap of the major topics:

- **APIs** are application interfaces, meaning that one application is able to interact with another application in a standardized way.
- **Web services** are a type of API, which must be accessed through a network connection.
- **REST APIs** are a standardized architecture for building Web APIs using HTTP methods.
- **Microservices** are architectural designs that separate portions of an application into small, self-containing services.
- **Containers** are standard units of software that package up code and all dependencies so an application runs quickly and reliably from one computing environment to another.
- **Stream processing** is a programming paradigm that allows some applications to more easily exploit a limited form of parallel processing.

For deeper dives into these terms and the concepts covered in this chapter we now offer references as well as some recommended resources.

References

Arbesman, S. (2013). *The Half-life of Facts: Why Everything We Know Has an Expiration Date*. Current Publishing, London.

Burk, S., & Miner, G. (2020). *It's All Analytics; Designing an Integrated AI, Analytics, and Data Science Architecture for Your Organization*. CRC Press, Boca Raton, FL.

Indrasiri, K., & Siriwardena, P. (2018). *Microservices for the Enterprise: Designing, Developing, and Deploying*, 1st ed. Edition. Apress, New York.

Petracek, N. (2020). *API Success: The Journey to Digital Transformation*. Technics Publications, Basking Ridge, NJ.

Additional Resources

Basic Terms Useful in This Chapter

XML [eXtensible Markup Language] is a standardized format for storing and sending data. Similar to HTML, XML stores data by wrapping it in descriptive tags.

JSON [JavaScript Object Notation] is similar to XML in that it also stores and enables you to send data in a standardized format. JSON just uses a different, object-based, methodology for systematically storing data.

HTTP [HyperText Transfer Protocol] is the foundation of transferring data and communications on the Internet.

SOAP is a messaging protocol used for exchanging structured information [XML data] over a network.

REST [REpresentational State Transfer] is a standardized architectural style that can be used when creating a Web API.

Web applications (Web app) are computer programs that are accessed over the Internet through a computer's web browser.

Additional Relevant Terms

API Management Systems, Complex Event Processing, Data Hub, Data Integration, Data Pipeline, Endpoint, Enterprise Message Service, ETL pipeline, Event Servers, Gateway (IT), IP Address, Interconnect, Java Message Service (JMS), JDBC, ODBC, Apache Kafka, Messaging and Event Processing, Microservices architecture, Open API, Point to Point Architectures, Representational State Transfer (REST and RESTful), SOA, SSL (Secure Socket

Layer), standards-based messaging system, Stateful and Stateless Interfaces, Trigger Event (related to messages), OLTP, information hiding

IT leaders and managers that want to know more about organizing and effectively administrating an API infrastructure should read "The Seven Make-or-Break API Challenges CIOs Need to Address" by Representational Keerthi Iyengar, Ling Lau, Srinivas Ramadath, and Vik Sohoni, McKinsey Digital, December 19, 2018. The seven key challenges addressed are:

Challenge #1: Where do I start?
Challenge #2: What should my API teams look like?
Challenge #3: What do I track?
Challenge #4: How do I ensure my APIs actually deliver business value?
Challenge #5: What technology tools do we need?
Challenge #6: Who owns which APIs?
Challenge #7: Where is the talent to do all this going to come from?

We also recommend a book by Nelson Petracek that covers microservices, events, and APIs as key enablers to a digital transformation. The book covers a great deal of useful information from monetizing APIs, to staffing and building the business case, to applying the API lifecycle and setting yourself up for the future and API management. As the title notes, the book is about educating yourself and executing the program that leads to your success. *API Success: The Journey to Digital Transformation* (Technics Publications; June 5, 2020).

Chapter 6

Data Stores, Warehouses, Big Data, Lakes, and Cloud Data

Errors using inadequate data are much less than those using no data at all.

Charles Babbage, mathematician, engineer, inventor, and philosopher

Every company has Big Data in its future, and every company will eventually be in the data business.

Thomas H. Davenport, American academic and author specializing in analytics

Introduction

In the last chapter, we discussed the technology that enables movement of data (APIs, messaging, business events, real-time processing and more). These are the pipes through which data flows or the highways on which data travels. These pathways are extremely important for two reasons:

1. Without data you cannot construct any analytics.
2. Analytic models incorporate data; we can move these models around as data and embed them in every business process and operational system in the organization.

DOI: 10.4324/9780429343957-8

We also concluded Chapter 5 with two methods for data movement important to this chapter:

- ETL (extract, transform, and load)
- ELT (extract, load, and transform)

Now we focus on options to store or park data – this is data at rest. This is data that sit until we use it. This data is vital to all forms of analytics from interactive and visual business intelligence (BI) to statistical analysis to AI and predictive machine learning models.

We cover many traditional data storage and "on-premise" technology options in this chapter, but we also speak about ways technology has adapted for Big Data, data lakes, cloud data, and hybrid environments. "On-premise" means we are storing data within the enterprise, in a data center or a set of distributed data centers.

Cloud data services offer data storage with less direct active management of infrastructure and typically describes data available to users over the Internet. These come in three forms:

- **Public clouds** are the most common type of cloud computing deployment; resources/hardware are owned and operated by third-party providers and delivered over the Internet.
- **Private clouds** consist of cloud computing resources used exclusively by one business or organization. The private cloud can be physically located with the organization's on-site data center or it can be hosted by a third-party service provider.
- **Hybrid cloud data services** refers to a mixture of on-premises infrastructure, private cloud services, and a public cloud.

We will see overlap in many technologies and we will contrast the advantages and disadvantages of these options.

We cover the following technologies in this chapter:

- Data storage technologies
- Data structures and formats
- Local file systems and network data storage
- Operational data stores, data marts, and enterprise data warehouse
- Distributed file systems (DFS) and Big Data
- High-performance data and DFS

- Cloud data storage
- "Other Big Data promises" data lakes, data swamps, reservoirs, analytic sandboxes and whatever we can think to call it tomorrow

Local file systems, network file systems, operational data stores, data marts, and enterprise data warehouses (EDWs) have been around for many years but are still very important to successful data design today.

Big Data was all the rage just a few years ago. It then ebbed in popularity and is now gaining a new resurgence due to some new technologies, including cloud architectures and optimized data stores. We briefly cover motivations, uses, benefits, and drawbacks in the paragraphs which follow.

First, we will begin with the "end in mind". We cover why data is so crucial to the success of the enterprise. We then cover two prerequisite areas essential to our understanding before we fully launch into these technologies. The first is volatile vs nonvolatile memory, the second is brief comments on data structures and formats that are important to understand the evolution of the data storage design.

Why Data Is so Crucial to the Success of an Enterprise

As the saying goes, data is the new oil! One of the key differences of oil and data is that oil is a finite resource and data seems to be limitless (Marr, 2018). Others, including *The Economist,* have said "The world's most valuable resource is no longer oil, but data".

We first source data in a variety of ways, then we move it through pipes and then we store it. We then convert raw data into usable information via analytic methods. This information is useful because it can be acted upon for more intelligent decision-making. These decisions make the data valuable.

Storing the data securely, efficiently, and cost effectively is important. We provide a high-level overview of some of the most common ways data is stored in an organization, along with some data basics. But it is always good to keep in mind that data is not an end unto itself but a means to drive value in the organization. Therefore, planning and designing your data architecture are critically important!

Data is important, because any planned success is built upon data. Even data that is only in your head; see the following gray box, "All Self-Improvement Is Relative and Based on Data":

All Self-Improvement Is Relative and Based on Data

If you are attempting to improve any performance or personal endeavor you have to measure outcomes across time to know how you are doing. You can't measure it without data. This data does not have to be recorded on a device or even a piece of paper. It could be recorded in your memory. But, you have to have data to make the determination. Imagine some simple self-improvement goals in your life:

- Maintaining an exercise schedule
- Eating healthy
- Reading more
- Keeping in touch with family and friends
- Limiting social media time
- Getting 8 hours of sleep a night

You have to know how you are tracking each of these to know how you are performing. Are you maintaining, improving, or falling short? You can only answer these questions if you have the data.

All organizational improvement is the same. You measure the things that matter. You measure the things you want to maintain or improve. Peter Drucker said it best – "What gets measured gets managed".

You might mentally track how you are performing in a particular area and compare this performance across time. You might write it down or record it. In the end it is data storage, it is measurement, and it is *All Analytics*!

We stated in the Part II Introduction that one of Scott's (author) favorite quotes was from the movie Sneakers (1992) where Cosmo says:

It's about the data…. Exactly! The world isn't run by weapons anymore, or energy, or money, it's run by little ones and zeroes, little bits of data. It's all just electrons.

But, it should not be forgotten that data by itself does nothing. It is just a cost. It is only when we turn data into usable information that we can act upon that we gain real value from it. One of the big costs of data is storing it safely, efficiently, and sustainably. That is what the rest of this chapter is about.

Before we begin discussing the various technologies to store data, we want the reader to clearly understand there are two designations of data storage; these are briefly explained in the next section.

Data Storage – Two Designations – Volatile and Nonvolatile Memory

Any electronic data is stored, at least temporarily. If you stream movies to your television, those movies are not stored permanently. They are streamed into temporary memory (cached) and as the movies play the already viewed cache is replaced with new cache to play.

This is **temporary** memory, or sometimes referred to as **volatile** memory, as it does not persist for long periods of time. You may have heard the term RAM (random access memory). Two common forms of this memory describe its nature – DRAM (dynamic RAM) and SRAM (Static); other forms also exist. Cached memory uses these forms of volatile memory.

This chapter also addresses **permanent** or **nonvolatile** memory. This used to be "disk" memory, but now there are many forms and formats for stored media like SSDs (solid-state drives). However, in all forms this non-volatile memory is available for the long term.

Many server products use a combination of volatile and nonvolatile memory. When the server is brought up, frequently stored data is copied from permanent memory into a volatile cache where it is resident for quick access and performance. The system will manage memory swapping between these two stores (the "permanent" and the "volatile") to optimize performance. One example is a self-service visual BI platform where used (permanently stored) data is frequently held in cache. When programmers develop a dashboard the most used data is sitting in volatile memory and is rapidly accessible.

Your PC or Tablet and Phone – Multiple Formats of Memory

Your PC or tablet and mobile phone (device) have multiple types of memory for multiple applications. Let's quickly talk about a few of them.

EEPROM – Electrically erasable programmable read only memory (see also flash memory) resides in a chip that ships with your device. This is fast, semipermanent memory meaning you can't easily update it. When you turn or boot your device this memory is used to start a basic set of instructions or firmware. Note: it used to be fairly common to update PC firmware (BIOS, basic input/output system), but it is less common these days. You had to run a process to first erase then second program the semiconductor (burn in); this the "erasable programmable". The ROM part means you can't easily do it, it is read only.

RAM – This memory is volatile, meaning once your device shuts down it is gone. It serves as very fast memory while you are using your device. You may run across SRAM – static RAM which is just an even faster form of general memory. VRAM is video RAM and allows all the graphic processing to be done separately by specialized video processor(s) and its own memory.

Nonvolatile Memory – Disk memory is for permanent data storage meaning that it is available after your shut your device off and then turn it back on. There are actual "disks" spinning very fast – 10K RPM or higher inside the drive. They are inexpensive and reliable. More commonly devices are moving to SSD where there are no disks or moving parts. Initially, the barriers for SSDs were the cost – in the 1990s when first introduced a 20 MB SSD sold for $1,000. They are now much less expensive and very common in laptops, computers, and phones. However, disk drives still have their place in larger computers and the data center.

Primer on Data Structures and Formats

Analytics data is stored, at least temporarily. All analytics development can be thought of as using data storage to build assets and models. The data structures and formats often dictate what method of storage is used, therefore we want to spend a couple of minutes outlining some of them. This is a very cursory and simplified introduction. There are entire books written on these subjects (see "Additional Resources" section at the end of this chapter).

1. **Structured data** – The best example of structured data is relational data. Examples are relational database files, as they go hand in hand with a specific database application (open source, MySQL). They can be stored on local devices or servers. They add structure to the data, as tables of the data are "related" with keys and can be merged/joined/ appended/transformed in various ways. These manipulations are normally done in structured query language SQL. SQL is a very accessible, yet powerful code base.
2. **Unstructured data** – Does not have a defined structure. Unlike the creation of a relational database where the creator defines the relationships, data types, and forms, in unstructured the data is in freeform. The most common form of unstructured data is text. Other examples include video, audio, images, and generally analog data in any form. It is estimated that text alone (structured and semi structured) accounts for at least 75%–80% of the entire world's data. This number may well continue to rise with the prominence of the Internet of Things (IoT).
3. **Semistructured data** is a form of structured data that does not obey the formal structure of data models associated with relational databases

or other forms of data tables but nonetheless contains tags or other markers to separate semantic elements and enforce hierarchies of records and fields within the data (see Buneman, 1997). Semistructured data does not have the same level of organization and predictability of structured data. The data does not reside in fixed fields or records but does contain elements that can separate the data into various hierarchies. Most people are familiar with CSV files that can be imported into databases and spreadsheets. They provide a minimal structure to the data. Extensible markup language (XML) is a format that has been around for 20 years, but its use has really taken off in the last 5–10 years. JavaScript object notation (JSON) is one of the most popular forms of semistructured data today. Graph databases are special types of databases; these are becoming extremely popular. They use graph structures for semantic queries with nodes, edges, and properties to represent and store data. Most of the value of graph databases is derived from these relationships.

4. **Data file formats and file compression**.
   a. A file format is a standard way that information is encoded for storage in a computer file. File formats may be either proprietary requiring licensed software to open/access or freeware in that the design information is freely available and no license is required.
   b. File formats have an extension (the characters after the '.' in the file name). Common examples are html, xml, log, txt, json, pdf, mp4, mov, jpeg, gif, tar, PY, PYC, and R. They typically dictate the applications that access these formats as defaults.
   c. File compression is used to reduce the file size. An algorithm is run against raw data and the redundancies and white space (blank space) are removed making the file smaller and quicker to load. Compression techniques are often applied to audio, video, and data that are being transferred between systems. This may be important to the analytics process as what might be considered redundant or nonrelevant to a data consumer may be important to a data scientist.

Data Stores Topology

For continuity, we return to the "the typical story of data growth, data complexity, and data needs" we presented in this section's introduction, **Designing for Data Success**, to provide perspective for this chapter and where it fits in this continuum.

The following bolded items are pertinent to this chapter:

- Operational systems and online transaction processing (OLTP)
- **Operational data stores (ODS)**
- **Enterprise data warehouse**
- Business intelligence (BI)
- New on-premise systems
- Special projects requiring special data sources
- RESTful and web APIs (Application Programming Interfaces)
- Self-Service and visual BI
- Message-oriented middleware and enterprise service bus (ESB)
- Software as a service (SaaS)
- **Big Data and data lakes**
- Data virtualization
- Streaming operational data
- **Cloud-based infrastructures**
- Third-party purchased data

Local File Systems and Network Data Storage

Local stores. There are huge amounts of data stored locally in devices such as computers, tablets, phones, smart watches, GPS sensors, and industrial sensors. These devices are adding to exponential data growth in two ways. The first is data volume per device as the storage capability of all devices has grown tremendously, see gray box "Amazing Facts and Figures about the Evolution of Hard Disk Drives". The second way is the volume and variety of devices. New "smart and personal" devices are being created every year and the adoption rate of these devices is growing as well. Local data storage in these devices accounts for the major increase of data in the data sphere.

Amazing Facts and Figures about the Evolution of Hard Disk Drives

There is a great article on the evolution and capacity increases of hard drives, see https://www.pingdom.com/blog/amazing-facts-and-figures-about-the-evolution-of-hard-disk-drives/.

Here is a comment on capacity increases:

It took 51 years before hard disk drives reached the size of 1 TB (terabyte, i.e., 1,000 GB). This happened in 2007. In 2009, the first hard drive with 2 TB of storage arrived. So while it took 51 years to reach the first terabyte, it took just 2 years to reach the second.

Fast forward 10 years, and in 2019 the largest commercially available HDDs can store at least 15 TB of data. The world of SSDs offers even more space of at least 100 TB.

Networked data stores. There are several options for networked data stores. These were the primary stores (hardware combined with software) for IT departments and data centers several years ago. While there has been a big movement to cloud and alternative stores, these storage methods are still popular and will remain for years to come. We outline the two most popular technologies.

Storage area network (SAN) is a combination of hardware and software. It grew out of data-centric mainframe architectures, where clients in a network can connect to several servers that store different types of data. A SAN is a way to provide users shared access to consolidated, block-level data storage, even allowing multiple clients to access files at the same time with very high performance. A SAN allows users to access multiple storage devices with mixed storage media types at the same time – they appear to users as if they were external hard drives on their local system. SANs are more expensive and more difficult to set up and maintain; they are deployed by medium to large businesses.

Network attached storage (NAS) is a computer connected to a network that provides file-based data storage services to other devices on the network. The primary strengths of NAS is how simple and inexpensive they are to set up. Therefore they are often the solution of choice by small- to medium-sized businesses. NAS devices offer an easy way for multiple users in diverse locations to access data, which is valuable when uses are collaborating on projects or sharing information.

Operational Data Stores

An ODS is a central database that provides a snapshot of the latest data from multiple transactional systems for operational reporting. It enables organizations to combine data in its original format from various sources into a single destination to make it available for decision support. An ODS contains lightly transformed and lightly integrated operational data with a short time window. It is used for real-time and near real-time reporting.

The evolution of many organizations is to start with an ODS and later develop data marts or an EDW. However, the EDW does not necessarily replace the ODS, they are architected differently and serve different purposes. See Contrasting the ODS and the EDW in the next section.

Data Marts and the EDWs

Data marts and EDWs were created to meet specific needs in the evolution of BI. While they have been around for many years they remain very important technologies for most organizations. They serve different roles from each other and they provide different data than the ODS just discussed (see following gray box, "Contrasting the ODS and the EDW").

Data marts are subject-oriented databases typically aligned with a particular business unit like sales, finance, or marketing. These are sometimes called "functional data marts" since they support specific business functions. Data marts accelerate business processes by allowing access to relevant information in a more timely nature since they are not aggregating the volume and variety (many data sources) that an EDW does. However, they are more transformed or normalized than an ODS.

Bill Inmon, the "Father of Data Warehousing", defines a data warehouse (DW) as, "a subject-oriented, integrated, time-variant and non-volatile collection of data in support of management's decision making process".

EDWs are normally highly transformed data sources. The data models are optimized and support online analytical processing activities like BI and interactive data slicing and dicing, i.e., interactive analytics/visualization. The EDW attempt to capture the "single version of the truth" in two ways:

1. Corporately agreed upon data sources for specific data elements
2. Corporately agreed upon definitions and transformation for data elements

These "corporate standards" ensure that data consumers are speaking the same language. This was the origin of data warehousing in the first place. Data consumers often produced reports that did not agree. The data was blamed for these differences, when in fact it was the sources and definitions that were the primary causes for the discrepancies. Other contributing factors were when the data was pulled, what time zone the consumer was in, filters applied and more.

Some sources try to distinguish the differences of data marts and EDWs by size. Size is a consequence and not a determinant. While EDWs are normally much larger, they are larger due to the fact they are pulling data from many sources and across business functions. As stated previously, data marts serve specific functional needs, as a rule, and therefore are beneficial to local business processes and projects. An EDW is designed to fulfill needs of the entire organization across all functions. We limit our focus on the benefits and drawbacks of the EDW.

Benefits and Drawbacks of the EDW

Benefits of an EDW

Single Version of the Truth

At least that is the goal. An EDW goes a long way into making that a reality. Major decisions on how data should be sourced, defined, and made available to consumers are agreed upon by the enterprise.

Enhances Productivity

The EDW standardizes, preserves, and stores data from distinct sources, aiding the consolidation and integration of all the data. Since critical data is available to all users, it allows them to make informed decisions. In addition, executives can query the data themselves with little to no IT support, saving more time and money.

Benefits Data Governance Activities

The EDW supports larger corporate data governance initiatives by providing standardization of data assets, feedback, and upstream quality improvements.

Drawbacks of an EDW

Fixed Costs

EDWs are costly to implement and these costs are multifaceted, often involving consultants, IT staff, business staff, and hardware expense if done on premise (we will see cloud options/benefits in an upcoming section). The expenses do not stop as new data is always being requested by users and added by IT.

There are ongoing license and hardware costs. As stated, the ROI on EDWs is typically substantial (dependent on adoption and use), but on-premises EDWs are associated with long-term fixed costs.

Native Data Is Not Available

Most data in the EDW has been transformed and/or aggregated. There are times when analytics consumers need non-aggregated and non-transformed data. The EDW does not support this need.

Security and Data Leakage

As the saying goes, "with much power, comes much responsibility"; the same is true here. Granting users access to data is fully controllable within these systems. However, what these users do with that information can be a risk to the organization.

A Taste Can Lead to Wanting More

Giving uses access to a wealth of information is a great thing, but it often spurs users into wanting more. "If I had this data, I could do that and that would be so cool". One of the criticisms of IT is that user requests to add new data into the EDW often takes 6 months or longer. This leads to everyone being frustrated. We will speak to how data virtualization can help with this in the next chapter.

Contrasting the ODS and the EDW

The architecture of the ODS is different from the EDW.

Depending on the data maturity or position in the data architecture life cycle, an organization may only have an ODS, only an EDW, or they may have both. An EDW is highly transformed and therefore may not be useful for many reporting applications. An ODS may include real-time data that is not accessible in the EDW. There are other differences, but in summary, here are other major divisions:

- An ODS is targeted for the lowest granular queries whereas a data warehouse is usually used for complex queries against summary/ aggregated data.
- An ODS is meant for operational reporting and supports current or near real-time reporting requirements whereas a data warehouse is meant for historical and trend analysis reporting usually on a large volume of data.
- An ODS contains only a short window of data while a data warehouse contains the entire history of data.
- In an ODS the frequency of data load could be real times, micro batch (every few seconds or minutes), hourly whereas in a data warehouse the frequency of data loads could be daily, weekly, or monthly.

Cluster Computing and Big Data

The promise of "Big Data" was all the rage a few years ago and some of it persists today, but in a more tempered view. Applications of all data sizes are not only alive and well but thriving. We offer this section to clear up some of the mystery of what "Big Data" means and describe technology that supports it.

What Is Big Data?

There are differing reports of who originally/officially coined the term "Big Data" and where it actually started. Part of the confusion revolves around the question, "Is Big Data a concept or is Big Data a technology?" Technology is most useful when it fits a particular set of needs.

Big Data as a Concept

We like the following as an easily understood description:

Big Data – a massive volume of data that is so large it is difficult to process using traditional technology (as of about 2005). In most enterprise scenarios the volume of data is too big or it moves too fast or it exceeds current processing capacity.

We revisit three factors which commonly characterize Big Data, the "**3 Vs of Big Data**":

Data volume – Data volume refers to the "width of the pipes" or the "number of lanes in the road-ways" if we use our previous metaphor of Chapter 5. The sheer amount of data from each source. There are many sources – different highways, HOV lanes, routes, roads, and alleys within the organization.

Data variety – Data variety is the number of disparate types, different structures, and formats of data that are flowing in the organization (see previous section in this chapter, **"Primer on Data Structures and Formats"**). Data variety can be thought of as analogous to different types of vehicles – busses, sedans, coupes, light trucks, tractor trailers, bikes, motorcycles, and self-driving cars.

Data velocity – Data velocity refers to the speed at which data is added to systems and how often the systems are refreshed. This is analogous to the rate of the various vehicles that are traveling along each road way.

Two more "Vs" are sometimes added to make it the "5 Vs of Big Data". The last two are more qualities of Big Data rather than terms that define or characterize Big Data. They are

- **Data veracity** – the assurance of quality or credibility of the collected data
- **Data value** – the return on investment for sourcing this data specific to the organization and the time it is being collected

There are a number of technologies that support "Big Data" such as data lakes, cloud architectures, data virtualization and we will get to these, but right now we want to focus on "game changing" technology when it comes to developing analytics and particularly training AI and machine learning models with very large data sets. These very large data sets will be in the form of DFS for training these models, rather than using traditional methods.

Big Data as a Technology

Big Data as a technology refers to "Cluster Computing". Cluster computing refers to a set of loosely or tightly connected computers that work together. From an end-user perspective they can be viewed as a single entity. Each computer that is connected to the network is called a node and there is a master node that orchestrates the workload for each worker node. Cluster computing offers solutions to solve complicated problems by providing faster computational speed and enhanced data integrity.

In the next section we develop the motivations for applying this technology to AI and machine learning problems. For interested readers, we first offer a brief contrast between cluster computing and Grid computing.

NOTE: Grid computing is another high-performance computing paradigm for computationally intensive problems (some references are suggested in the "Additional Resources" section at the end of the chapter).

Cluster Computing, Distributed Computing, and Grid Computing

Distributed computing is an environment in which a group of independent and geographically dispersed computer systems all take part in solving a complex problem, each by solving a part of the solution and then combining the result from all computers. These systems are loosely coupled systems coordinately working for a common goal. An example is a telephone or cellular network.

Cluster computing can be thought of as a special form of distributed computing where there are interconnected nodes (computers) with worker nodes completing individual tasks. These tasks are orchestrated via master node. An example is Hadoop machine learning (see gray box, "Quick Note on Apache, Hadoop, and Spark").

Grid computing is a broader form of computing that subsumes distributed computing. Grid computing is focused on the ability to support computation across multiple (administrative) domains that sets it apart from traditional distributed computing. Its support for multiple administrative policies and security authentication and authorization mechanisms enables it to be distributed over a local, metropolitan, or wide-area network. An example of Grid computing is computing infrastructure devoted to biomedical research (http://www.gpugrid.net/).

Why the Push to Big Data? Why Is Big Data Technology Attractive for Data Science?

The technologies of Big Data came about to support the massive collection and lengthening of processing time when dealing with these huge volumes of data. Users needed to access the data, and analyze and model the data more expediently. From an analytics and data science perspective, there was a major technology and practice shift when adopting Big Data technology. Traditionally, most analysis and machine learning involved moving data from large data repositories (and most of these distributed) into a single "sand box" for analytics. This involved increasingly more time as the volume of the data increased; it was taking more and more time to move the data across the wire. It also was a security risk since you were moving this data across a network, thus making it easier for someone to tap into sensitive data.

You were also creating a duplicate copy of all this data on another server or servers, which increased costs and added additional security risks. What if you could instead move the algorithms (machine learning and other) to where the data lives in the first place? Move the algorithms instead of the data? This was the brilliance of Big Data technology. We will call this "in-cluster, in-database or in-memory machine learning" for short. A cluster refers to a group of servers that are grouped together to work on the same computational set of problems and can be viewed as one computer resource. Our examples will focus on Hadoop and Spark, two open source technologies available as part of the Apache (see gray box on Apache, Hadoop, and Spark) scalable in-database and in-cluster processing. For in-cluster, in-database computing, we are referring to moving the algorithms to the cluster where the data lives

(Disk, Hadoop HDFS and MapReduce). In-memory computing refers to moving the algorithms to faster, volatile/RAM which is much faster (Spark).

> **Quick Note on Apache, Hadoop, and Spark**
>
> The Apache Software Foundation (www.apache.org) was incorporated in 1999 as an American nonprofit corporation. Our focus has to do with Big Data systems that support scalable cluster computing or in-database and in-cluster processing of Big Data – Hadoop and Spark as examples.
>
> *Hadoop* was initially released in 2006 and was widely adopted (with its commercial derivatives) by 2012. According to the Apache Foundation (http://hadoop.apache.org/).
>
> The Apache Hadoop software library is a framework that allows for the distributed processing of large data sets across clusters of computers using simple programming models. It is designed to scale up from single servers to thousands of machines, each offering local computation and storage.
>
> It offers a software framework for distributed storage (HDFS, Hadoop distributed file system) and processing of Big Data using the MapReduce (a parallel, distributed algorithm) programming model.
>
> *Spark* was initially released in May of 2014. It was developed by University of California, Berkeley's AMPLab and was later donated to the Apache Software Foundation. Spark and its resilient distributed dataset were developed in response to limitations in the MapReduce cluster computing paradigm (e.g., Hadoop). Spark's advantage over Hadoop is speed and performance. The main way it accomplishes this is using its in-memory data processing. In-memory data processing means slower disk access is eliminated and replaced by RAM or flash memory. This is more expensive, but according to the Apache Website, it can run up to 100 times faster (see http://spark.apache.org/ for logistic regression in Spark vs Hadoop).

Pivotal Changes in Big Data Technology

We should note that in the last year, we have witnessed some major changes in Big Data technologies, particularly in Hadoop and commercial vendors supporting Hadoop-based infrastructures. We have talked with colleagues that are shutting down their open source Hadoop clusters (and commercial analogs) and opting for cloud and other technologies. We do not think this is the end of Hadoop as many companies have realized the value of their investment. However, it has meant the shuttering or downsizing of commercial providers, and some companies that had not realized the value of their investment are making sharp pivots into cloud and hybrid cloud (see Park, 2019, for names, trends and consolidations). We have seen other writers and bloggers offer the same sentiments. See Sivalingam (2019) for his perspective on whether the death is Hadoop or Big Data.

Data is valuable everywhere it is meaningfully applied to real problems, i.e., where good analytics are performed. We need Big Data, small data, and everywhere in between. However, the view "just throw it all in and we will use it someday" is a losing proposition. This "throw it all in" applies in data warehousing as well as data lakes.

One more time – *if data is not used it is just a cost and of no value.* It costs money to store it, secure it, back it up, and it is a liability. To paraphrase Ben Franklin, "an ounce of planning is worth a pound of success".

Big Data and the Gartner Hype Cycle

For many years "Big Data" was the rage, it was a major hype cycle. You will still hear the term, but it is now considered part of the landscape and not the technology that will "ever change the world", as it once was. In machine learning, it is still important to qualify the difference in technology as to where the models are trained. Are you moving data from a database into an analytic system or moving the code / algorithms to the data?

We have mentioned Gartner several times. Gartner Inc. is a global research and advisory firm providing information, advice, and tools for businesses in IT, finance, HR, customer service and support, legal and compliance, marketing, sales, and supply chain functions (see www.gartner.com.). It is a member of the S&P 500. According to Gartner's Website

> Gartner Hype Cycles provide a graphic representation of the maturity and adoption of technologies and applications, and how they are potentially relevant to solving real business problems and exploiting new opportunities. Gartner hype cycle methodology gives you a view of how a technology or application will evolve over time, providing a sound source of insight to manage its deployment within the context of your specific business goals.

There are five phases of the hype cycle

> Each hype cycle drills down into the five key phases of a technology's life cycle:
>
> **Innovation trigger**: A potential technology breakthrough kicks things off. Early proof-of-concept stories and media interest trigger significant publicity. Often no usable products exist and commercial viability is unproven.
>
> **Peak of inflated expectations**: Early publicity produces a number of success stories – often accompanied by scores of failures. Some companies take action; many do not.

Trough of disillusionment: Interest wanes as experiments and implementations fail to deliver. Producers of the technology shake out or fail. Investments continue only if the surviving providers improve their products to the satisfaction of early adopters.

Slope of enlightenment: More instances of how the technology can benefit the enterprise start to crystallize and become more widely understood. Second- and third-generation products appear from technology providers. More enterprises fund pilots; conservative companies remain cautious.

Plateau of productivity: Mainstream adoption starts to take off. Criteria for assessing provider viability are more clearly defined. The technology's broad market applicability and relevance are clearly paying off.

A hype cycle graph would look like the following with expectations in the y-axis and the five key phases would be along the bottom (see Figure 6.1). Each technology would appear somewhere on the continuum and labeled as to when the technology would reach the phase of "Plateau of Productivity". Here we have provided one technology (normally there would be a few dozen) for Big Data. This approximates where Big Data was in 2014.

It is interesting to note that Big Data dropped off the hype cycle early – in 2015. In 2014 it had been listed as "Peak of Inflated Expectations" (see Woodie, 2015) – "as big data-mania set in, the technology was near the

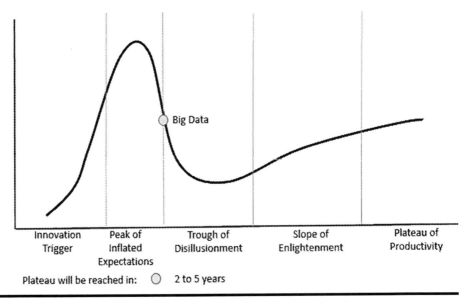

Figure 6.1   Example of Gartner hype cycle with Big Data location in 2014.

'Peak of Inflated Expectations'. A year later, as the shine started wearing off, Big Data started slipping down into the 'Trough of Disillusionment'". It would have been expected to be near the bottom of the trough in 2015, but instead it was totally absent. "I would not consider Big Data to be an emerging technology", Betsy Burton (Gartner Analyst) said "This hype cycle is very focused. I look at emerging trends".

So in 2015 Big Data had lost its emerging technology status and was considered mainstream.

To look at the pressure on CEOs and CIOs to adopt Hadoop and Big Data we can see what views were being expressed in late 2011. Dan Woods, in *Forbes* (see Woods, 2011), explains how to pitch the pros and cons to the CEOs. Big Data was all the rage and organizations had a real fear of missing out; a fear of letting competitors leapfrog them with the mysterious wonders of Big Data that would revolutionize business models – or so went the hype! Big data technology was hot!

Optimized Big Data

We mentioned the advantages of Hadoop as a Big Data architecture for efficient AI and ML development. We also mentioned Spark as being even faster due to its in-memory data processing. We even detailed the performance gains from "volatile" vs "nonvolatile" memory early in this chapter.

The reader should be aware there are a number of commercial providers of platforms built upon Hadoop and Spark. These providers often cite enhanced speeds and performance over Hadoop and Spark. These are attained via proprietary "memory optimization" which is memory swapping and caching.

Organizations should carefully investigate alternative technologies and big data tech is a prime example. Please see our commentary on Build, Buy, or Outsource in Part I.

Cloud Data – What It Is, What You Can Do, Benefits, and Drawbacks

Clouds services have been growing rapidly for the past several years and this growth will continue (see gray box, Growth of Cloud Services). Cloud technologies offer many benefits such as reducing infrastructure and personnel costs, dynamic sizing and scalability, and business continuity, to name just a few.

Cloud offers data storage in almost every flavor we have outlined in the previous chapter on data movement and continuing into this chapter on data storage designs. From cloud-based data warehousing to in-memory data stores, it is available around the world from one of the four public cloud providers.

Growth of Cloud Services

According to Louis Columbus in Forbes, public cloud will be soaring to $331B by 2022. Cloud technologies have been growing rapidly and this growth is expected to not only continue but accelerate. Gartner predicts the worldwide public cloud service market will grow from $182.4B in 2018 to $331.2B in 2022, attaining a compound annual growth rate of 12.6% (see Columbus, 2019). There are various aspects discussed in this report, but the point is that cloud is huge and getting bigger. Another point made is that when it comes to data storage, cloud is shifting storage from inside the data center, i.e., on-premise to hosted services.

CLOUD – DATA STORAGE OPTIONS

Cloud offers virtually every data format and data interface that we have covered. From relational databases (typical of transactional systems) to NoSQL databases (useful for software developers) to Binary Large OBject storage (BLOB, useful for images, audio and media objects) major cloud providers offer options. There are also options for loading these data stores via web services or bulk transfer. Cloud is offering those big technologies as well and some are using these architectures. There are some purporting scalable sensor (IIoT) data storage and analysis systems using cloud computing and big data technologies (Aydin et al., 2015).

Cloud also provides options for streaming data (see Chapter 5) as well as graph databases (see previous section in this chapter).

So, it is not a question of whether cloud offers a solution.

It is whether it is the right solution.

In general, here are some major considerations:

Cloud Benefits and Drawbacks

Options to store data in the cloud are diverse and support all the various types of data we discuss in this chapter – structured and relational, semistructured and unstructured, and even streaming data which will be discussed soon. All of these options are supported in cloud repositories, so virtually any analytics application consuming data can keep their data in the cloud.

So why are people moving data to the cloud? Here are just a few examples:

1. **Cost savings** – there are no hardware investments with cloud. You can normally expense rather than capitalize these costs. No long-term commitments required, except human capital to change strategies. Service costs are offset by fewer highly specialized personnel.
2. **Scalability** – your enterprise can scale up or scale down your operation and storage needs quickly to suit your situation, allowing flexibility as your needs change.
3. **Business continuity** – specialized human resources are taken care of by the cloud provider so losing a key database administrator or similar role is not the issue it can be with owning all aspects of the data center.
4. **Data security** – cloud offers many advanced security features that guarantee that data is securely stored and handled.
5. **Mobility** – employees who are working on the premises or at remote locations can easily access all their cloud services. All they need is Internet connectivity.
6. **High reliability** – cloud environments are distributed across the globe and have near 100% availability. The cloud provider handles disaster recovery, backups, and more. However, you must consider your network and Internet connectivity (see #1 drawback of cloud).

It would be unfair not to mention a few of the drawbacks with cloud:

1. **Requires connectivity** – *this is a big one*. No Internet connectivity with public cloud, or network connectivity with private cloud, makes cloud technologies useless.
2. **Security** – while cloud offers some security advantages, it opens up others. There have been examples where administrators of cloud services have created data breaches.
3. **Control** – since the cloud infrastructure is entirely owned, managed, and monitored by the cloud provider, it limits control of the customer. If you have technical issues, you can be at the mercy of the provider.
4. **Unexpected charges** – if (virtual) machines are left running the meter is running. Also, you may be charged for data movement and

other fees. Companies that do not manage these services can be surprised by expenses.

5. **Vendor lock** – of course, this can happen with any IT product or service, but it should be considered up front. If you move everything to a specific cloud provider, there is a lot of inertia and it takes a lot of effort to move to another vendor.

Cloud Storage

Cloud storage is a model of computer data storage in which the digital data is stored in logical pools. In other words, the data may not exist in the same physical unit, but it appears to be from a user perspective. The physical storage spans multiple servers (sometimes in multiple locations), and the physical environment is typically owned and managed by a hosting company. These cloud storage providers are responsible for keeping the data available and accessible, and the physical environment protected and running. People and organizations buy or lease storage capacity from the providers to store user, organization, or application data. This provides many benefits as well as limitations which we briefly elaborate upon in this chapter.

Time will tell, but we think cloud is the way forward for many enterprise programs and projects, so it will be the major public cloud providers that likely pave the way for technology.

"Other Big Data Promises", Data Lakes, Data Swamps, Reservoirs, Muddy Water, Analytic Sandboxes, and Whatever We Can Think to Call It Tomorrow

The authors are skeptical of marketing hype (possibly marchitecture, portmanteau of the words marketing and architecture) and hyperbole often presented by software providers, bloggers, consultants, social, broadcasting, and news media. You might think that we have a cynical disposition, we like to think we are "data driven". We have seen much buzz over the years that often results in empty promises, misspent money, and regrets.

The data lake appeared as the next evolution beyond EDWs and in-memory cluster computing. It was set to overcome some of the drawbacks of the EDW. For example, the EDW is highly normalized (transformed and aggregated) and does not support some of the features of the original data. There is merit in this goal of "Data Lakes". Further, there are likely some data lake success stories somewhere.

However, we have seen time after time, stories of failures. We have heard of data lakes turn into data swamps. Lakes that have deteriorated and become unmanageable, with substantial negative return on value over time. Our recommendation is to be very careful in trying to support all organizational goals in large monolithic technologies. We believe so many data store options still thrive because there is utility in nearly everyone and it is best to invest across them with specific goals – keep the end in mind, plan and execute carefully.

Summary

Whew, that is a lot of information. Interestingly, much of the storage and technology foundations that supported the early days of data and analytics are still around. Moreover, they support some of the organization's data foundations today. Nevertheless, there have been great advancements and some newer technologies are poised to really take off. So, what we have more than anything else is a large variety of technologies that support various initiatives and functions of the enterprise.

Organizations are still supporting local and networked file systems, just not in the volume they once did. Not everyone may have an ODS, but they are very likely to have an EDW. They may have dipped a toe into DFS/in-cluster storage or they may have skipped it or even abandoned it for the cloud.

So almost every organization is a hybrid of some sort.

In the next chapter, we cover a very interesting technology. One that is exploding. It promises to take all the technology that we discussed here and extend them to serve them all to data consumers (machines or humans) from a single platform. Moreover, it appears they are pulling any and all data they desire via a monolithic system that has the blessing of IT and adheres to all the corporate standards.

It is a very cool technology that can use ALL these technologies and extend them: data virtualization.

References

Aydin, G., Hallac, I. R., & Karakus, B. (2015). Architecture and implementation of a scalable sensor data storage and analysis system using cloud computing and big data technologies. *Journal of Sensors*, 2015, 1–11. doi:10.1155/2015/834217.

Buneman, P. (1997). "Semistructured data". Symposium on Principles of Database Systems.

Columbus, L. (2019). Public Cloud Soaring To $331B By 2022 According To Gartner, Forbes. https://www.forbes.com/sites/louiscolumbus/2019/04/07/public-cloud-soaring-to-331b-by-2022-according-to-gartner/#6d3066d35739.

Lasker, L., Parkes, W. (Producers) & Robinson, P. A., (Director), (1992). Sneakers, United States, Universal Studios.

Marr, B. (2018). Here's Why Data Is Not the New Oil. Forbes. https://www.forbes.com/sites/bernardmarr/2018/03/05/heres-why-data-is-not-the-new-oil/#39b12ecf3aa9.

Park, H. (2019). The Death of Big Data and the Emergence of the Multi-Cloud Era; KD Nuggets. https://www.kdnuggets.com/2019/07/death-big-data-multi-cloud-era.html.

Sivalingam, J. (2019). What does the death of Hadoop mean for big data? TECHWIRE ASIA; https://techwireasia.com/2019/07/what-does-the-death-of-hadoop-mean-for-big-data/.

Woodie, A. (2015). Why Gartner Dropped Big Data Off the Hype Curve, Datanami, https://www.datanami.com/2015/08/26/why-gartner-dropped-big-data-off-the-hype-curve/.

Woods, D. (2011). How Real-Time Marketing Technology Can Transform Your Business; https://www.forbes.com/sites/ciocentral/2011/05/06/how-real-time-marketing-technology-can-transform-your-business/?sh=6748fa176fff.

Additional Resources

Two seminal books for data warehousing:

1. Inmon, W.H., (2005) *Building the Data Warehouse*, 4th Edition. Wiley Publishing.
2. Kimball, R. (2013, July) *The Data Warehouse Toolkit: The Definitive Guide to Dimensional Modeling*, 3rd Edition. Wiley Publishing.

Useful, Interesting Podcast on Single Source of the Truth – The Data Skeptic – http://dataskeptic.libsyn.com/single-source-of-truth.

Data Lakes and Architecture

There is a great deal of confusion and promise of technology. We cover the differences of big data concepts and big data technology more in our first book. But the issues remain of "promises vs delivery" of solutions to very big problems. An interesting LinkedIn post by Bill Inmon on late

January 2021 https://www.linkedin.com/pulse/data-lake-architecture-bill-inmon/.

We are big fans of Bill's emphasis on architecture while recognizing that distributed computing and HDFS-type technology has its place.

Some Terms to Consider Exploring

ETL (Extract, Transform, and Load), ELT, Contextual ETL, Database, Data Warehouse, Operational Data Stores (ODS), Cloud, Data Cache, Big Data, Graph DBs, Nodes and Edges (Network Analytics), Cluster Computing, Grid Computing, Computing as a Service, Distributed Computing, Apache, Hadoop, HDFS, Spark, HIVE, MapReduce, MLlib (Apache Spark's scalable machine learning library)

Kumar, Sunil; Shankar, Hari; Ali, Navae;

SETI@HOME:

Application of Grid Computing – A Survey. http://www.mitpublications.org/yellow_images/1361441444_logo_Untitled2.pdf.

Bright Hub as an interesting website that includes an introduction to Grid computing information on the SETI project. https://www.brighthub.com/environment/green-computing/articles/67601/

Two Books on Grid computing:

1. Kiat-An Tan, Frédéric Magoulès, Jie Pan, & Abhinit Kumar. (2009). *Introduction to Grid Computing*. CRC Press.
2. Grandinetti, L. (2005). *Grid Computing : The New Frontier of High-Performance Computing*. Elsevier.

Following are four more technical sources that speak to technology to do near-memory computing to speed up model training for complex problems:

1. Huskin, Edward In-Memory Computing and the Future of Machine Learning (August 30, 2019), The Data Warehousing Institute (TWDI), https://tdwi.org/Articles/2019/08/30/ARCH-ALL-In-Memory-Computing-and-Future-of-Machine-Learning.aspx?Page=1.
2. Lapedus, Mark; (Feb 2019) New approaches are competing for attention as scaling benefits diminish. Semiconductor Engineering. https://semiengineering.com/in-memory-vs-near-memory-computing/.

3. Singh, Gagandeep; Chelini, Lorenzo; Corda, Stefano; Javed Awan, Ahsan; Stuijk, Sander; Jordans, Roel; Corporaal, Henk; Boonstra, Albert-Jan; (November 2019) Near-memory computing: Past, present, and future; Microprocessors and Microsystems, Elsevier Publishing.

4. Singh, Gagandeep (Aug 2018) A Review of Near-Memory Computing Architectures: Opportunities and Challenges. IEEE, Conference Proceedings: 2018 21st Euromicro Conference on Digital System Design.

An interesting *Wall Street Journal* paper on the new Stanford IoT hospital – Rosenbush, Steven (Nov. 16, 2019) New Stanford Hospital Takes Holistic Approach to Technology, *The Wall Street Journal CIO Journal*, https://www.wsj.com/articles/new-stanford-hospital-takes-holistic-approach-to-technology-11573905600.

Chapter 7

Data Virtualization

Things get done only if the data we gather can inform and inspire those in a position to make a difference.

Mike Schmoker, Results

The plural of anecdote is not data.

Marc Bekoff

Introduction

The enterprise data warehouse (EDW, Chapter 6) has been useful for many years and will be for many years to come. However, there are major gaps in the EDW. These gaps are widening with time, and data-driven organizations will have to address them if they want to be successful in realizing the promise of modern analytics.

What is the problem? New technologies and rapid adoption of those technologies. As an example, take a technology like software as a service (SaaS). These platforms are cloud-hosted systems where users most often interact and create queries via a web interface. Suppose we have a CRM (customer relationship management) system like Salesforce. We can query a SaaS database that is part of the platform and we can download thousands of rows for analysis, but you can't put all your Salesforce data into an EDW. Additionally, there are cloud and big data technologies that don't fit well in a data warehousing paradigm.

DOI: 10.4324/9780429343957-9

One of the most exciting data technologies today is data virtualization (**DV**). It is not new; it has been around in enterprise form for about 20 years. However, it has not been universally adopted, but is coming of age. Organizations of any size, across industries, are considering it as a solution to many of their data challenges.

Another reason for the interest in this technology is that data is becoming more varied. In brief, data variety describes the disparate data sources, data types, different structures, and formats of data (see Burk & Miner, 2020 for a more detailed discussion of data variety).

The Typical Story of Data Growth, Data Complexity, and Data Needs

As we noted in Chapter 4 section overview, there exists a broad and varied set of data sources and types. Additionally, data volume is constantly growing, and data structures are changing with technology. Let us recall a typical evolution of data architectures in an organization. We will see that DV was created to help sustain organizations in this ever changing landscape.

Here are bullets from our evolving data ecosystem taken from Chapter 4 (you can review details in Chapter 4, if helpful):

- Operational systems and online transaction processing (OLTP)
- Operational data stores (ODS)
- Enterprise data warehouse
- Business intelligence (BI)
- New on-premise systems
- Special projects requiring special data sources
- RESTful and Web APIs
- Self-service and visual BI
- Message-oriented middleware and enterprise service bus (ESB)
- Software as a service (SaaS)
- Big data time and data lakes
- Data virtualization
- Streaming operational data
- Cloud-based infrastructures
- Third-party purchased data

DV can help aggregate and make available all of these data sources in a unified, sustainable manner. It is easily extensible or adaptable to new technologies that don't exist at this point in time. It can also help the organization more easily evolve from existing (legacy) systems to new systems by simultaneously sourcing and comparing both at the same time without interruption of operations.

DV – What Is It?

DV was created not to supplant the EDW but to extend its reach and capabilities. With virtualization, there is no physical re-creation or copying of data, as needed with data warehousing. An apt, concise definition on which we agree was provided by techopedia:

> *Data virtualization* is the process of aggregating data from different sources of information to develop a single, logical and virtual view of information so that it can be accessed by front-end solutions such as applications, dashboards and portals without having to know the data's exact storage location. (https://www.techopedia. com/definition/1007/data-virtualization)

For those readers wanting a more technical definition, van der Lans (2012) offers this definition:

> *Data virtualization* is the technology that offers data consumers a unified, abstracted, and encapsulated view for querying and manipulating data stored in a heterogeneous set of data stores.

He covers a detailed treatise with definitions of abstraction, encapsulation, and federation. These details are beyond the scope of this book. However, we add some basic descriptions of relevant terms in the "Additional Resources" section at the end of this chapter for you to consider/investigate. Note, however, in this chapter we assume that the data in the DV platform has been curated and federated when we speak about its capabilities and advantages.

A graphic illustration of DV is provided in Figure 7.1. At the bottom of the figure are the various data sources. These are rich sources, beyond traditional data sources. Indeed, DV platforms can support all the data sources mentioned in the "The Typical Story of Data Growth" section above.

In the middle of Figure 7.1 is the virtualized layer. This is not a persistent copy of data, but instead, it is data brought into fast, virtual memory, thus making it immediately available for the user. When a user or application (we label both here as a data consumer) requests data, this data is queried from the source and presented into this virtual layer.

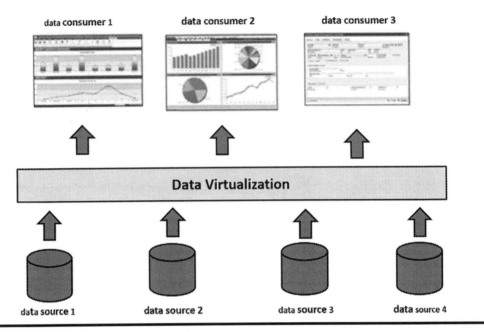

Figure 7.1   What is data virtualization?

To be clear, an important feature of DV is that a separate "write to disk" (persistent) copy of this data is never made, thus the data is not duplicated. While there are a myriad of data sources being queried and brought into this virtualized layer, *the consumer perceives that they are accessing one very large integrated data source.*

Briefly, some of the capabilities that define DV and benefit the organization are:

A Platform Connecting to Hundreds of Data Sources

DV is a platform that connects to "virtually" any data source. But that is not the reason for its name. The process is termed "data virtualization" because there is no persistent copy of the data. The sources of data you can acquire seem nearly limitless. These can be data warehouses, data marts, operational data stores, cloud-based platforms, SaaS, streaming sources, web and restful APIs, local databases, network drives and much, much more.

A Platform with Searchable Data and Rich Metadata

Users can easily search all available enterprise data that they have permission to access. If there are multiple instances of the same data elements (example patient or customer ID) they can easily see where the different elements are located and which they should use from each application. As an example, if a data consumer is wanting to calculate lifetime customer value they can not only search and find the applicable data elements, but they can make sure they are using the corporate standard for their particular business case. These capabilities are made available via a system catalog which provides additional capabilities (Pullokkaran, 2013).

A Collaboration Tool for Functional Areas and Users

The system catalog also allows business users, IT users, and even third parties to communicate and collaborate in regimented/defined ways. You can make forums open to everyone or allow only group restricted conversations. This offers many benefits, but one of the great benefits is a boost to data quality and IT productivity.

A Pathway for New Systems and System Migration

One of the major hurdles that organizations face is moving from old, existing (legacy) systems to new systems. Often this migration is delayed for years because it requires so much time and money. An enterprise resource planning system conversion often takes years and millions of dollars to fully implement. There is a huge amount of effort mapping old data to new data and quality checks. DV can greatly reduce the time and effort and therefore money to bring on new systems.

An IT Tool for Rapid Prototyping

Another way that DV saves IT time and money is by its quick prototyping of data management processes. As stated, DV is not meant to replace the EDW but to augment it and extend its reach. So, new elements are always being sourced into the EDW and this takes time and effort of which DV can greatly assist.

A System for Enhanced Security of Data

DV allows for additional security between the data consumer and the data source system. When the data is made available in DV, the administrators can give access permission to individuals or to groups of users. These security measures can be defined in very granular ways, for example:

- Permission to the column (variable) level
- Permission to the row (record or case) level
- Permission limited to a date range
- Permission by rules – combinations of all of the above

What Is in a Name?

As we stated in our first book, marketers and technologists have a vested interest in creating new terminology so they can differentiate and sell. The reason we named this chapter "Data Virtualization" was because there is a growing mixture of terms, concepts, and hype around DV. While there may be subtle differences, there is a great overlap in terms being thrown around in the following technologies:

- Virtual data layer
- Logical (or virtual) data warehouse
- Data-as-a-service (DaaS)
- Data fabric

Virtual data layer is part of DV. It is the layer that exists between the underlying data sources and the business user or data consumer. **Note that these data consumers can be human or services** that automatically feed into other systems including operational analytic dashboards, machine learning and predictive models, rules-based systems, and even events and messaging services (see Chapter 5 for further information).

A **logical data warehouse** is another name for an implemented and operational system enabled via DV technology. It is called a "logical" data warehouse because there is no replication of data, i.e., there is no physical copy of the data other than data that may have been cached, but that data is not cached on traditional physical disks, but in fast, volatile (RAM) memory.

Data-as-a-service is a paradigm or business-centric strategy that seeks to leverage data as a business asset and make that asset available quickly and easily. The term has been around over a decade and followed the many labels of "as-a-service" that started with SaaS. Any "as a service" (noted "Xaas") is SaaS. Technologists and product marketers use it as a way to extend SaaS down to specific uses for consumers or customers.

DATA FABRIC

In the last couple of years, there has been a lot of buzz about data fabrics. In February 2019, Gartner noted "Data Fabric" as one of the data and analytics technology trends (see Gartner Press Release, 2019):

> Data fabric enables frictionless access and sharing of data in a distributed data environment. It enables a single and consistent data

management framework, which allows seamless data access and processing by design across otherwise siloed storage.

Through 2022, bespoke data fabric designs will be deployed primarily as a static infrastructure, forcing organizations into a new wave of
cost to completely re-design for more dynamic data mesh approaches.

(From: Gartner, 2019)

We are anxious to see if new technology plays out to support this data fabric or if it is just a natural evolution of the data virtual technology that has
been around for over a decade.

In our opinion, we see most of the above as **paradigms and strategies**
whereas DV is a **technology** that supports these paradigms.

The Continuing Quest for the "Single Versions of the Truth" – Motivation beyond the EDW

We mentioned in Chapter 6 that the EDW was created to provide a single
version of the truth to solve the problem of individual reports that did not
agree because the numbers were pulled from different data sources. By
creating a central hub from which all numbers were sourced the idea is that
everyone would be "on the same page". While this worked fairly well for
many years, as data variety grew and technology solutions expanded (cloud,
SaaS, and data lake), the EDW began to experience shortcomings. DV can
help organizations overcome these weaknesses.

Organizations have been moving to SaaS platforms and this will likely
accelerate. SaaS is a cloud-based service where instead of downloading
software for your desktop PC or business network to run and update, you
instead access an application via a web browser. The software application
could be anything from office software to enterprise resource platforms.

Can you effectively load data that is resident in a SaaS into a data warehouse?
No. But, people still need access to this data in near real time to make intelligent decisions. DV can provide connections into SaaS platforms and the user
can access and even merge this data from other sources, easily and effectively.

Or, data may be sitting in a source such as a data lake. Data lakes are
nonrelational data stores and it typically takes IT or a data engineer to query
this data. These are very large, optimized stores that a business analyst does
not normally query. DV can provide access to this data for the analyst as
the query logic and transformations are embedded inside of DV and hidden
from the user. The user simply gets the data elements requested.

DV is a technology that can offer the single version of the truth of the
EDW while overcoming all these other challenges. DV became an extended,

enhanced version of the EDW with near real-time query ability. In the next section, we explore these as well as other advantages of DV.

Can You Tell Which of These Dashboards Is Wrong?

Take a look at Figure 7.2. One of these dashboards is wrong, can you tell which one? It shows two visual BI dashboards side by side; there are minor

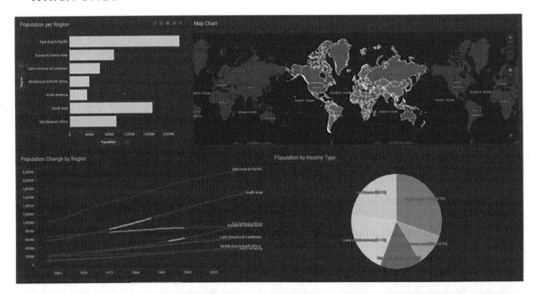

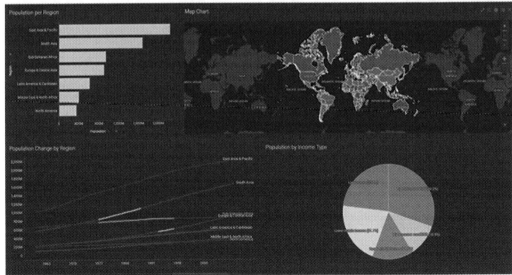

Figure 7.2 Which one of these dashboards is wrong?

differences between the two. Which one is wrong? The one that Suzy produced? The one that Bob produced? The one produced with the marketing template or the one based on the finance template? This illustrates a very important problem that has existed for years! It is not the development of the chart. You cannot tell which is wrong by looking at the chart design! It is not the chart, but instead it is the data used to create the chart. What we need is clean data and agreed upon data definitions! It is the data!

The following gray box describes **Three Ever Present Problems with Data** that lead to such discrepancies that DV can help organizations overcome.

NOTE: We are highlighting data issues that DV can help overcome in this section. It is important to note that the producer of visual BI can always game the system and consumers should be aware of these challenges when reviewing these dashboards. We cover this in our first book in the analytics literacy section (see Burk & Miner, 2020). The truth can be manipulated by the producer of the chart, "gaming the system" or it can be done unintentionally with inaccurate data.

Three Ever Present Problems with Data and How DV Can Help

Three of the most likely reasons for inaccurate data are:

WRONG DATA SOURCE

Suppose that customer address is being sourced for a marketing project. There may be many sources of a customer's addresses such as financial system, sales system, support or warranty system, or marketing system. Which one should be used? Best practice is to have identified the "golden record" for each pertinent data value. This will identify which source system is to be used for each specific business case based on organizational or committee review. The "golden record" for the customer address in marketing use cases may be the cloud-based marketing or **CRM system**. The "golden record" for a patient ID may be the master patient index system. DV can be configured to source the appropriate systems for the appropriate use case so no data consumer pulls data from the wrong source. Furthermore, it sources data on local network drives, cloud, SaaS, data lakes, and the EDW dynamically, thus greatly extending and improving the accuracy and veracity of the data.

LACK OF DATA QUALITY DUE TO INPUT ERRORS

There are numerous reasons for poor data quality. For data that is manually input by humans there is often a misalignment of incentives. Humans are incented to "do things fast" or "just get it entered" rather than make sure the data is accurate. For automated systems, such as sensor- or camera-based systems, the sensor or network can lead to data problems. DV is not the best solution for these problems; instead moving quality control and validation at the point of entry is best. However, since DV can source multiple systems and create reports to identify problem areas, you can use them to improve data quality.

DATA FRESHNESS

One issue with the EDW is timeliness of the data. As data expands it becomes more difficult to load the data warehouse. IT often loads tables incrementally, as available, and then does a full load at best once a day, but more typically once a week and sometimes once per month. So, what is an analytics consumer to do that needs up to the minute data? With DV the query can produce near real-time data, sourcing the freshest data required for the analysis. The value of data degrades very rapidly (see Arbesman, 2013). Better still, DV can pull those optimized queries from the EDW that stores the largest breadth of data and append any gaps from data coming in from the more recently updated data in operational systems.

What Are the Advantages of DV?

A Sustainable Architecture for the Ever-Increasing Complexity of Data

We hope that the simple diagram in Figure 7.3 illustrates some of the advantages of DV, but to contrast more explicitly look at the figures after Figure 7.3. The figure below demonstrates what data consumers would need

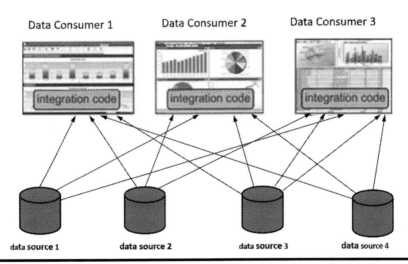

Figure 7.3   Traditional spaghetti – multiplicative data connections and different results.

to go through to produce analytics without DV technology. Each would need to create unique queries across multiple systems; it is spaghetti. This simple example is four data sources and three data consumers/applications. Thus, with this *multiplicative relationship* there are 4 * 3=12 data connections that have to be created and maintained. Many organizations today have 50 or more data sources and 10 or more applications. That is 50 * 10=500 data connections that have to be created and maintained as consumers require more and more data access. This becomes unsustainable. That is the reason many IT EDW requests take 6–12 months to fulfill, if they are fulfilled at all. Moreover, the results of each data consumer may be different based on the way they are querying the source.

Integrating data stores without a DV server leads to duplication of integration code.

Figure 7.4 shows the same user queries utilizing DV technology. The data sources are brought in the DV layer in a consistent, agreed upon fashion approved and governed by the organization. This is similar to a "bus architecture" that computer chips (semiconductors) offer. All the data comes in the bus or channel and then is routed to the correct destination. In our example above there are 50 sources and 10 applications requiring 500 connections using previous methods; but now, with DV, it only requires 50+10=60 connections in this *additive relationship*. This is a much more manageable situation, plus each data consumer is accessing consistent, coherent data.

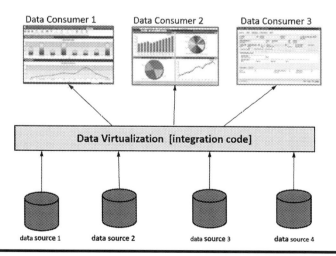

Figure 7.4   DV technology – additive data connections with consistent results.

Simplified User Experience

DV greatly simplifies the user experience in a variety of ways. We now highlight a few of these:

1. DV consumers have access to a wealth of data without worrying about the technical details of the queries. Whether they are joining or merging the data properly is not a concern as these queries are centralized and the user sees the use case and data available without having to worry with constructing the query.
2. They do not have to worry about whether they are pulling data from the proper source. For example, there are many data sources that can present customer information; traditionally a business consumer or analyst can pull from any of these sources. But it may not be the correct source for the task at hand. With DV, the source is approved by the organization for various use cases. This eliminates confusion, minimizes missteps, and simplifies the work of the user.

More Collaborative and Productive User Experience

1. **Simplifies communication and collaboration within the data community** – When data errors are found, questions arise or feedback is needed instead of going to an outside source of communication like email or a business communication platform it can be done inside the DV platform. You can annotate, communicate, and share information at the point of concern rather than externally.
2. **Simplifies finding needed data elements** – This enhances productivity. Data consumers can spend hours trying to find relevant data for analytic projects. However, data within DV becomes part of a catalog that can be searched. All reference information can be made available. No need to search across dozens of systems or send dozens of emails.

Data in Near Real Time

Many virtualized data services can operate in real time (or close to it) to surface fresh data that might be time sensitive for business processes during the day. This allows DV to enable users and embed analytics into operational applications. Compare this to a traditional EDW where users and systems are lucky to have data from yesterday or last week.

Source Data and Combine Data Easily

We mentioned that you cannot load a cloud-based SaaS into a data warehouse. Traditionally, a data consumer would need to perform a query on the SaaS system, pull that data down and then join or merge it with existing data and hope they do it correctly. But, with DV, this is done automatically, correctly, and efficiently saving a lot of time and money.

No Need to Replicate and Make Physical Copies of Data

With DV, the data available is virtual in nature. It is not sitting on a physical disk waiting to be accessed. Instead there are high-performance queries that are available on demand that can pull data from multiple sources, join, and merge the data appropriately within the system.

Improved Security and Administration

With DV you are not moving data, so it is less likely to be compromised. You also have an added security permissions layer for role-based or user-based security that allows for both column- and row-level access that is easily governed outside the database. Thirdly, a business-centric metadata repository or catalog exists where users can search, collaborate, and understand the enterprise data.

Positive Impact on the EDW, IT, and the Business

IT is continuing to increase staff to keep up with data-related service requests, but even with additional resources it takes up to 6 months to get data into the data warehouse or an access point for analytics users. If IT can fulfill the request, since DV offers many self-service features, tighter integration with IT and rapid prototyping it can lower the burden on IT. It also reduces the frustration of business analysts waiting for months for particular data. It also allows for functional efficiency with communication and workflows between business units and IT.

Governance and Data Quality

DV affords better data governance, data management, and data quality. Two examples are consistent compliance of regulations like the General

Data Protection Regulation and the Health Insurance Portability and Accountability Act. DV allows data stewards and IT to work together on remediating data quality issues via a single platform and workflow.

DV Is Scalable – Scales Up and Scales Out

As the enterprise grows and as data volumes grow, DV can scale up with it. As new systems come online and disparate data sources from APIs, cloud and SaaS are enabled; DV can scale out with these new sources.

Enabling Future Data and Even Technology

Data needs are constantly changing. Business users have new projects that require new data. The organization can bring on new systems and even purchase third-party data. DV is very adaptable to source these new data forms. You can be sure as technology changes, DV will change to enable it.

Digital Transformation, the Story of the Elephant and DV

Let's consider digital transformation and how DV fits in. First, a non-curated definition, Wikipedia (11/20/2020) states:

> Digital Transformation (DX) is the adoption of digital technology to transform services or businesses, through replacing non-digital or manual processes with digital processes or replacing older digital technology with newer digital technology.

When business leaders hear that the organization is undergoing a DX program they may think of it in very different ways than IT leaders. This is very similar to the parable of the blind men and the elephant or the poem by John Godfrey Saxe, "The Blind Men and the Elephant". After a boardroom presentation on DX, the thought of various leaders might go something like:

Business Leader #1 – This is great! This DX will lead to **data democratization**. We are finally going to be tearing down the walls of the data silos. The business will finally be able to get access to the data we have desperately wanted.

IT Leader #1 (sitting across from Business Leader #1) – sees the same slide and thinks we finally are able to have **control and governance**; we can enforce some data policy and keep data leaking out and hearing, "these reports don't match".

Business Leader #2 – This will lead to **creativity**. We can explore and launch new ideas since we have data that we have wanted for years to launch new business strategies.

IT Leader #2 (sitting across from Business Leader #2) – sees the same slide and thinks we finally have **data consistency**. I get beat up all the time for data quality, no more.

Business Leader #3 – This will lead to **disruptive business models and innovation**. I can now invest in new business models because I can join external data that I never had with internal data to expand into new avenues.

IT Leader #3 (sitting across from Business Leader #3) – sees the same slide and thinks "protection". Our data assets are locked and we can feel safe in keeping the organization running without threat.

These three contrasts are presented in Figure 7.5. None of these thoughts is incorrect.

Business leaders and IT leaders often see things differently because they have different business objectives and challenges. Business leaders are challenged to grow the business or expand into new products, services, or geographies. They are forced to risk the status quo. IT leaders are challenged with keeping the business running securely and efficiently. IT often sees business innovation (not technical innovation) as a threat to their ability to sustain operations. These different objectives cause friction.

However, when it comes to data, the technology of DV can minimize these tensions, such that business people feel free to be innovative and IT does not feel exposed to data-related risks.

DV can bridge these divides with authorization, curation, and federation. Authorization means that IT can provide the control it needs to so that it can enforce data policy and keep data leaking out. At the same time DV affords the business the entire wealth of the data to the organization, subject to privacy, security, and compliance constraints.

The Meaning(s) of Digital Transformation

Democratization	Control
Creativity	Consistency
Disruption	Protection
Business	IT

Figure 7.5 The meaning(s) of digital transformation.

Bridging the Gap of the Business and IT with Data Virtualization

Democratization	Authorization	Control
Creativity	Curation	Consistency
Disruption	Federation	Protection
Business		IT

Figure 7.6 Bridging the gap of the business and IT with data virtualization.

It also allows IT to be consistent. The combination of source and specific business case are cross referenced, predetermined, and accepted as standards within the organization. These are the facts/data elements presented to data consumers (people and applications). At the same time, the business user no longer has to worry, "am I pulling the information from the right database with the correct query logic for this business project?" The organization has already defined it and analytics people can use their energy and time to work in creative ways.

It also affords IT protection. IT does not have to worry that if they allow access to certain data, the user will "bring down the system" with a rogue query. Yet, the business people can be pioneers and explore and use data in disruptive, cutting edge ways. IT is no longer killing the party.

These are three of many ways DV can allow IT and the lines of business to not only coexist but thrive. These three contrasts are presented in Figure 7.6.

What Are the Drawbacks of DV?

While there are many advantages of DV, you should be aware there are drawbacks as well.

Some of the Major Disadvantages of DV

1. Lack of open source technologies. Contrast this to streaming, APIs, scripting languages, etc. where there are open source options.
2. Overall investment. While the return on DV is easily justified, the returns come in over a period of years. Depending on the implementation, some companies do get some returns within 3 months, but there

are multiple expenses – the system itself, services, internal personnel, and related resources.

3. DV is a difficult platform to "dip a toe into" with a test project unless you can work out a proof of concept with a vendor. The vendor may want you to cover expenses.

4. Lack of performance in the DV platform. While there are ways to remediate performance issues, they do exist. The advantage of having up to the minute data is countered by the fact you are making a query with DV into the source system. One way around this is caching data, but caching costs $ for volatile (RAM) memory. Also, whether you can cache every 4 hours, or every hour, there is a tradeoff in processing that data into cache vs data availability.

5. Impact on operational systems. May impact response time; however, this can also happen without DV if users are not trained properly and the correct systems parameters set to limit rogue queries like requests for 50M rows of data.

6. To be effective, it requires a big commitment. This commitment requires the necessary investment in the technology, active sponsorship of projects using the technology, training of users as well as data literacy education, and patience. The last two pieces are critical – you must create an analytics culture – it is not simply training users in tools and this will take time.

7. Governance, change management, and systems administration may seem high, especially in the beginning when DV will shine the light on all the "bad data" and "bad processes" upstream that need to be remediated. The cost of bad data is extremely high, estimated to be $3.1 trillion per year in the US (Redman, 2016). DV can significantly reduce these costs. The business processes should also greatly improve based on the DV impact.

> The cost of bad data is extremely high, estimated to be $3.1 trillion per year!

Database Views, Materialized Views vs the Virtualized Layer

We want to prevent confusion. You may have heard of a virtualized database query or materialized views. Although similar in one regard, there are major differences between these and DV. The one way they are similar is that no physical duplication of data is made. They are different, because the database/materialized view is only using its own platform to source data, the Relational DataBase Management System itself, whereas DV can consist of hundreds of data sources outside the DV system itself.

Are You Ready for DV?

DV is one of the most promising technologies around. It has a good history and shining future, but that doesn't mean it is right for everyone. It may not be a good fit if

- You don't have the budget or need to invest in shorter term programs. The overall total cost of DV for medium and large companies is typically easily justified. However, smaller and fast-growing companies must balance the fact that the dividends DV pays are over the life cycle and not immediate. You must weigh out time horizons, cash flow, and other investments.
- Your business runs primarily on one platform and your data sources are not expanding. We would argue this is not likely or you are not seizing strategic opportunity. However, it is possible.
- Your organization is very limited in analytics knowledge. You would receive a return on investment based on the employee's contribution. Until there is sufficient cultural support and data/analytics literacy it would not be a wise choice to invest in DV. We suggest you start investing in that knowledge and recommend our first book on data and analytics literacy (Burk & Miner, 2020) and additional research on how to get started.

Summary

While DV is not a new technology, it is gaining acceptance, especially since you can integrate SaaS, data lake, and cloud data not found in the EDW. It offers many additional benefits including tighter collaboration, functional efficiency, and self-service features.

In the next chapter we cover data governance, data management, and metadata management. These topics are very important in getting the most return on investment from your data infrastructure.

References

Arbesman, S. (2013). *The Half-life of Facts: Why Everything We Know Has an Expiration Date.* Current Publishing, London.
Burk, S., & Miner, G. (2020). *It's All Analytics! The Foundations of AI, Big Data, and Data Science Landscape for Professionals in Healthcare, Business, and Government.* CRC Press, Boca Raton, FL.

Gartner Press Release, (2019, Feb 18). Gartner Identifies Top 10 Data and Analytics Technology Trends for 2019. https://www.gartner.com/en/newsroom/press-releases/2019-02-18-gartner-identifies-top-10-data-and-analytics-technolo.

Pullokkaran, L. J. (2013) Analysis of Data Virtualization & Enterprise Data Standardization in Business Intelligence, Working Paper CISL# 2013-10, Composite Information Systems Laboratory (CISL), Sloan School of Management MIT.

Redman, T. (2016, September), Bad Data Costs the U.S. $3 Trillion Per Year. *Harvard Business Review.*

van der Lans, R. F. (2012, August). *Data Virtualization for Business Intelligence Systems: Revolutionizing Data Integration for Data Warehouses.* Morgan Kaufmann, Burlington, MA.

Additional Resources

For an interesting historical account and application of DV related to BI and comparison to extract, transform, and load (ETL) and EDW, see Pullokkaran's MIT Thesis: "Analysis of Data Virtualization & Enterprise Data Standardization in Business Intelligence" https://dspace.mit.edu/handle/1721.1/90703. It offers some nice illustrations and context on how multiple pieces of the technology chain fit together.

For those interested in history and origins of ideas. Please see a seminal paper on federating data – McLeod and Heimbigner (1985). "A Federated Architecture for information management". *ACM Transactions on Information Systems*, Volume 3, Issue 3. pp. 253–278

A very good book on DV can be found in the references (van der Lans, 2012). It is more for a development or technical audience but provides a good business context at the same time.

Consider researching the following terms. We have provided brief definitions to support our intention.

Data curation involves annotation, publication, and presentation of the data such that the value of the data is maintained over time, and the data remains available for reuse and preservation.

Abstraction – Abstract the technical aspects of stored data, such as location, storage structure, API, access language, and storage technology.

Virtualized data access – Connect to different data sources and make them accessible from a common logical data access point.

Transformation – Transform, improve quality, reformat, aggregate, etc. source data for consumer use.

Data federation – Combine result sets from across multiple source systems.

Data delivery – Publish result sets as views and/or data services executed by client application or users when requested.

Semantic data layer – A semantic layer is a business representation of corporate data that helps end users access data autonomously using common business terms.

Data virtualization software may include functions for development, operation, and/or management.

Chapter 8

Data Governance and Data Management

Good Governance cannot remain merely a philosophy. Concrete steps have to be taken for realizing its goals.

Narendra Modi, Prime Minister of India

What gets measured gets managed

Peter Drucker, Father of Management Thinking, Author

Do your little bit of good where you are.

Desmond Tutu, Anglican cleric and theologian

Introduction

Data governance involves people, processes, and information technology; all these are required to create consistent and proper handling of an organization's data across the enterprise. Data management and data governance work hand-in-hand. Data is a vital asset to every organization and therefore it is critical to manage and secure it effectively.

In this chapter we lay down the foundations of data governance and provide references and resources for further study. We break the chapter into two major divisions:

DOI: 10.4324/9780429343957-10

■ the policies, procedure, and process side of data governance, and then
■ the technology that supports data governance.

If we have one takeaway we would say that a consistent, strong message from leadership on **how vital data and information are to the organization** is essential. The most successful businesses for the last 20 years are ones that have capitalized and seized opportunity from their investment of data. Moreover, **accessible, usable data is everyone's responsibility**.

The Cost of Bad Data Estimated to Be $3T

It is estimated that bad data costs $3 trillion. Yes, trillion dollars (Redman, 2016). Redman states:

> The reason bad data costs so much is that decision makers, managers, knowledge workers, data scientists, and others must accommodate it in their everyday work.

We will talk about moving data quality upstream in this chapter, but for now, consider many business processes. Departments do not work in isolation, but in a chain of departments that are interconnected. If data quality is poor in department A, then bad decisions are made there: additionally then (downstream) department B works with the same bad data and the upstream bad decisions, and makes further bad decisions. Then department C which is downstream from both departments A and B … and so forth. This is within one enterprise. You then have enterprises, private, and public interacting and the problem gets larger.

Data Governance – Policies, Procedure, and Process

Mid- to large-size organizations often have a data governance program that includes a governance team. This governance team consists of a steering committee that acts as the governing body and additionally data stewards that continually examine their incoming and stored data to make sure it complies with the governance policies. Both the steering committee and the data stewards work together to create standards and policies for governing data. It is very important to have participation from the leadership team and every business operation represented. IT should not be considered solely responsible for data governance. Everyone in the organization has a responsibility for ethics and quality in the data of that organization.

If the organization has a chief data officer (CDO) they will be the senior executive who oversees a data governance program. The CDO is responsible for the design and budget of the program and will routinely report to the board of directors on the program's status. If the organization does not have CDO, the program is typically led by another c-level executive, possibly the CIO. If the CIO is the leader, it is imperative that the program not be considered an IT program; instead it must be a corporate program.

The **data governance team** (sometimes called the data governance office) may be led by the CDO or by another executive that has some operational authority with data (director of data management, director of data quality, etc.). This data governance team is dedicated full time to data governance activities. It coordinates the process, leads meetings and training sessions, tracks metrics, manages internal communications, and carries out other management tasks.

The **data governance committee** is a separate entity that is responsible for setting policy and procedural standards. This committee is primarily made up of business executives and other data owners. The committee approves the foundational data governance policy and associated policies and rules on things like data access and usage, plus the procedures for implementing them. It also resolves disputes, such as disagreements between different business units over data definitions and formats. The data governance team often attends meetings and makes recommendations to the data governance committee but does not have a formal vote in the process.

Data stewards have the responsibility of overseeing data sources and data stores of the enterprise. These data sources include operational systems on premise, in-the-cloud, and data purchased from third-party providers. They also ensure that the policies and rules approved by the data governance committee are understood by the enterprise and followed.

Professionals with knowledge of particular data assets and domains are generally appointed to handle the data stewardship role. It might be a full-time or part-time job depending on size and industry. Stewardship works best when there are a mix of IT data stewards and business data stewards.

It should be noted that everyone in the organization should be a data steward at a fundamental, informal level. Each person is part of the organization's success and must know that useful, available data is core to the way a business operates, competes, and improves.

Who's Part of the Data Governance Program?

Figure 8.1 illustrates the importance of all roles (adapted from TechTarget, Margaret Rouse). It takes a village to be a smart data-driven organization. It all starts top leadership that includes the CDO and a highly visible and

Who's part of the program on data governance?

Data Governance Team
A data governance manager heads a program office that may also include data architects and governance specialists.

Data Governance Council or Committee
Typically made up of executives from all business units. It sets data policies and standards and resolves issues

Data Stewards
Stewards oversee data sets and are in charge of implementing governance policies and monitoring compliance with them.

Chief Data Officer
CDOs often have overall responsibility and accountability for their organization's data governance program..

Data Quality Analysts and Engineers
They work with the governance team and data stewards to fix data errors and track data quality metrics.

Figure 8.1   Who is part of the data governance program?

respected data governance team and a data governance council or commit-tee. It percolates down the organization that involves everyone, chiefly, data stewards and data quality analysts and engineers.

Data Management for Advanced Analytics Is a Team Sport

In a survey conducted by Philip Russom, Senior Director of TDWI Research for Data Management, in 2018, an interesting question comes up that applies directly to data management for advanced analytics:

The people who contribute most to the design and implementation of data management focused on analytics have job titles such as "Data Engineer", "DataOps", "Data Architects", and "Data Analysts". Additionally many other people in other job titles contribute. A snapshot of these job titles and proportion given to this task is captured in Figure 8.2. There are a number of positions involved and there are a number of "catch all" buckets in the table below. From this we think you, the reader, can determine that data management for advanced analytics is a team sport.

Goals of Data Governance

The goals of data governance are multifaceted. We have outlined a few, but let's jump into a few specifics. Again, this is not a full treatise, but we offer a framework and many jumping off points for the reader to explore more deeply.

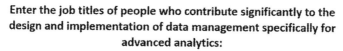

Enter the job titles of people who contribute significantly to the design and implementation of data management specifically for advanced analytics:

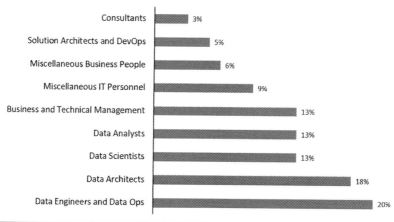

Figure 8.2 Roles supporting design and implementation for data management specifically for advanced analytics.

Let's do a simulated white board session. If we attended a whiteboard meeting, we would write down many of objectives we have heard over the years and we would gather yours. It might look something like the following.

Goals of Data Governance include:

Data integrity
Data security
Data consistency
Data confidence
Compliance of regulations and data privacy laws
Adherence to organizational ethics and standards
Risk management and data leakage
Data distribution
Value of good data
Moving data quality upstream reduces costs
Technology and structure that minimizes the cost of the DG program
Data literacy education

In our session we would discuss each in turn in an interactive dialogue. We would note that there are significant overlaps in many of these terms and initiatives. But we would probably spend most of our time brainstorming the pain points, the gaps, and begin planning the requirements for moving your data governance program forward.

Our discussion might include some of the comments for each goal, as described below. In our exchange we would interact and make sure we are all on the same page and moreover we would list whether we can achieve the objective primarily through a function that is described in policy and procedural standards. We would also be concerned about whether technology has a primary role or whether it had to be a merger of function and technology.

Data Integrity

The term data integrity is broad in scope and may have a widely different meaning depending on the specific context. Generally data integrity means the assurance of data accuracy and consistency over its entire life cycle (Boritz, 2011). We want to understand what the data means today and whether it will mean the same thing tomorrow.

This might seem simple on the surface, but sales districts change, physician networks change, and diagnostic code listings change (see ICD9 vs ICD10 in a following gray box, Diagnosis Code Changes Costs Healthcare Organization Big!). How organizations follow these changes is important. In fact, in IT there is a specific term, "Slowly Changing Dimensions" – a dimension that stores and manages both current and historical data over time in a data store. We discuss technology that can help with this in a later section of this chapter on master data management.

Data Security

Data security addresses many questions, including the following:

1. Who has access to what data?
2. What policies and procedures are in place to prevent unauthorized data access?
3. What systems are in place to prevent unauthorized data access?
4. What are the regulations across the globe that we have to adhere to control data access?
5. What are our internal processes that cover the discovery of inappropriate data access? In other words, if an organization finds out that a team member or someone outside the organization has accessed data they should not have accessed, what is the response?

This is a mixture of technology and policy. We cover technologies that support data security. But it should be noted that security needs to be handled at every level – corporately, and in each division and department, and additionally in each information system.

Data Consistency

Consistent data systems provide the same relevant information across geographical time zones, boundaries, business units, and use case. It should include integrity – the data means the same thing today as it did last year. Business rules provide the data governance across all the dimensions within an enterprise.

Data Confidence

Data confidence is broader than the accuracy, integrity, and consistency of the data. Data confidence is psychological. It is paramount. First, data is rarely 100% accurate – moreover, no one agrees to a common definition of what accuracy even means! The question should be, "Is this data accurate and consistent enough to make good decisions?" We have seen projects derailed over insignificant fractions.

Yes, data should be as accurate and precise as possible, but less than 100% does not mean you cannot make good decisions with it. Do not let zealots derail projects, make them prove the opposite case – that you cannot make a good decision based upon the data at hand.

Compliance to Regulations, Data Privacy Laws

We covered "Trustworthy AI" in an entire chapter. We will just state some of the obvious cases here and let you focus on your interest. Data privacy regulations were created for obvious reasons. Individuals did not want to suffer negative economic or social consequences based on their biology, nature, or inclinations. Privacy should mean privacy.

Two popular regulations:

HIPAA – *Health Insurance Portability and Accountability Act.* This is a US regulation for protection and privacy of an individual's healthcare information. It was initiated in 1996 and is well adopted. It was created primarily to modernize the flow of healthcare information, stipulate how personally identifiable information maintained by the healthcare and healthcare insurance industries should be protected from fraud and theft, and address limitations on healthcare insurance coverage.

GDPR – *General Data Protection Regulation.* The Europe Union (EU) is a leader in privacy and data protection. GDPR is a regulation in EU law on data protection and privacy in the EU and the European Economic Area (EEA). It also addresses the transfer of personal data outside the EU and EEA areas. The GDPR's primary aim is to give control to individuals over their personal data and to simplify the regulatory environment for international business by unifying the regulation within the EU.

Adherence to Organizational Ethics and Standards

Organizations are setting their own standards. They want to move beyond what is required. Employees are demanding organizations to be involved in privacy and ethical treatment of data. With the explosion of social media and the Internet it is paramount for organizations that have behavioral data to be aware and sensitive to access of this data. Therefore, internal standards and controls are necessary to protect it.

Risk Management of Data Leakage

This is an adjunct topic to data security and organizational standards. However, even the best security systems and policy will not keep a rogue team member from exposing organization data to the world that should be kept private. Organizations face huge fines and negative consequences to their reputation if they do not firmly control the data within their organization, have strict policy, and are willing to act severely against any infringement including prosecution to the maximum for violation.

Data Distribution

This is covered by policy and technology and is an adjunct to security. However, it is big enough to point out in a separate vein.

Access to data imports power and responsibility. Under ideal circumstances, every employee would be granted access to all corporate data allowable by law and internal policies. Data protection would be safeguarded by policy and procedure. In reality, a majority of the risk for organizations is via employee misuse of data and not external data hacks. How do you unlock the value of the data without putting yourself at risk?

Organizations have to carefully consider how to set guidelines for who is granted access to what data, when, and where. They must define and verify data distribution policies including the roles and accountabilities of involved internal and external entities. Organizations should adopt technology at every level to support these dams and filters to prevent data getting into the wrong hands.

Value of Good Data

With the "end in mind" we should garner value from data. What are the corporate and departmental objectives? They could be cost containment, revenue growth, capture market share, or maximizing profitability.

As we have said data is the new oil, but oil and data do nothing until you do something with them. They are costs to the organization. So, what is the ROI on different data types? If you can buy data (see next chapter) what are you willing to pay for it such that it provides a positive return?

How much should you spend on cleaning your data? How much on storing and maintaining old data? Organizations need to assess the value and make hard decisions about the data they source, cleanse, and keep.

Moving Data Quality Upstream Reduces Costs

Process outputs can be services, goods, products, or even data can be an output of a process. A well-founded quality paradigm is to ensure quality of the output upstream, i.e., in the early steps of the process. If quality issues are identified in earlier steps they can be corrected there, rather than being identified downstream where there is additional scrap, time, and money (see following gray box example). Data is no different. A good governance program will provide mechanisms to facilitate this practice upstream.

Cost Avoidance of Moving Quality Upstream

There are a number of interesting case studies of cost avoidance by removing defects after a product is manufactured and the results are staggering. For example:

> A study, by TRW Emeritus Professor of Software Engineering Barry Boehm, assessed that the average cost of fixing a defect increases 100 fold between the initial Design Phase of a project and the deployment

to Production. So where a defect found in that initial phase will cost $140 to fix, it will increase to $500 during Build, $1,000 during Unit Test, $2,500 during Integration Test, $4,500 during System Test, $7,000 during Operational Readiness Testing/UAT and ultimately $14,000 in Production.

Data Literacy Education

Many of the topics we have just white boarded and discussed will need developed and supported via a multitier data literacy program. In fact, the data literacy program is fundamental to every aspect we discuss in

"Poor data literacy" is the second biggest internal roadblock to success, as ranked by respondents to Gartner's CDO survey.

this chapter. We stress multitier because it is an entire educational program, a mini university offered organizational specific certifications and degrees based on business case and roles.

Technology to Support Data Management and Governance

We stated in the whiteboard session that one of the goals should be for a "Technology and Structure that Minimizes the Cost of the Data Governance Program". The enterprise must carefully consider its choices of technologies available to support the spectrum of data governance functions and activities.

There are companies that market dedicated data governance platforms. These platforms may cover some of the needs of certain organizations. However, in our experience, most organizations require several platforms across vendors to support their functions and activities. We believe it is most beneficial to the reader to outline process and technology requirements that will bring the organization forward in becoming a "data-driven" organization. As previously stated, data management goes hand-in-hand with data governance. We outline technology that supports both these activities, specifically we cover technology considerations for data management, data quality, and security.

Data Management

Ask 100 people what data management means and you are likely to get 100 answers. According to DATAVERSITY (dataversity.net)

Data Management is a comprehensive collection of practices, concepts, procedures, processes, and a wide range of accompanying systems that allow for an organization to gain control of its data resources. Data Management as an overall practice is involved with the entire lifecycle of a given data asset from its original creation point to its final retirement, how it progresses and changes throughout its lifetime through the internal (and external) data streams of an enterprise.

We have already covered some of what is encapsulated by this definition. What we have not covered is metadata (*data about data*) management or specifically reference data management and master data management. These are extremely useful technologies that are available and should be considered by any data governance program.

Master data, along with reference data and metadata, is a key organizational data asset. While far more complex definitions for master data can be found on the Internet, to simplify, master data are the entities that drive business processes, are evaluated by analytics, and are controlled through governance processes.

Master Data

A simple example of master data in a business process would be the data that represents a business transaction. When a customer buys a product at a store location, we have at least three tables of master data. As an example, the product has an ID (SKU) that is part of a large product master. This product master is a part of a hierarchy (men's clothing -> shirts -> long sleeve -> button collar, etc.). There are hierarchies for location and possibly customers as well. This data changes across time so the organization can find that the management of all the relationships can become complex very quickly.

We covered this above, in the data integrity whiteboard session when we mentioned "Slowly Changing Dimensions". You need the ability to track and manage all the metadata that changes over time.

From an analytical standpoint, how do you view sales across locations, product groups, and customer designations? You cannot create reports, dashboards, and predictive models without relevant and consistent master data. From a regulatory standpoint or governance perspective, master data allows you to implement and enforce controls. As a simple example take accounting: rules like generally accepted accounting principles must be followed.

Reference Data

Reference data is another form of metadata that is sometimes equated with master data. However, it is a newer and separate data form. Reference data management is about managing classifications and hierarchies across systems and business lines. For effective reference data management, companies must set policies, frameworks, and standards to govern and manage both internal and external reference data. Platforms are available to manage all these structures.

Some examples of reference data are country codes, units of measure, currencies, time zones, industry classifications, legal entities, charts of accounts, and conversion rates. Most often there are dependencies within these classification systems. As organizations grow and time evolves reference data is extremely important to analytics supporting the business: acquisitions, mergers, sales, and organizational changes. Reference data is constantly evolving; good reference data management allows for consistent analytics across time.

Diagnosis Code Changes Costs Healthcare Organization Big!

The US healthcare uses a system of medical coding for diagnosis called International Classification of Diseases (ICD). Prior to October 2015 the version was called ICD-9 with approximately 13K diagnosis codes. ICD-10 was mandated by the US Center of Medicare and Medicaid Services (CMS) with over 70K diagnosis codes. This represents a case study of the difficulty of changing reference data across time periods as well as geographic zones. Unless you have a good reference data management policy and technology platform that can handle the translation across these dimensions, all forms of data analysis and analytics have to be scrapped and new ones implemented for the new classification system.

Data Quality

The authors have been involved with analytics for decades. Data quality was a problem when we started and it still remains a problem today. It can be introduced anywhere along the chain of business processes and once it gets introduced it normally persists. For commercial businesses it is difficult to remediate some of these issues. For local, state, and federal governments remediation can be much more difficult. Add the inter-exchange that many organizations have with other organizations and it just gets extremely difficult.

Cleaning Data: Most Time-Consuming, Least Enjoyable Data Science Task, Survey Says

According to Gil Press for *Forbes*, a 2016 survey conducted of data scientists found:

Data scientists found that they spend most of their time massaging rather than mining or modeling data (often stated by many analysts as taking 90% of the time in an analytics project).

Seventy-six percent of data scientists view data preparation as the least enjoyable part of their work

So, not only does dirty data cost organizations $3T, it also leads to job dissatisfaction!

One thing that organizations can do to alleviate data quality issues is planning and process. The default answer for what data organizations want to track and store is "keep everything". It is like a household the more you keep the messier things are going to get and the more difficult the cleaning efforts are going to perpetually be. It is the nature of entropy.

Another planning and process step falls to the internal procedures you will adopt to facilitate moving data quality issues upstream. These are work processes assisted with technology. Your data needs to be easily tagged in any system and annotated. The technology should allow collaboration between users identifying problems and system administrators with oversight responsibilities. Convenient messaging with annotated data should be communicated between these parties as well as the data stewards.

There are other technologies that can assist with improving and maintaining your data quality. However, in the end, data quality is not one omnibus system that does all the cleaning, even if it has a master data catalog with great workflow mechanisms and data versioning. From a technical standpoint you need the ability to remediate data at any and every point in the enterprise. You will then need technology that is plugged into your governance system and that can communicate with the data stewards.

Security

No one needs to be told how big an issue data security is for modern enterprises. From small to the largest businesses, from public to private organizations, securing your data is paramount. Good policy and procedure are important as we mentioned in section one of this chapter.

Controls to safeguard your data should be done at every level. However, you do not want users to have to have individual credentials to each and every system. Most employees have access to dozens of systems. There are technologies to assist with this. We list a couple in the "Additional Resources" section.

Most commercial databases can be locked down by row and by column for both "work function/role" and by named user. We spoke to the powerful security features that are available in Chapter 7.

IT usually takes the lead with system security. When IT plans systems for "anything data", including data security, they should include the data governance committee and data stewards.

Summary

No organization of any size can compete or be run effectively today without a solid data strategy. Data governance is the glue that binds the second most important asset of the enterprise; the first being the people involved.

Data governance is not just a technology platform. It is planning, strategy, and controls around data and the people that interact with that data. It is about ensuring that not only all the investment that has been made to source, transform, and store that information and make it available is recouped, but the organization actually makes a return on that investment.

This is data monetization. We will speak briefly about this in the next chapter as well as in Part 3, Design Considerations for Analytics Architecture.

References

Boritz, J. (2011). IS practitioners' views on core concepts of information integrity. *International Journal of Accounting Information Systems*, 6(4), 260–279. Elsevier.
Redman, T. (2016). Bad Data Costs the U.S. $3 Trillion Per Year. *Harvard Business Review*.

Additional Resources

There are great articles on the TechTarget Website (techtarget.com) relating to data governance and data management. Per the author's experience, TechTarget is a reliable source of high-quality information. Margaret Rouse does a great job on writing on the subjects in this chapter.

TWDI is another great, high-quality, vetted reference for articles and even training – https://tdwi.org/Home.aspx. As they say on their website – "25 Years of Leading Research and Education for Data and Analytics".

Some Terms Related to This Chapter to Consider Exploring

Master Data Management, Metadata Management, Reference Data Management, Data Quality Management, Data Retention/Archiving, Data Privacy/Security, Data Architecture, Data Strategy, Data Management, Governance, Stewardship, Data Policy, Slowly Changing Dimensions, CDO, CTO.
Two interesting articles relating to the CDO:

1. Experian (2019). The Chief Data Officer, Powering business opportunities with data. https://www.edq.com/resources/data-management-whitepapers/the-chief-data-officer-powering-business-opportunities-with-data/.
2. Dobinson, C. & Williams, H. (2019, November 21). What is the difference between a CIO and CDO? https://www.cio.co.uk/it-leadership/cio-cdo-differences-3644709/.

Data Quality Resource

Larry English was considered by many to be "The Father of Data Quality". He wrote books and offered conferences for tens of thousands. He founded the TIQM (total information quality management) movement. We recommend his book:

English, L. P. (2009, October). *Information Quality Applied: Best Practices for Improving Business Information, Processes and Systems*, 1st Edition. Wiley Publishing.

Chapter 9

Miscellanea – Curated, Purchased, Nascent, and Future Data

If we have data, let's look at data. If all we have are opinions, let's go with mine.

Jim Barksdale, CEO Netscape

Data is the New Bacon!

Anonymous

Introduction

We have discussed a great deal in the last few chapters, Part 2 Overview, Data Design for Success. We want to end this part with a few parting thoughts, some important terms the reader may encounter, and a look toward the future of data.

Data strategy is one of the three pillars of a successful AI and analytics program. Your analytics strategy builds upon your data strategy. So if you get the data wrong, even the brightest people, the most efficient processes, and the greatest analytics technology cannot make up the gap. It is crucial to get the data strategy correct.

DOI: 10.4324/9780429343957-11

Part of that strategy will likely include *supplementing* your internal data. This would most likely be purchasing data in some fashion from a broker or an exchange. It is important to consider these costs into your soft ROI or hard ROI calculations when you assess the value of your analytics programs.

Another part of data strategy is *monetizing* your own data. This could be done in several ways including outright selling of your data to an exchange or monetizing in other ways. We offer some brief comments on this topic in this chapter.

We want to make sure that we explain that it is extremely important to be constantly preparing for tomorrow.

> Every organization will face new problems, face new problems and generate new data. Successful ones have a strategy in hand to source new pipelines for the data.

Finally, data is constantly evolving. The adoption of new technologies to analyze various types of data is evolving. We offer a few trends and things to look out for.

Zero-Party Data; A Gift from Customers

Forrester Research's definition of zero-party data – "Zero-party data is that which a customer intentionally and proactively shares with a brand. It can include preference center data, purchase intentions, personal context, and how the individual wants the brand to recognize [them]".

Forrester's Fatemeh Khatibloo, VP principal analyst, notes that zero-party data "is gold. … When a customer trusts a brand enough to provide this really meaningful data, it means that the brand doesn't have to go off and infer what the customer wants or what [their] intentions are".

Data Outside Your Organization

In the last several chapters we have been discussing ways to acquire data within your organization; ways to use it internally for your organization. We now focus on the idea of supplementing your data with sources outside your organization. Why would you consider data outside information? We offer two considerations:

■ supplemental data and
■ meaningful data.

Supplemental Data

Companies could often use data that is outside their ability to source themselves. For example, retailers would like information about customer discretionary spending habits and behaviors they cannot collect in their internal operations. The retailer only collects the customer transactions but would like more information on their customers so that they can target offers and advertisements more successfully. This data is sometimes available for purchase through outside marketing companies. The company can merge this outside data with its internal data to make better decisions and take more effective actions.

Meaningful Data

Most organizations collect lots of data. In fact, they collect far more than they ever use because a lot collected is not the right data or the data is not meaningful. We offer three things to consider to get you thinking about rich and meaningful data to support your analytics program. Do you have:

1. **The right data for the right job?** The historical data you have within your organization may not be *rich* enough for a particular business case. For example, your business objective is to predict a rare event within your organization. Fraud is a great example of a rare event. Fraud is a major concern for many companies. Any financial transaction in a public or private enterprise can fall victim to fraud. It can be very expensive (CMS, Center for Medicare and Medicaid, estimated in 2019 that Medicaid alone reached $60B for improper payments). Fraud perpetrators may garner a large payout with a single case or amass large dollar amounts over a long period of time with numerous cases. But, fraud doesn't happen often when considering millions of transactions. So training predictive models is difficult. You can oversample and do other statistical things to remedy the lack of "hits", but nothing beats good data to train a model; cases like this is where companies should consider paying for data. Strategic decisions, new product lines, and new territories where your company does not have data are additional examples where you may want to purchase outside data.
2. **Clean Data?** We spoke about data in the last chapter, "Data Governance and Data Management"; we also spoke to data quality and cleaning or

remediating data. Nevertheless, there are times when your data is too messy for an important project. You are lacking time, knowledge, or tools to get it prepared to meet a deadline. This is a time to carefully consider purchasing outside data.

3. **Unbiased data?** We discussed trustworthy AI in Chapter 3. For now, it is important to know that bias pervades any organization in many ways, and thus will also manifest itself in your data. We have spoken over and over about the fact that processes generate data. Processes often reflect the way things are and not the way things should be and result in that bias. AI is very good at training specifically to the data. Examine your data carefully, especially paying special attention to under and overrepresentation in variable categories. If your data is not providing the right signal you should consider purchasing data from an external source.

A Data Review – Part of Data Strategy

As we stated in the beginning of Part II, organizations collect far more data than they ever use, we referred to this as "dark data", in the introduction (Chapter 4).

> And maybe only 15%–30% of data collected is ever used (see Priceonomics, 2019; Barrett, 2018); it sits there and does nothing (it is called "Dark Data"). So, it is only when your action is based on data that you gain value from it; therefore – It's about the analytics and *It's All Analytics!*

An effective data strategy will include a governance policy and periodic reviews of data architecture and what data is being retained. "Keep it all, forever" is not an effective data strategy. The most effective data strategies limit both data collection and data retention.

Data for Free

There are a number of sources where organizations can acquire free data. Healthcare data is often made available by federal and state agencies. Some free data can be downloaded in batch files, normally formatted in comma-separated values (*.csv). Other data can be accessed via an API as we discussed in Chapter 5. We outline a few sources here as examples.

Publically Available Data

There are terabytes of government data available and more is coming everyday as the government opens up in the name of transparency. However, while there are vast amounts of data available from the government, the usefulness of this data is often limited. As an example, there are volumes of data available from the Centers of Medicare and Medicaid, but it is mostly payment data with limited sets of variables, so its uses are very limited for improving healthcare. This data is typically available for download only, no APIs. Some example sites:

https://www.medicare.gov/download/downloaddb.asp
https://developer.cms.gov/data-medicare/
https://data.cms.gov/provider-data/?redirect=true

States are following the federal governments lead to open up data for citizens and researchers. The state of Texas has a "Texas Open Data Portal" that offers information from state permits and licensing, business and economy, government and taxes, social services, and much more (https://data.texas.gov/).

The FDA has downloadable datasets as well as APIs available (https://open.fda.gov/). It is widely used, with millions of downloads and API calls. For the 30 days prior to 1/16/2021 there were over 7.5 million API calls made for data. The graph in Figure 9.1 was adapted from the FDA website and illustrates the quantities of these downloads.

Data Available from Commercial Entities and Universities

Most commercial providers of free data offer it in a *freemium* version. Meaning they offer a limited selection or limited volume for free, or they might provide researchers and organizations using data for public good (usually non-profit foundations) free data. These are sometimes referred to as freemium pricing models. Freemium (a portmanteau of the words "free" and "premium") is a strategy where a basic product or service is provided free of charge, but if a consumer wants additional features or services there is a fee.

Data provided by these organizations have data for download like government entities, but often offer APIs for data access as well. An example of

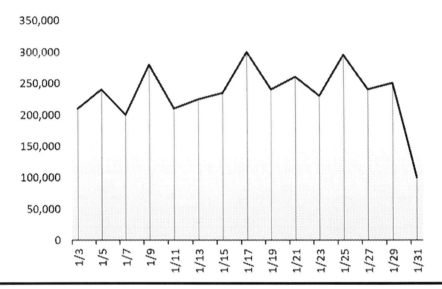

Figure 9.1   openFDA API calls in the past 30 days.

a freemium service with data available for easy access is *data.world*. This company offers a rich set of getting started data sets for people interested in learning and applying AI and analytic methods to real world data. The data can be downloaded in a couple of clicks. They even categorize the data for consumers (https://data.world/datasets/free). Note, you will see that several of these data sets come from public sources, like the City of Austin, Texas, and universities, that you could access from other sites.

There are several universities that offer data sets. One of the earliest providers that provided data specifically for machine learning was the University of California at Irvine, UCI. They have offered their Machine Learning Repository (https://archive.ics.uci.edu/ml/index.php) for years:

> The archive was created as an ftp archive in 1987 by David Aha and fellow graduate students at UC Irvine. Since that time, it has been widely used by students, educators, and researchers all over the world as a primary source of machine learning data sets, as an indication of the impact of the archive.

The data on the site is downloadable. It offers a great resource for developing data and analytics skills as well as prototyping solutions.

DATA FOR GOOD

There are major corporate initiatives underway to improve society. There are various names for this shared value, corporate social responsibility, or data for good. One interesting project is *Data USA*, a collaboration between Deloitte, Datawheel, and MIT professor, Cesar Hidalgo.

MISSION

"Data USA provides an open, easy-to-use platform that turns data into knowledge. It allows millions of people to conduct their own analyses and create their own stories about America – its people, places, industries, skill sets and educational institutions".

BEGINNING

In 2014, Deloitte, Datawheel, and Cesar Hidalgo, Professor at the MIT Media Lab and Director of Collective Learning, came together to embark on an ambitious journey – to understand and visualize the critical issues facing the United States in areas like jobs, skills and education across industry and geography. And, to use this knowledge to inform decision making among executives, policymakers and citizens.

CAVEAT

It is possible with any data aggregator to create bias by commission and omission. This can be done with intent or without intent. Aggregators select data sources – thus by commission they determine what to include and by omission determine what not to include – based on access constraints, content, or other criteria.

Data for Sale

Data for sales is a hot topic! The global data monetization market size is expected to reach USD 7.34 billion by 2027, registering a CAGR (compound annual growth rate) of 24.1% from 2020 to 2027, according to a study conducted by Grand View Research, Inc.

Buying data is important for two reasons. First, you may be buying data already, and if so you are in good company. Or, as your organization matures, there will be projects when you want to invest in data. Either now or down the road, it is very likely you will be investing in data.

Second, you may be monetizing your data or considering ways to monetize your data. One way to monetize is to sell it wholesale, outright. Alternatively, you can use AI and analytics to enhance your data and sell it at a premium.

Traditionally, a data supplier is a data broker, data syndicator, or open data provider. But increasingly, it is any company that wants to share or sell its own data. A data consumer is any individual or company that wants to collect or purchase data.

There is significant overlap of data brokers, exchanges, and marketplaces. We expand a bit in this section allowing the reader to dive in deeper where they deem fit.

Data Syndicators

Data syndication dates back to television syndication and tracking of consumer behavior. While syndicated data is used by many industries, it is most commonly affiliated with the consumer packaged goods and related industries. Syndicated data is an aggregated collection of product retail sales activity across a chosen set of parameters. It's often compared to retail direct data, but it has the potential to track industry trends along product categories and geographic markets.

Data is typically provided in a more direct or raw format such as store data that gathers product information – syndicated store data. This data is sometimes lacking in quality. It is also available in a more intelligent form – syndicated panel data that tracks consumer behavior such as consumer demographics, brand loyalty, store loyalty, purchase frequency, and any number of conceivably useful shopping preferences.

Data Brokers

According to the Federal Trade Commission (Ramirez et al., 2014), a data broker is defined:

> Data brokers—companies that collect consumers' personal information and resell or share that information with others—are important participants in this Big Data economy.

There are more nefarious interpretations of what data brokers do. Big tech and social media companies have received a great deal of attention and scrutiny for spying, selling, and biasing data results. Several of the largest companies have appeared several times in recent years before congress to testify how they are using data they acquire. In fact an apt quote that applies:

> If you're not paying for the product, you are the product.

Data brokers can collect data from individuals' behavior across websites, where they visit, what they post, who they interact with, and more, and/or they can also aggregate data from public records and private sources, including census and change of address records, motor vehicle and driving records, voter registration lists, and web browsing histories.

Data Exchange and Data Exchange Platforms

Data exchange is the process of taking data structured under a source schema and transforming it into data structured under a target schema, so that the target data is an accurate representation of the source data. Data exchange allows data to be shared between different computer programs (Doan, 2012).

A data exchange platform is used to describe a place for buying and selling third-party data. Data acquirers and data providers need a secure and compliant environment to both leverage the potential of their data and meet the provider that will best answer their data needs. The major cloud-based providers offer data exchange platforms. These platforms make it easy to find, subscribe to, and use third-party data in the cloud.

Data Marketplaces

In the past 5 years, dozens of data companies have launched data marketplaces serving every industry, functional area, and role with a diversity of data sets in every conceivable format.

The biggest potential data marketplace players are cloud platform vendors.

A data marketplace is a public data exchange open to any company that wants to supply or consume data. They can span every industry or very specific, even niche industries – boutique data marketplaces.

Data consumers that have used market places may have had bad experiences with third-party data. Modern data exchanges have to overcome this unfortunate legacy by providing data integrity, quality, and consistency. Unless data consumers trust the data available they will not engage.

Should You Monetize Your Data?

We have said, possibly too often, that if you are not using your data you are spending needless money collecting data. The only way to make sense of the investment of collecting, storing, and securing your data is to use it. The most obvious way to justify these expenses is to use the data in your internal processes and programs: using AI and analytics to improve your processes and execute strategic initiatives.

Additionally, you can sell your data either outright or via a data exchange, thus creating new revenue streams for your organization. This is sometimes referred to as "direct monetization", or you could monetize your data by adding value to it and then selling it. By applying analytics to your data, you create more value and can garner a higher return. This is sometimes referred to as "indirect monetization".

Should Citizens Be Paid for Their Data?

CNBC reported on 2/12/19

- Gov. Gavin Newsom proposes "a new data dividend" that could allow California consumers to get paid for their digital data.
- Some tech experts have suggested that companies like Facebook and Google should pay consumers for their information.

"California's consumers should also be able to share in the wealth that is created from their data", Newsom said from the State Capitol in Sacramento. The governor said tech companies that "make billions of dollars collecting, curating and monetizing our personal data have a duty to protect it".

Future Data

Future data takes two forms. The first is based on technology and innovation – we describe that in the next paragraph. The second is internal to your organization – what projects will you be supporting with data in 2, 3, and 5 years? You have to be well ahead of the curve. It is part of your *data strategy*. You need to be thinking about what data you will need in the future so you can support it with new technology or new collection methods.

Keep an Eye Out for Nascent Technologies and Trends in Applications of Analytics

We want the reader to know there are evolving technologies and new data types to support new analytic methods. At the same time, some data types and technologies that have been around for a while have seen a meteoric rise in application. We outline three here and encourage the reader to continually keep an eye on changes in the data landscape and track it over time so that you can discern the hype from reality. These three data technologies are not new but are growing rapidly. Something to keep an eye on and consider investing in; these three (Geographic Information System (GIS) and Geo Analytics; Graph Databases; and Time Series Databases) are discussed in further detail below:

GIS and Geo Analytics

Geo analytics is nothing new. However, the use of this data has been consistently growing for several years, and the growth is not slowing. Geo mapping data has improved and the data itself may be reaching a greater maturity level. However, applications of this data is still growing. AI and analytics models are being deployed to new sets of problems that are spatially related. Furthermore, the use and consumption of predictive models overlaid on top of geo data. This makes the models much more intuitive and meaningful.

> Specialized data science programs in GIS, geospatial, and related data are becoming popular. Several top US schools are offering programs with a Master of Science in Spatial Data Science.

Additionally, maps of facilities, machines, and even products are being used in predictive analytics. As an example, in the semiconductor industry, maps of wafers are being constructed and then AI algorithms are applied to see if defects are being systematically produced based on the same locations of the wafer maps.

Graph Databases

We briefly mentioned graph databases in Chapter 6. Graph databases show relationships between entities. A graph is composed of two elements: a node and a relationship. Each node represents an entity (a person, place, thing, category, or other piece of data) and each relationship represents how two nodes are associated. This general-purpose structure allows you to model all kinds of scenarios – from a system of roads, to a network of devices, to a population's medical history, or anything else defined by relationships.

Graph databases excel for apps that explore many-to-many relationships, such as social networking, fraud detection, contract tracing, recommendation, and personalization systems. These systems use graph structures for semantic queries with nodes, edges, and properties to represent and store data. Most of the value of graph databases is derived from these relationships.

Time Series Databases

A time series is a sequence of numerical data points in successive order. Time series databases (TSDBs) make it possible to efficiently and continuously add, process, and track massive quantities of real-time data with lightning speed and precision. While you can store time series data in a relational database or even flat files, TSDBs utilize specific algorithms and architecture to deal with their unique needs. TSDBs have been outpacing all other database models by a wide margin over the past 2 years.

TSDB systems have been a multibillion-dollar business for years and a mainstay in process-manufacturing plants since the 1980s.

So why are they outpacing all other database models now?

Primarily because, time series data volumes are huge. Back in 2010 manufacturing companies were generating 1,800 petabytes of data per year (twice as many as the next closest vertical, government) and much of that was time series data. Manufacturing data volumes have only continued to grow in recent years thanks to new Internet of Things and Industrial Internet of Things deployments.

Today Is the Time to Start Collecting Data for the Future

As the adage goes, the best time to plant a tree was 30 years ago. And the best time to start collecting the data you will need in 5 years is today. Suppose an interesting project is presented at a company meeting. Will you have the data to support the initiative? If it is forward looking or strategic, likely not. That is why part of your data strategy must be forward thinking and strategic in nature.

Your Data Strategy must be Aligned with your Corporate Strategy! Design and Align!

What questions would you like to answer in the future?

As part of your data infrastructure and analytics programs you should be constantly asking that question. There are often questions you would like to answer, but you just don't have the data available internally or for purchase externally. It can take months or years to collect enough data for AI training models. You should constantly be thinking forward about what questions you want to answer and what data you will need to answer these questions.

Data Strategy and Data Paradigms

There are many, in fact very many new terms popping up on the data landscape. It is confusing and in our estimation this is going to get worse – from data hubs, data lakes, data lakehouses, data fabrics, data as a service, data concierges, and much more. There are tons of architectural diagrams that outline some differences in the technologies. The hope is that a "mature" data architecture that covers all the needs of the organization will emerge. We don't know of any companies that have been successful in a monolithic platform for all their data needs. In fact, with respect to data fabrics, even Gartner states

> No existing stand-alone product contains all the capabilities needed to fully implement a data fabric architecture. As a result, data and analytics technical professionals will have to stitch together a data fabric using multiple solutions (Build) or examine data management solutions that deliver parts of the data fabric promise, knowing that some elements will be missing (Buy).

As an example of confusing definitions, consider a contrast of a top-rated analyst firm, International Data Corporation (IDC) who defines Data as a Service (DaaS) as:

> data delivery and access services that result in the trade in machine readable data. This data can include raw data or value-added information derived from the raw data and/or from aggregated third-party data. The requirement for machine readability expressly excludes long-form text, pictures or photos, video, and sheet

music or musical performances. However, IDC's definition of DaaS includes metadata from human consumable content such as books, magazines, newspapers, movies, TV, and recorded music but not that content itself.

Contrast that to Wikipedia that defines it as:

> In computing, data as a service, or DaaS, is enabled by software as a service (SaaS). Like all "as a service" (aaS) technology, DaaS builds on the concept that its data product can be provided to the user on demand, regardless of geographic or organizational separation between provider and consumer. Service-oriented architecture (SOA), and the widespread use of API, has rendered the platform on which the data resides as irrelevant. DaaS began primarily in Web mashups and, since 2015, has been increasingly employed both commercially, and within organizations such as the United Nations.

Confused? We are too.

Summary

You will hear a great deal of data hype and the promise of technologies that solve all data problems in the enterprise. Whether it is data fabric or data hub or DaaS we do not believe there is a single platform that can provide all your data needs. You need to carefully architect your data technology around a carefully planned, cogent data strategy. You need to provide process and controls, i.e., governance, to secure and sustain these investments. If you do, you can drive a high return on your data investments.

References

Barrett, J. (2018, April). Up to 73 Percent of Company Data Goes Unused for Analytics. Here's How to Put It to Work. https://www.inc.com/jeff-barrett/misusing-data-could-be-costing-your-business-heres-how.html.

Doan, A., Halevy, A., & Ives, Z. G. (2012). *Principles of Data Integration*. Elsevier/Morgan Kaufmann, Burlington, MA.

Priceonomics (2019, Aug). Companies collect a lot of data but how much do they actually use? https://priceonomics.com/companies-collect-a-lot-of-data-but-how-much-do/.

Ramirez, E., Brill, J., Ohlhausen, M. K., Wright, J. D., & McSweeny, T. (2014). Data brokers a call for transparency and accountability. Federal Trade Commission, May 2014.

Additional Resources

Curated Data is a very hot topic. Here is an introductory resource: Data Curation 101: The What, Why, and How by Dataversity (Nov 2017, https://www.dataversity.net/data-curation-101/)

Terms related to this chapter – Zero-party data, Curated Data, Data Profiling, Data bias, Selection bias, Supplemental Data, Marketplaces, Data Monetization, Private Data Exchange, Syndicated Data, Open Data Provider Synthetic Data, Data Exchange, Data Exchange Platforms, Data Brokers, Geographic Information Systems, GIS, geo analytics, Graph Data(bases), Time Series Data(bases), TSDB, DataOps.

What Is DataOps?

DataOps is an automated, process-oriented methodology, used by analytic and data teams, to improve the quality and reduce the cycle time of data analytics. While DataOps began as a set of best practices, it has now matured to become a new and independent approach to data analytics.

DESIGNING FOR
ANALYTICS SUCCESS

Chapter 10

Technology to Create Analytics

In God we trust, all others must bring data.

W. Edwards Deming

Introduction

In previous chapters, we examined the importance of business strategy, culture, and digital decisions. To briefly recap, before beginning any data or analytics initiative, it is important to have a clear business strategy, strategic priorities, and have objectives and key results defined. Then, one needs to align the entire organization to support those objectives by establishing an analytics center of excellence (CoE) and staffing the CoE. Once the organization is aligned to support the program and cross-functional teams are assembled, one can then focus on automating digital decisions.

Prior to automating digital decisions, having a clear, well-defined understanding of the business decision to be made is probably the single most important factor for the business. For example, business decisions could include – "should we offer a mortgage to this individual?", "what is the next-best offer that we can present to an individual given his or her past purchase history and digital habits?", "what discount should we offer to this person?", or "how many and which medical staff do we need in the healthcare facility next week?" Once we understand the business decision to be made, the team needs to understand how data and analytics can be used to improve that decision whether it be in terms of speed, accuracy, optimization, simulation, or prediction. After we understand how analytics can help improve or accelerate the decision making process, it is paramount to understand how the organization's actions and behaviors will change as a result of the digital business decision. If using data and analytics to make a digital decision doesn't change the actions and behaviors of the business, then it may be necessary to step back and rethink the process. After all, we are attempting to use data and analytics to optimize outcomes and make the best decisions possible. If the organization doesn't respond to the analytic output with a change in behavior, why bother?

After the team considers how the business will change its behavior as a result of the digital decision, they will need to consider the architecture that is required to support that business decision.

Figure 10.1 outlines the steps required before beginning any analytics project.

Analytics Maturity

As organizations begin their analytics initiatives, there are several different types of analytics that they may employ. Broadly, they are categorized as follows (Table 10.1).

Now that we understand the various types of analytics an organization may employ, let's take a look at an analytics maturity model. There are several different maturity models available, but one of the most popular comes from competing on analytics (Davenport & Harris, 2017) which is illustrated in Figure 10.2.

In the maturity model (Figure 10.2), the y-axis denotes the relative competitive advantage an organization may achieve by deploying the different categories of analytics – progressing from reactive to prescriptive analytics.

Greater competitive advantage may be achieved as one moves up the *y*-axis. The *x*-axis illustrates the broad categories of analytic techniques associated with the analytic types. Reactive analytics are similar to looking in a rear-view mirror of an automobile; these typically include summary statistics and ad-hoc reports. The degree of sophistication, complexity, and automation increases as one moves from left to right on the *x*-axis.

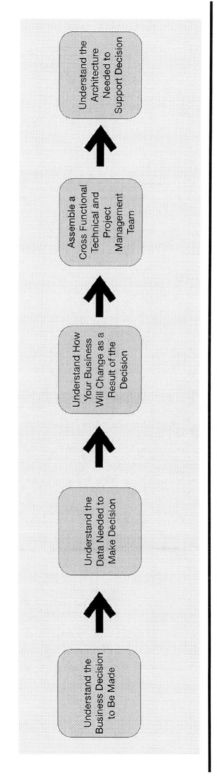

Figure 10.1 Steps required for business understanding for analytics projects.

Table 10.1 Analytic Types, Questions, and Methods

Analytic Type	Questions Answered	Example Use Case	Analytic Methods
Descriptive	What happened?	How many patients were in the hospital yesterday? What were our sales for the past week? How many widgets did the factory produce last month?	Aggregations, Summary Statistics, Reports, Dashboards
Diagnostic	Why did it happen?	What caused the increase in number of patients compared to last week? Why did our sales increase from the previous week? What were the top ten defect types that prevented us from producing the widgets according to our target?	Aggregations, Summary Statistics, Paretos, Root Cause Analysis, Statistical Process Control
Predictive	What will happen?	What is the probability that the anomaly on the CT scan is a tumor? Taking into account seasonality, what do we think our same store sales will be during the holiday season? When do we think the equipment is going to fail?	Data Mining, Predictive Analytics, Forecasting, Machine Learning, Clustering, Text Analytics, Video Analytics, Audio Analytics
Prescriptive	What should I do?	Given the forecast, we recommend increasing/decreasing staffing levels Based on our predictions, we recommend shipping more of a certain product to prevent a stockout Based on our prediction, we recommend performing maintenance on the equipment before it breaks down and causes a line disruption	Data Mining, Predictive Analytics, Forecasting, Machine Learning, Clustering, Text Analytics, Video Analytics, Audio Analytics, Business Rules, Optimization, Simulation

HOT SPOTTING IN HEALTHCARE, DOES IT REALLY WORK?

In 2011, *The New Yorker* featured an article discussing the notion of hot spotting (Atul Gawande, 2017) in healthcare. The article claimed that 1% of the patients in Camden, NJ, accounted for 30% of the hospital costs. Dr. Jeremy Brenner compiled data from the three main hospitals in Camden. As he began to analyze the data, he noticed that certain locations within the city accounted for more emergency room visits than others. As an example, Brenner's analysis highlighted the fact that there was one specific building that accounted for three million dollars in healthcare bills from serious falls. The article noted the following:

> The two most expensive city blocks were in north Camden, one that had a large nursing home called Abigail House and one that had a low-income housing tower called Northgate II. He found that between January of 2002 and June of 2008 some nine hundred people in the two buildings accounted for more than four thousand hospital visits and about two hundred million dollars in health-care bills. One patient had three hundred and twenty-four admissions in five years. The most expensive patient cost insurers $3.5 million.

Armed with this data, Brenner eventually assembled a cross-functional team of doctors, healthcare experts, and social workers. The primary goal of this team was to create mitigation and intervention strategies to help the people with the most need. Helping people was the primary motivation, but if the interventions were successful, they would also result in lower healthcare costs. The initial results were quite promising. In 2009, Brenner's program reduced hospital costs by 56% (approximately $1.2 million per month to $672,000 for the targeted group). This program has been widely touted as a model for other cities to follow. But does it really work?

In January of 2020, the *New England Journal of Medicine* released the results of a randomized, controlled trial of healthcare hot spotting (Finkelstein et al., 2020). After tracking 800 patients within the study, they concluded the following:

In this randomized, controlled trial involving patients with very high use of health care services, readmission rates were not lower among patients randomly assigned to the Coalition's program than among those who received usual care.

The study authors mention that this was a very localized study and that more research needs to be conducted in this area. The point worth mentioning is that even though the hot spotting has been in use for over a decade with programs being replicated around the world, the current research suggests that it may not be as effective as initially thought.

Not only is hot spotting popular in healthcare, we see other examples including:

■ Predictive policing
■ Prioritizing and identifying buildings that need inspection with constrained resources
■ Prioritizing and identifying restaurants that may fail health code violations
■ Epidemiological monitoring of disease outbreaks to deploy healthcare workers

One of the core elements across all of these examples are the use of data, analytics, and geographic information systems for spatial analysis.

One of the falsely drawn conclusions of Figure 10.2 is that one must progress up the maturity curve in a stepwise manner similar to ascending a staircase. In other words, many organizations originally interpreted this to mean that they needed comprehensive reporting and dashboards before we can use predictive analytics, forecasts, or optimizations. However, this isn't necessarily the case. We have seen many organizations use various combinations of these different elements without fully exhausting all of the opportunities for an analytics category that is lower on the maturity scale. The key, as previously mentioned, is to understand the business decision to be made (and ensure it is in alignment with corporate strategic goals) and map the analytics functionality that needs to be in place to support the decision process.

Additionally, when assessing an organization's analytic maturity, there are also a few other elements to consider that are beyond the technology realm. Namely,

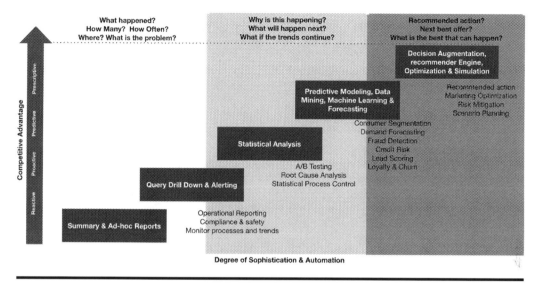

Figure 10.2 Analytic maturity model.

- Organizational commitment
  - Does the organization treat data as a critical business asset?
  - Is analytics considered a core strategic business process?
  - Is there an executive sponsor and champion assigned to the projects?
- Data literacy
  - What is the level of analytic and data literacy within the organization?
  - Are there training and upskilling programs in place?
  - What percentage of the population has access to dashboards and reports to analyze data?
- Data foundation
  - Is there a solid foundation of data and a continuous data quality improvement program in place?
  - Does the organization trust the data and analytic results generated from the data?
  - Usage and span
  - How broadly and often are analytics being used to make everyday decisions?
  - Are the results trusted by the organization or are they often overridden by intuition or "gut feel"?

WHAT IS DATA LITERACY?

According to former Gartner Analyst and CEO & Founder of The Data Lodge, Valerie Logan defines a data literacy as the following (Logan, 2020):

> *Data Literacy:*
> *The ability to read, write and communicate with data in context - in both work and life.*
>
> *Including an appropriate level of understanding of: (vocabulary):*
> *- data terms and concepts*
> *- analysis methods and concepts*
> *- value drives, outcomes and actions*
>
> *combined with the ability to: (skills):*
> *- think critically*
> *- engage with others collaboratively*
> *- and apply data constructively"*

Additionally, Logan defines any good data literacy program as "an intentional commitment to upskilling the workforce and culture (Logan, 2020)".

As with anything, when beginning any initiative, it is useful to think of things through the lens of people, process, and technology. Before diving into the architectural components which will be discussed in the upcoming section ("Analytics Architectural Components"), there are a few items to consider as it relates to the data science and machine learning (ML) process that will influence the final implementation of the architectures. We present these considerations for data science practitioners to consider in the next section.

Architectural Considerations for the Data Scientist

Now that we have an understanding of data and analytic maturity levels and models, let's examine the data science and ML process. In the first book, *It's All Analytics*, we reviewed the CRISP-DM (cross-industry standard process for data mining) model that was popularized by SPSS in the mid-1990s. Although the methodology is still widely used, we have made several refinements to the model based on our experience. Figure 10.3 outlines the common steps associated with the data science and ML process.

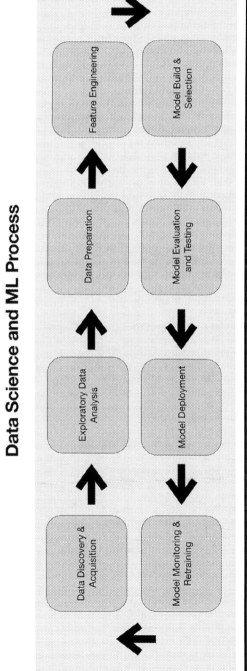

Figure 10.3   Steps for the data science and machine learning process.

Since the basic elements of the data science and ML process have been well documented in other works, we will not provide a review of what happens for each of the process steps. However, as it relates to architecture, we will provide some considerations and things to think about for each of the steps.

Data Discovery and Acquisition

With a solid understanding of the business decision to be made and the ramifications to current business processes, the project team needs to understand the various data sets available to make that decision while respecting privacy rules, internal policies and procedures, as well as external regulations. Before building models, the team should understand any limitations or restrictions that may impede the integration of the final model into the business process. For example,

- Will the data be available in the run-time environment?
- Is the data sourced internally, externally, or both?
- Are you legally and ethically entitled to use the data?

Now, data scientists are very clever people and are always innovating on how to use novel methods for analytics. We recommend that the organization begin with a minimum viable data set and use the tried and true algorithms before attempting to use more novel methods. This is where the old KISS acronym comes in handy, "Keep it Simple Stupid".

THE $1M ALGORITHM THAT WAS NEVER IMPLEMENTED

(Amatriain & Basilico, 2012)

In 2006, Netflix, who started as a mail-order DVD rental company, launched a $1M multiyear competition to improve the accuracy of its movie recommender algorithm by 10%. After 2,000 hours of work, the team won a "Progress Prize" for delivering an ensemble algorithm which consisted of 107 algorithms that improved upon the existing system by 8.43%. When Netflix examined the underlying code, there were two primary algorithms that were primarily responsible for the improvement.

They were singular value decomposition and restricted Bolzman machines. After refactoring the code to be more scalable (the original was designed to score 100 million records and Netflix had more than 5 billion to score), they implemented the two algorithms. Fast forward 2 years, and a different team claimed the $1 million prize. However, the algorithm was never implemented into Netflix's production systems. Why? The winning algorithm was an ensemble of hundreds of different algorithms and in part, Netflix stated:

> We evaluated some of the new methods offline but the additional accuracy gains that we measured did not seem to justify the engineering effort needed to bring them into a production environment.

It goes to show, just because a model is more accurate and provides additional value to the organization, the complexity of the implementation was simply not worth the technical effort. "Keep It Simple Stupid".

Exploratory Data Analysis

During this phase, the data scientist will use statistics and visualizations to gain an overall understanding of the structure and nature of the data being used for analysis. Many statistical techniques have assumptions on the underlying structure of the data. The data scientist will need to examine the data and make sure that the data is of the right shape and format for methods that will be employed. A few considerations are:

■ How similar is the training and test data to the data that we will see in real life when the model is in production? (Sweenor et al., 2020)
■ Will the production model be able to access similar data structures to those that occur in the training and test environment? (Sweenor et al., 2020)
■ Are there redundant variables?
■ Is there target or data leakage that may not be available at the time of prediction? In other words, are there correlated variables to the predictor variable that are in the training and test data set that may not be available in the run-time environment at the time of prediction?

Data Preparation

When preparing the data for training and testing, the data scientist may impute missing values, remove values (or select outliers of interest), apply transformations to the variables, and group or bin variables. Additionally, there may be specialized processing required for nontraditional data such as text, image, and audio data. Architectural considerations include:

- How performant does the data prep sequence need to be in the production environment?
- Where will the data be processed? For example, if you are doing image analysis and recognition at the edge, is there enough processing power?
- Is there sensitive or personally identifiable information present in the data? Does it need to be masked, obscured, removed, or can it be used at all?

Feature Engineering

Now, feature engineering may be considered part of data prep but we consider it a separate step in the process as it requires specific architectural considerations such as a feature store (see "Feature Stores"). Many data scientists consider feature engineering as much of an art as it is a science. The main goal is to find the variables that are most predictive of the target, but then further combine, calculate, and create new variables that will give the analytic model more predictive power.

- How can we gain consistency of feature generation across the organization?
- Are the features reusable?
- How variable are the input data streams? How often will our data pipeline be disrupted?

Model Build and Selection

In the model build and selection phase, the data scientist or ML engineer will iteratively train, test, and evaluate several models in their relation to the problem at hand. They may select one or more models or may even combine the models which are known as ensemble modeling (also known as voted prediction). There are several things we want the models to be able to do:

- How sensitive are the models to changes in the incoming data streams?
- Are the models scalable to large data sets? Do they need to be?
- How complex are the models, are they understandable
  and interpretable?

Model Evaluation and Testing

In the model evaluation and testing phase, the analytic professional will move from the sandbox environment to one which may be closer to the production run-time environment. Architectural considerations include:

- What are the business, accuracy, and performance requirements for the model inference or prediction?
- How big or complex are the models? Can they be processed on an edge device if needed?
- Are the models free from bias?

For example, in regards to performance requirements, if the target is predicting a cancer in a patient we want the absolute greatest accuracy with false positive and false negatives being essentially "zero". If it is a manufacturing process where we can tolerate 5% error, then 95% accuracy is satisfactory. So, when one thinks of model evaluation, they need to go beyond performance and accuracy type metrics. An often overlooked consideration is the business performance of the model – is it improving the business in the way it is supposed to?

Model Deployment

Model deployment generally consists of taking the code and exporting it in a language that is appropriate to the target run-time environment. For example, if the model is expected to run in a database the optimal score code may be SQL (Structured Query Language) or PMML (Predictive Model Markup Language). Other formats may include Java, C#, C++, PFA (Portable Format for Analytics), and ONYX (Open Neural Network Exchange).

- How many computational resources will we require to run the models?
- Will the data pipelines be included in the score code or are they separate?
- What dependencies does the model require to run?
- Where will the results go? A dashboard, another control system,
  a database, an automated process?

Model Monitoring

After the model is deployed, it is important to have a system and framework in place to monitor the model. Monitoring may include tests for model accuracy, performance metrics, and business metrics. Architectural considerations include:

■ What metrics will we be using to monitor model performance?
■ Do our results need to be reproducible? Do we need to version the models and the data?
■ Where will we store the metadata associated with the model runs?
■ What are the criteria for which we will update models, either retraining or complete remodeling?
■ Who responds to model failures? Do we have data scientists on call?

Legality and Ethical Use of Data

In addition to the considerations of each step in the data science and ML process, there are specific legal and ethical considerations that one must think about throughout the process. For example,

■ Are we allowed to use certain variables given geography and jurisdiction requirements?
■ Are we compliant with the generalized data protection regulation (GDPR) that exists in Europe?

For those unfamiliar with GDPR, this is a good starting point to learn more about the regulation (https://gdpr.eu/).

Automation and ML

As vendors continue to invest in developing software for data science and ML systems, automation is becoming increasingly important. In fact, an entire discipline has emerged known as automated machine learning (auto ML), although the name is a bit misleading. Automated machine learning helps data scientists to be more productive by automating some of the mundane and monotonous tasks associated with data science and ML.

Auto ML is a capability that automates key steps of the data science and ML process. Auto ML automates:

1. Data prep and cleansing routines
2. Selection of most important features
3. Creation of new features (feature generation) to be used in ML models
4. Selection of which parameters are to be used in the model
5. Model identification and selection
6. Hyperparameter tuning

By reducing some of the tedious parts of data science activities, data scientists can spend more time on higher value and innovative activities. In addition to improving data science productivity, auto ML is used by beginners and nonexperts to quickly get started with data science and ML.

Other benefits of auto ML include:

■ More rapid identification on which areas or projects may be most valuable for further exploration by data science experts
■ Increased accuracy of final solutions by allowing data scientists quickly explore a wider range of analytic approaches and data prep strategies

When evaluating various data and analytic software applications and packages, there are many capabilities to consider. Table 10.2 shows auto ML capabilities across the data science and ML lifecycle.

The Real World Is Different Than University

For organizations who are just beginning their data and analytics initiatives, we need to be careful on how we approach projects, especially if you plan on hiring data scientists who have recently graduated from college or are early in their career. Not to diminish or disparage their skills or ability, but they often suffer from a bit of naïveté and overconfidence. As they say, you don't know what you don't know.

Typically, newly minted data scientists will be assigned their first project from their manager. Now, we have seen on all too many occasions, where the task or problem they are assigned is not in alignment with strategic priorities but let's assume for the time being, it is an appropriate

Table 10.2 Automation Considerations for Data Science and Machine Learning

Data Discovery and Acquisition	Exploratory Data Analysis, Preparation, and Feature Engineering	Model Build, Selection, Evaluation, Testing, and Inferencing	Model Deployment, Monitoring, and Retraining
Automated schema detection and suggested joins Automated data profiling, quality checks, and cleansing Automated and suggested data transformations Automated data prep and feature engineering Automatically identify lineage, metadata, and enrichment recommendations	Ask questions in plain language Automated brush linking across visualizations Interactive AI to suggest visualizations and surface insights Auto ML (feature generation, selection, model build, selection) Built-in anomaly detection Seamless team collaboration and coordination Advanced spatial analytics One-click data science for common uses	Automated predictive model code generation Models (pipelines embedded in AI infused business applications) Model Ops: model deployment, management, governance Natural language explanations of visualizations Streaming data science for real-time decisions Automated alerting based on statistical or predictive models and business rules	Dynamic learning for self-updating models Automated champion-challenger testing and model recommendations Explainable AI to increase understandability and transparency, and reduce bias Automated model monitoring, retraining, and updating

project to work on that will provide tangible business outcomes when completed.

Excited about their first project, the data scientist will typically select their favorite open source software package (Python and R) and begin building models. After all, they were able to solve a number of increasingly complex problems using these languages and techniques in college, so why wouldn't it work in business?

The real word is quite a bit different than the problems that one solved in an academic setting. Many of the problems that were addressed in college are simply too contrived. The problems that were solved in an education

Table 10.3 Points of Difference between the University and the "Real World"

Academic Setting – The Artifice	*Corporate Setting – The Real World*
Data sets generally provided and are relatively "clean"	Data needs to be ingested/integrated from a wide variety of sources which you may or may not have access to and are typically quite messy
Analytic output are typically not integrated and deployed to a business system	One needs to coordinate with a IT and DevOps to deploy and integrate with production systems
Performance characteristics are not fully tested	Scalability and performance need extensive testing
End result is usually a prediction that stands by itself	End result needs to be integrated with a business system and one needs to ensure that end users are fully brought into the new process
Model is static and is not retrained	Model needs to be monitored, retrained, updated, and potentially remodeled in a corporation
Bias and ethics are often not addressed	It is critical to understand the business implications of what you are doing. Just because you *can* do something doesn't mean you should do something
Governance requirements are often not addressed	There are many rules and regulations to which corporate needs to adhere

or university setting are very different from business problems in several important ways. These are shown in Table 10.3.

Based on Table 10.3, we can see that when working in a corporate setting, we need to access and integrate disparate datasets, do extensive testing, integrate with production systems, determine model monitoring and retraining processes, be cognizant of ethics, and ensure that governance requirements are adhered to. Now that we understand some of the key differences between academic and corporate settings, let's discuss some considerations for analytic projects.

THE CRITICALITY OF ANALYTICS

Way back in the year 1965 *anno domini*, if a company was fortunate enough to achieve Fortune 500 status, they could expect to remain in this category for over 30 years (Perry, 2016). Fast forward to current times and experts agree that we are now squarely in the Fourth Industrial Revolution, which is characterized as "a fusion of technologies that is blurring the lines between the physical, digital, and biological spheres (Schwab, 2016)". Data volumes are growing at exponential rates and there is no end in sight. And sadly, as soon as the data are created, the information value contained within it begins to decay. This is why it is imperative to use data science and ML to find the hidden gems contained within your data and share this with the right person or system, within the right context, as rapidly as possible. The need for advanced analytics is no longer a nice-to-have, it is a requirement. Organizations need to treat analytics and analytic output as a core strategic asset if they are to survive. If not, the risk of becoming irrelevant is all too real. As an example, once household names in 1965, Fortune 500 companies like American Motors, Detroit Steel, Polaroid, Xerox, and Zenith Electronics are no longer in business. It is anticipated that one-half of today's Fortune 500 will be gone within 10 years, and the rate of change is accelerating (Bock et al., 2017). However, there is hope, companies like Boeing, Campbell Soup, IBM, and Proctor and Gamble (who were also listed in 1965) are still alive and well. Additionally, companies who were not conceived of yet, like Microsoft, eBay, Netflix, Home Depot, and Target, are currently thriving. To succeed in the new era, every company must become a data and analytics company (if they're not already).

Do You Know How to Bake Bread?

For most people, when they hear any of these words – "analytics", "data science", "machine learning", "artificial intelligence" – their mind quickly races to models and algorithms. Now, the math is certainly important but there are certainly many other factors to consider. Here's a quick analogy to help level set.

There are many home cooks who can bake a decent loaf of bread. After all, it's fairly straight forward. One needs to simply combine four simple ingredients: water, flour, yeast, and salt. To make bread, you mix the four ingredients together, knead it, let it rise, and then put it in the oven for the allotted baking time. After you take it out and cool the loaf, you have some edible bread. For new data scientists, they often think that it is quite simple to build a model similar to how simple it is to make a loaf of bread in your kitchen.

> Similar to transitioning from a home cook to a full-fledged baker, a business will require additional capabilities to industrialize and **scale** their data and analytics initiatives.

However, let's imagine for a moment– that instead of cooking one loaf of bread in their kitchen, that you want to become a full-fledged baker. If you were to become a baker, you may need a few different things compared to your kitchen. You may need larger quantities of ingredients, bigger mixers, more ovens, a quality control system, an invoicing system, a distribution channel, and maybe even a retail location. The point is, if you want to become a baker, you certainly need much more than you would have if you simply made bread in your kitchen.

Analogously, this is equivalent to what is required for organizations to get into the analytics and data science game. They need a bit more than running Python or R on their laptop. They may need data pipelines, model factories, model repositories, model monitoring systems, metadata systems, business rules, integration technologies, app developers, edge processing, streaming technologies, and so forth.

Now that we have an understanding of the basic difference between academic and corporate settings, as well as what's needed to become a baker, let's look at different types of analytic capabilities and architectural considerations within an organization.

Analytical Capabilities and Architectural Considerations

As mentioned in Chapter 1, a robust data and analytics platform will need to service different functional areas of the business such as customer experience, partners, Internet of Things (IoT), and the enterprise. To further build this out, we have contextualized the framework in Figure 10.4 (Gilbert, 2020) to the healthcare domain. As illustrated, one can see all of the different areas that the data and analytics platform will service and some of the use cases that may be applicable for the healthcare ecosystem.

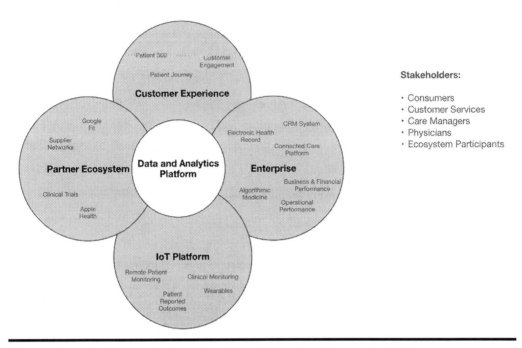

Data and Analytics Platform Service Areas
Healthcare Contextualization

Stakeholders:

- Consumers
- Customer Services
- Care Managers
- Physicians
- Ecosystem Participants

Figure 10.4 **Analytics platform for a "Real Time Healthcare Facility".**

Data Management as a Prerequisite

To have a more complete understanding of data and data management-related technologies, please refer to Part 2. Data is critical to data science and ML initiatives, thus it is an extremely important topic. As they say,

$$\text{Garbage In} = \text{Garbage Out}$$

Now, much has been debated as to where organizations should start as it relates to analytics projects. Do we start with the data architecture or the analytic architecture? We have seen both approaches in the field and either is appropriate. The real key is to understand the decision to be made and then work backward from there.

Starting with the Data

For many organizations, starting with the data is a natural starting point for data science and ML initiatives. From extract, transform, and load (ETL) or extract, load, and transform (ELT), to data warehousing, to data virtualization, and master data management, there are a myriad of technologies to consider. When one starts with the data, the organization needs to ensure that the project is appropriately scoped and that they don't fall into the never-ending data management projects. After all, your data is never perfect, so the organization needs to know when the requisite data is accessible and of suitable quality. These projects tend to have a longer cycle time which tends to test the patience of many business executives. Organizations can become discouraged in the absence of quick wins, analytic outputs, and changes to business processes.

Starting with the Analytics

When organizations start with the analytics, the data scientists will need to build the data pipelines required for the project. However, on the positive side, being able to achieve some quick wins by demonstrating how analytics can be used to solve business problems may outweigh the risk. But, the organization needs to be cognizant that data scientists may not build enterprise-grade data pipelines. The pipelines created may be brittle with and saddled with technical debt (which we will discuss later in the chapter "Technical Debt"). After the analytics are integrated with the business process, the IT team may need to rebuild or refine the pipelines that were built by the analytics team.

Data and Analytics Architecture

Figure 10.5 identifies some of the common components that will be in the data and analytics architecture. Many of the data-related technologies have been discussed in Part 2, so will provide a brief recap.

Data Sources

There are many but the common types include:

■ **Streaming** – data in-motion, often coming from a sensor or click stream. For example, GPS data from your cell phone or data being collected from your FitBit.
■ **Operational** – these are typically used to run the business, without operational stores, some business functions would top. Examples

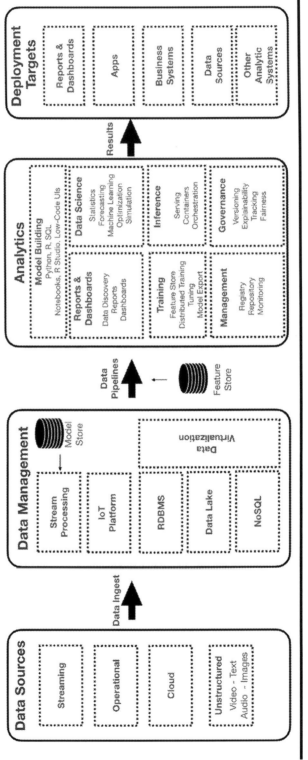

Figure 10.5 Data and analytics functional architecture.

include Customer Relationship Management, Manufacturing Execution Systems, Human Resources, and Finance Systems.

- **Cloud** – cloud could include the above but they are generally accessed via application programming interfaces (APIs) and may not be owned by the organization.
- **Unstructured** – data that is not "numbers". These are generally stored as key-value pairs and may include text data, image data, video data, sound data, and so forth.

Data Management

These include:

- **Stream processing** – this is generally an event or complex event processing engine that can ingest, aggregate, and perform calculations and analytical functions on data in-motion.
- **IoT platform** – the IoT platform allows organizations to process data near the source of where it's generated. This will be discussed in the section "IoT and Edge Analytics".
- **RDMS** – Relational Database Management Systems provide the data foundation for many organizations and have been around since the 1970s. Data is generally stored as rows and columns and is easily queryable via SQL.
- **Data lakes** – data lakes are generally stored in Hadoop Distributed File System (HDFS) and provide a low-cost approach to storing data. Data generally stored in HDFS without the rigor of ETL processes that occur in RDBMs.
- **NoSQL** – Not only SQL (NoSQL), these are more general than RDBMs databases and allow for data storage and retrieval beyond rows and columns. They may be organized as key-value pairs, document, column, and graph styles (IBM Cloud Education, 2019).
- **Data virtualization** – this is covered more thoroughly in Chapter 7, but this is essentially a technology that allows organizations to access and query multiple data sources but it looks, acts, and behaves like a single data source. It provides a common view across all of the data sources.
- **Model store** – this is a storage system for data science and ML models that may be used for stream processing. The models are often generated by data scientists or ML engineers.

Analytics

There are many capabilities provided by the analytics architecture. Functionality includes technology to create and visualize analytic output such as reports and dashboards. It also includes components to build models, train models, score (infer) workflows, manage, and govern models. We will provide a brief summary of each of the components below.

Model Building

To build data science and ML models, organizations will typically rely on open source code such as R and Python which offer users a wide variety of libraries and frameworks for data scientists to use. In addition to R and Python, many data scientists will access data using SQL. To author the workflows, individual development environments like Jupyter Notebooks or RStudio are frequently used. Many organizations also rely on vendor-provided low or no-code user interfaces that allow users to drag nodes on a canvas to build workflows.

Example technologies:
Languages: R, Python, Julia, Scala
User Interfaces: Notebooks (Jupyter or Zeppelin), RStudio, PyCharm, Atom

Reporting and Dashboards

Many organizations will most certainly have a need for reports and dashboards. These allow executives, managers, knowledge workers, and front-line professionals with information that is needed to make data-informed decisions. Organizations typically begin with internally facing dashboards but they can just as easily have an external focus as well. Additionally, many of these reports and dashboards are increasingly becoming embedded in mobile apps so that the end user may not even realize they are interacting with analytic output.

What's the Difference Between Reports and Dashboards?

"*Reporting* is the practice of collecting, formatting, and distributing rich information in a readily digestible and understandable fashion (Stupakevich et al., 2019)". Reports can be thought of as a set of preconfigured navigational flows. The reports can be interactive and the user may drill down but there are only certain paths that users can generally take. In general, reports are designed for users to consume the output, not analyze the data. Think of a simple credit card statement. On the credit card statement you may have a summary of spending for the billing period along with a list of the detailed transactions. Most of the major credit card issuers have online portals where they can search through the transactions or look at spending habits by category (i.e., amount spent on groceries vs. restaurants vs. car/auto). In general, you can search for and find whatever the designer of the report prebuilt for you. But you cannot look at things that were not predesigned.

A dashboard on the other hand is similar to a report but generally offers more interactivity. Users create dashboards to analyze the data to find hidden patterns and surface new insights that may have otherwise gone unnoticed. Dashboards often have a starting point for analysts but

> "Brushing" allows an analyst using a dashboard to "click through" and drill across different data visualizations.

users may be able to create specific types of reports that the designer didn't originally prebuild into the system. This allows the user to create new views of the data to solve specific problems.

Example technologies:

JasperReports, JFreechart, Pentaho, BIRT, and others.

Data Science

Data science functionality consists of a wide variety of capabilities which span statistics, forecasting, ML, optimization, and simulation (Burk & Miner, 2020, provide foundations and comparisons of these and other subjects).

Statistics

Descriptive statistical summaries and aggregations generally form the backbone of reports and dashboards and are frequently used in conjunction with data science and ML. Statistical (parametric) methodologies may make assumptions (e.g., assumption for normality) about the data that must be checked prior to employing specific methodologies.

Forecasting

Forecasting involves using data from the past to foresee what the future value of the variable may be at some other time period in the future. Typical use cases include predicting demand for products and services or predicting future sales.

Optimization

More precisely known as mathematical optimization, it is a technique to find the best possible outcome to a problem. In general, you are trying to maximize or minimize an objective function within a given set of constraints. Optimization may be used to optimize shipping routes or maximizing the return on investment from a set of marketing campaigns.

Simulation

A technique that essentially runs a sequence of "what-if" analysis to understand the behavior of a real-world system. For example, Monte Carlo simulations may be used to understand the risks and behaviors of financial instruments such as options and derivatives.

There are a variety of open source libraries and technologies that can be used for statistics, forecasting, optimization, and simulation. We chose not to list specific packages as the landscape is broad and continually rapidly evolving.

AI, ML, Deep Learning – Oh My!

There have been many questions on the differences between artificial intelligence, ML, and deep learning. The diagram below proves to be a useful schematic to visualize how the terms are interrelated (Serokell, 2020) as identified in Figure 10.6.

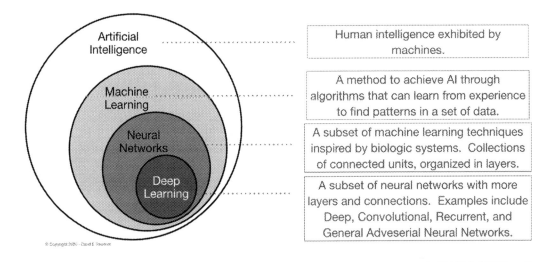

Figure 10.6   Interrelationships of AI, ML, NN, and deep learning (Serokell, 2020).

The term artificial intelligence is not new and was coined in the 1950s. For the scope of this chapter, we will consider the realm of narrow artificial intelligence, that is, artificial intelligence designed to solve a very specific problem. We will shy away from HAL in the 1968 film classic *2001: A Space Odyssey* as well as the manipulative *Ex Machina* in the 2014 film. As it relates to analytics infrastructure and technology, narrow AI generally involves technologies like computer vision, audio analytics, natural language processing, text analytics, and other similar technologies.

VIDEO GAMES AND SELF-DRIVING CARS

Traditionally, computer code is deterministic in nature. That is, it can be thought of a series of "if-then" rules that dictate everything the computer will do now and forever into the future. Now, these rules can be quite complex and may come close to simulating "intelligence" but in the end, it is still a series of "if-then" rules.

When we speak about AI, self-learning computer code is written. Instead of using a series of "if-then" rules, one can construct the code in such a way that it "learns" from doing. For these use cases, data scientists and ML experts typically turn to reinforcement learning (RL). The concept is surprisingly simple and we can use the example teaching a computer to play the classic arcade game Frogger.

For those of you not familiar with Frogger, the concept is surprisingly simple. There is a highway with moving vehicles that the Frog must cross to earn points. Generally, the cars, trucks, and busses move either way in the x-direction (left to right or right to left) while the Frog can move in all four directions (x – left, right and y – up, down). If the Frog gets hit by the truck, he is penalized −1 point (or the RL algorithm is) and if the Frog finds a present, he is rewarded with +1 point.

Unity (who makes video a video game development platform) has posted a nice YouTube video teaching the computer to play Frogger. They did this "tabula rasa" or from a clean slate. After playing the game over and over via simulation, after 6 hours of training, we have a super Frogger. It does raise some interesting questions, why does the Frogger move in a "forward" direction? After all, the only thing the algorithm knew was that it was rewarded from finding a package and penalized for getting hit by a car. Why doesn't it go backward more often to grab more presents? Computer scientist Danny Lange, currently at Unity and who has led AI and ML efforts at Uber, Amazon, Microsoft, and IBM, describes this phenomena as emergent behavior which is dictated by the rewards function. If you pick the wrong rewards function for your AI system, you may have emergent behavior that is unwanted.

In the Frogger example above, we used ML to train the Frogger to get the most gifts without getting squashed by a car. However, if we wrapped that engine in an autonomous vehicle then we'd be getting a bit closer to AI (still narrow AI).

Example Technologies:
Frameworks: Microsoft CNTK, Google TensorFlow, Amazon SageMaker, Pytorch
Libraries: Spark MLLib, Scikit Learn, Keras

Model Training

Includes technology like feature stores, distributed frameworks, hyperparameter tuning, and export formats.

Feature Stores

This is covered in more detail in the forthcoming "Feature Store" section. Feature stores are essentially reusable repositories to store and call features (also known as variables which can be derived or computed) in data science models. Feature stores ensure reusability and consistency across the organization. A comparison can be found at https://www.featurestore.org/.
Example technologies:
Hopsworks, StreamSQL, Feast

Distributed Training

When creating data science and ML models, there may be scalability challenges with libraries like Pandas and NumPy. If you need an intergalactic (or internet) scaling of your models, you may need a distributed training environment.
Example technologies:
Apache Spark, Ray, Horovod

Tuning

Hyperparameter tuning is needed when the parameters for the model cannot be derived from the data. Optimally tuned parameters can improve the performance (accuracy) of your models.

Example technologies:
Hyper opt, Raytune, Talos

Model Export

After the models are created and tuned, you may need to export them to a framework agnostic format. These model export formats allow you to take the models and run them in different computing environments.

Examples technologies:
PMML (Predictive Model Markup Language), ONNX (Open Neural Network Exchange), Neuropod (from Uber)

Model Inference

After the models are trained, they will make predictions (inference) on new data that the model has never seen. To accomplish this, organizations will need serving, container, and orchestration technology.

Serving

Model serving (typically via an API) separates the running of the model from both how the model was created and the target environment to which it will be deployed or integrated.

Example technologies:
Kubeflow, MLRun, MLFlow, Airflow, Luigi, Seldon, BentoML

Containers

Containers are a way to deploy applications in an on-premise or cloud environment without the application build focusing on environment-specific variables. Simply put, this allows you to run the application reliability across different environments.

Example technologies:
Docker

Orchestration

Going hand in hand with containers, organizations will need technologies to orchestrate and manage the deployment of containers.

Example technologies:

Kubernetes, Apache Mesos, Netflix genie

Model Management

As models proliferate across an organization, it becomes increasingly important to have a common location to store and track models across the organization. In addition, you will need a way to manage and monitor the models as they are used (or not) across the enterprise. Model management is essentially an overarching term that results from the combination of the model registry, model serving, and model monitoring.

Repository and Registry

The repository is a centralized database that can be used to store models. The model repository and registry provide this functionality. The repository and registry provide versioning of both the models and metadata. Additionally, the registry can associate specific runs (experiments) and hyperparameters to the models. This provides a foundation to be able to recreate the experiments if need be.

Example technologies:

ModelDB, MLFlow Model Registry

Monitoring

When models are deployed into real-world environments, the organization needs a way to monitor their performance to understand when they need to be updated, retrained, or remodeled. Chapter 11, "Model Ops", will cover this need in greater detail.

Example technologies:

Amazon Sagemaker Model Monitor, Hydrosphere,

Governance

In addition to being able to build, infer, train, and build models, separate care must be taken to ensure that your models can be governed. To accomplish this, organizations will need to consider versioning, explainability, tracking, and fairness.

Versioning

Organizations should have technology to make sure that the model code, data, and even specific runs in the model actually work and are accurate (see Model Management).

Code Versioning

As data scientists build models, the code should be versioned to organizations that can understand who changed what, where, and why.

Example technologies:
Git

Data Versioning

Includes both workflows and scripts to retrieve the data as well as the data snapshot itself. This allows organizations to be able to trace predictions back to the source.

Example technologies:
dotmesh, DVC, Pachyderm, Quilt

Tracking

In addition to being able to version the code and data, organizations need to be able to track the specific runs of the model.

Example technologies:
MLFlow Tracking, ML Run

Explainability

As data science and ML models proliferate, there are requirements to be able to explain why specific predictions are being made. Depending on the industry, there may be legal requirements to have explainable models. This is an active area of research but as of this writing, there are several technologies that are being developed.

Example technologies:
AI Explainability 360, Microsoft InterpretML, Lime, Lucid, SHAP, TreeInterpreter

Fairness

Related to being able to understand why a specific prediction is being made, organizations are required to ensure the predictions are fair (see Chapter 3). Essentially, organizations need to make sure that the models are not biased and that they do not run afoul of regulations.

Example technologies:
Aequitas, AI Fairness 360, Audit AI, DeepLIFT, Fairlearn

Streaming Analytics

Streaming analytics has certainly been increasing in popularity over the past few years. Streaming analytics is an event processing engine that allows businesses to capture real-time data, in-motion, and perform analytical functions on the data. Streaming engines generally have a persistent data store that is configurable and allows the user to define how long the data shall be held. This allows organizations the ability to deal with out of sequence events, compute aggregates and summary statistics on windows of data, and more importantly, apply data science and ML models to the data as well.

Use cases for streaming analytics:

- Real-time financial transaction processing and fraud detection
- Real-time monitoring of health data to improve patient care
- Real-time processing of industrial equipment sensors to monitor and predict changes or breakdowns of equipment
- Monitoring of logistics fleets whether they be trucks, trains, or cargo ships

Example technologies:
Kafka, Flink, NNStreamer, Apache Storm,

IoT and Edge Analytics

IoT and edge analytics (to be clarified below) are useful when one needs to process events and data as close to the point of creation and impact as possible. As an example, suppose you have developed a computer vision algorithm for an anti-collision system within a self-driving car. The amount of data generated by the images captured from cameras is enormous. There is no feasible way to use a traditional processing architecture where you would collect the data, transport it to a central server or cloud service for analysis, and then send the result back to the warning system within the car. This simply takes too long, thus you need a computational engine and data science model to process the data as close to the camera as possible.

Use cases include:

- Predictive maintenance of submersible pumps in areas where Internet does not exist
- Healthcare monitoring of patients on a wearable device
- Audio and image analysis from security cameras
- Acoustical monitoring and vibrational analysis from wind turbines to understand if things are running normally
- Precision farming to maximize crop yields by applying specific fertilizer regiments for each plant
- The "Internet of Cows" – ability to track each individual livestock, prescribe individual care, track and monitor feeding habits, and general health (Schwartz, 2017).

When considering IoT and edge analytics, there are three different areas to consider, edge, platform, and enterprise as illustrated in Figure 10.7.

The IoT and edge analytics framework (Making Your Business Thrive With IoT, 2018) consists of the following:

- **Edge** – this is the "real" world where there is interaction between the physical components (e.g., sensors) and the rest of the IoT ecosystem.
- **Platform** – platform are the components that are used to collect and process data near or at the edge.
- **Core** – often referred to as enterprise, this is where you "normally" work, there are business applications and processes.

IoT and Edge Analytics Framework

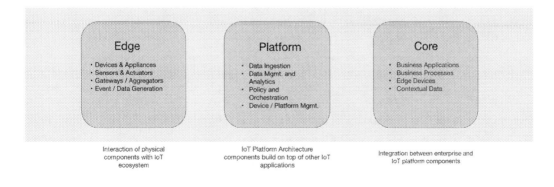

Figure 10.7   IoT edge analytics platform.

Cloud Ecosystems and Frameworks

As cloud ecosystems and frameworks become more "en vogue", the cloud providers have done a nice job of creating an ecosystem of tools that can be used. However, one consideration is the notion of vendor lock-in. If you orient around one particular cloud ecosystem, how easy is it to switch to another? If you want to use the compute and storage capabilities of one cloud vendor but the algorithms, streaming capabilities, and BI tools from another, can you do that?

Cloud ecosystems are generally orienting around the following megavendors, many if not all who offer storage, compute, algorithms, analytics, and IoT frameworks:

- Microsoft azure
- Google cloud computing services (GCP)
- Amazon web services (AWS) Alibaba cloud

Since these providers are rapidly evolving and adding new services, we will not try to provide a detailed treatment of the architectural components since they change so quickly and will probably be out of date by the time you read this book.

A Few Example Architectures

Now that we have an understanding of architectural considerations and capabilities that may be needed, let's take a look at some real-world example architectures from some of the leading companies.

Uber

The popular ride-share app Uber thinks about data science and ML and have developed a system named "Michaelangelo". As illustrated in Figure 10.8 (Hermann, 2017), Uber has a clear delineation between online (real time) or offline usage. Another interesting insight about the architecture is the need for a feature store to facilitate reusability as well as performance requirements.

As you can see in Figure 10.8, Uber's Michelangelo spans the phases of the analytics flow which includes data ingest, model training, model evaluation, and deployment and monitoring. One interesting note is that Uber

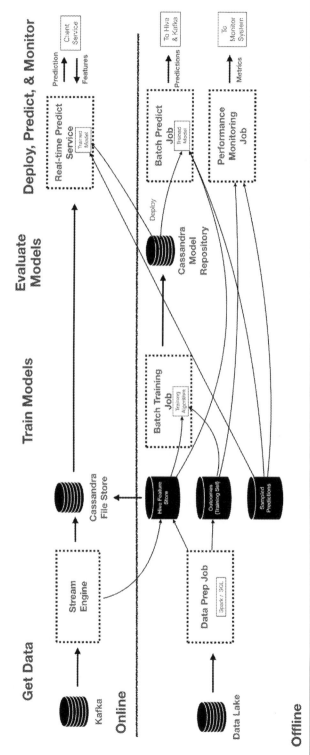

Figure 10.8   Uber's data science and ML architecture.

has included a feature store (which will be discussed in the next section "Feature Stores"). Another item of interest is the distinction between online and off-line usage. For a detailed treatment of this, we recommend you dive into the Uber Engineering Blog (https://eng.uber.com).

Facebook

In Figure 10.9, adapted from Robinson (2019), we see a similar architecture at Facebook which consists of online and offline usage, open source frameworks, and features stores.

Similar to the previous example, we see the data science flow which consists of data ingest, feature creation, model training, model evaluation, and deployment (which leads to inference) and monitoring (not shown). Again, similar to the Uber example, we see the distinction between offline and online usage. Additionally, various frameworks like Caffe2, PyTorch, and ONNX have been specifically identified. For a more detailed treatment, consider following the Facebook Engineering Blog (https://engineering.fb.com).

An Evolution of CRISP-DM

For those familiar with the CRISP-DM methodology, we see that there have been several developments since using the proprietary data science and ML software paradigm pioneered by SAS Institute, SPSS, and Statistica. We see more use of open source technology and frameworks from cloud providers and a more extensive use of APIs and abstractions. Also, the concept of feature stores is relatively new and we expect this space to continue to evolve.

Feature Stores

After reviewing a few of the real-world architectures, we recommend considering a feature store as a part of the architecture. The feature store will allow for consistency, reusability, and be more performant rather than having to calculate features for each inference or prediction of the model. Figure 10.10 (Dowling, 2020) illustrates the concept of a feature store.

As systems become more complex and interdependent, it is important to create layers of abstraction in the data science and ML technology stack. One such abstraction is the feature store. One of primary benefits of the

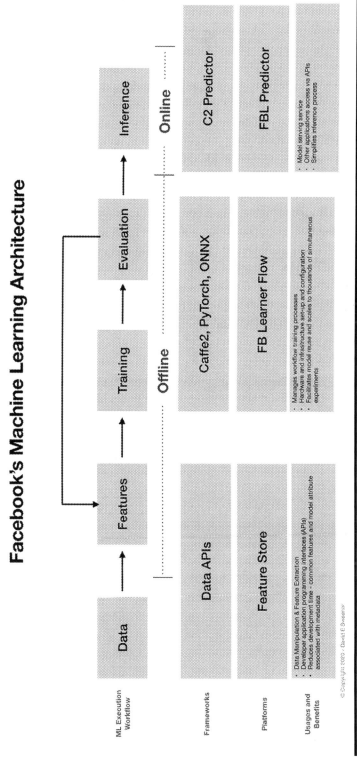

Facebook's Machine Learning Architecture

Figure 10.9   Infrastructure diagram of Facebook's ML architecture and flow.

Analytics Flow with Feature Store

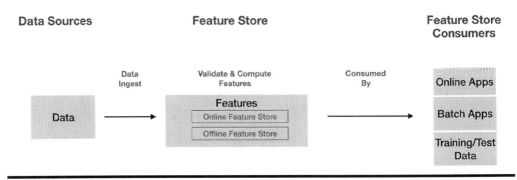

Figure 10.10   Analytics flow with online and offline feature store.

feature store is that it allows for consumers (other data scientists and app developers) to simply call the feature store via an API to provide the features needed for analysis. This eliminates the need for each app or ML workflow developer to write code to calculate features within their application. It promotes reuse and consistency across the enterprise. We will explore additional benefits very shortly in Table 10.4.

Drilling down to more level of detail in Figure 10.11 (Dowling, 2020), we look at a little more detail on the flow of the feature store and relevant technologies.

Hopsworks is an open source platform for creating ML platforms (logical-clocks/hopsworks, 2020). Beyond Hopswork, there is a comparison table of features stores at (https://www.featurestore.org).

When we look at the feature stores being used, beyond reusability and consistency, capabilities and benefits include the following identified in Table 10.4 (Indrayudh, 2020).

Table 10.4   Feature Store Capability

Capability	*Description*
Input Correctness	Ensure data integrity and semantic clarity
Feature Computation and Performance	Mechanisms for development of transformations using execution frameworks (e.g., Pandas and Spark)
Trust and Discovery	Mechanisms to document discover, and validate features
Serving and Monitoring	Serving the computed features

Feature Store Detailed Flow

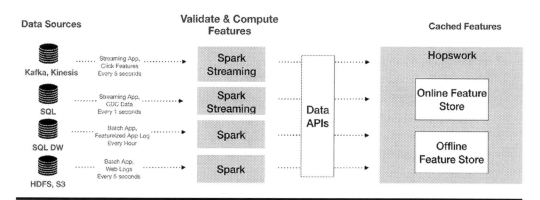

Figure 10.11   Flow to create online and offline feature stores.

HELP! HOW DO I ACTUALLY USE A FEATURE STORE?

Since feature stores are relatively new, we will provide a brief technical overview of how developers and data scientists use them as provided by Dowling (2020). Here is some code of the flow:

```
import hsfs

# "prod" is the production feature store
conn = hsfs.connection(host="ea2.aws.hopsworks.
ai", project="prod")
featurestore = conn.get_feature_store()

# read raw data and use Spark to engineer
features
raw_data_df = spark.read.parquet('/
parquet_partitioned')
polynomial_features = raw_data_df.map(lambda
x: x²)

# Features computed together in a DataFrames
are in the same feature group
fg = featurestore.
create_feature_group(name='fg_revenue',
version=1,
type='offline')
```

```
fg.create(polynomial_features)
g.compute_statistics()
```

In this code snippet, we connect to the Hopsworks Feature Store, read some raw data into a DataFrame from a parquet file, and transform the data into polynomial features. Then, we create a feature group, it's version is "1" and it is only to be stored in the "offline"' feature store. Finally, we ingest our new polynomial_dataframe into the feature group and compute statistics over the feature group that are also stored in the Hopsworks Feature Store. Note that Pandas DataFrames are supported as well as Spark DataFrames, and there are both Python and Scala/Java APIs.

Dowling also provides a second code snippet to gather and retrieve features from a data science and ML workflow.

```
import hsfs
conn = hsfs.connection(host="ea2.aws.hopsworks.
ai", project="prod")
featurestore = conn.get_feature_store()

# get feature groups from which you want to
create a training dataset
fg1 = featurestore.get_feature_group('fg_
revenue', version=1)
fg2 = featurestore.get_feature_group('fg_
users', version=2)

# lazily join features
joined_features = fg1.select_all() \
.join(fg2.select(['user_id', 'age']),
on='user_id')
sink = featurestore.
get_storage_connector('S3-training-dataset-
bucket')
td = featurestore.
create_training_dataset(name='revenue_
prediction',
version=1,
data_format='tfrecords',
```

```
            storage_connector=sink,
            split={'train': 0.8, 'test': 0.2})
            td.seed = 1234
            td.create(joined_features)"
```

So, we can see from the above code snippet, one can use a small bit of code and an API to create and join features on a data set of interest in a data science and ML pipeline.

Technology

There are a myriad of technologies that are used in data science and ML projects. The Linux Foundation has assembled a nice landscape with a listing of various AI, ML, and data science projects. Figure 10.12 (LF AI & Data Landscape, n.d.) is an overview of the AI and Data Landscape provided by the Linux Foundation. When you view the website, the landscape is dynamically generated upon each page load so we encourage you to visit the website for yourself.

Cost Considerations

When embarking on any data and analytics initiative, many organizations question whether they should build or buy a solution. For the builders, freely available open source software comes to mind and for the buyers, there are many commercially supported packages that span the capability spectrum for data and analytics.

When considering costs, Maha Shaaikh and Tony Cornford of The London School of Economics and Political Science (LSE) proposed a framework (Shaikh & Cornford, 2011) to evaluate the costs which are identified in the Table 10.5.

In addition to the above, there may be a few costs and risks that are unique to the data and analytics space. Namely,

1. Opportunity costs associated with developing something that you could otherwise purchase
2. Refactoring and technology change costs
3. Privacy, regulatory, and governance costs
4. Costs and risks associated with key talent leaving for competitor

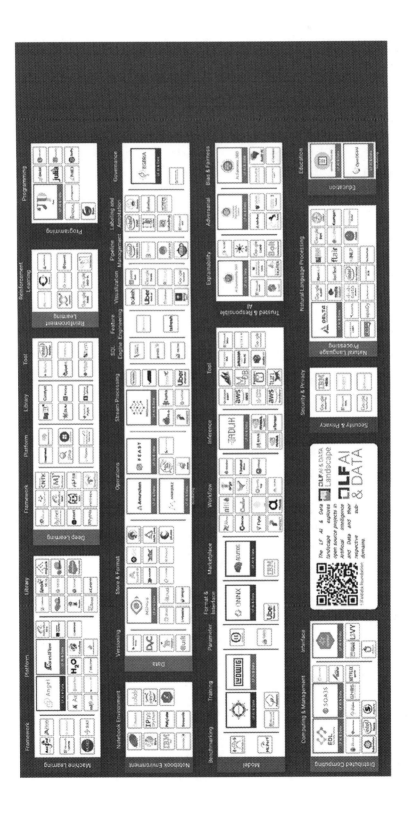

Figure 10.12   The AI and data landscape from the Linux Foundation (https://landscape.lfai.foundation/).

Table 10.5   Costs Considerations for Open Source Software

Cost Category		
Search	Cost of upfront evaluation study	
	Cost of upfront proof of concept evaluation	
Acquisition	Cost of software	
	Cost of customization for business needs	
	Cost of integration with existing platform	
Integration	Cost of data and user migration	
	Cost of training	
	Cost of process and best practice change	
Use	Cost of in-house support services	
	Cost of contracted support services	
	Cost of maintenance and upgrades	
	Software scalability costs	
Retire	Exit costs for software and hardware	
	Exit costs for change over and retraining	

5. Documentation costs
6. Cost of technical debt (to be discussed in the next section)
7. Indemnification and culpability

Now, each technology selection is unique to the set of initiatives that the organization wishes to pursue. From our practical experience in the data and analytics space, we see organizations using a hybrid approach that includes both COTS (commercial off the shelf) software as well as open source software.

Other Open Source Considerations

One of the primary benefits of open source software is the community. Having a robust community is extremely important in the data and analytics space. If you select the right framework with an established or growing community, you will have new features and capabilities to take advantage of that no single software vendor could ever match. However, with open source, there are also risks of selecting the wrong framework or package. If there are critical bug fixes required for the software or updates that will be the responsibility of the adopting organization to fix. If you work in a regulated industry which requires certainly validation and verification of software development practices (or numerical validation in the case of analytics required by the US Food and Drug Administration (FDA)), that will also be the responsibility of the adopting organization. Additionally, if questions of indemnification or culpability arise, your organization may be responsible for those. Lastly, there are a dizzying array of different licensees that one needs to investigate and understand.

In the end, if you hire expensive data scientists or statisticians, you want them to be productive and use the software that they are comfortable using. We've often used the analogy, you wouldn't tell a Michelin Star Chef what type of ingredients or equipment he or she should use. You want them to be creative and innovative. For organizations interested in adopting open source software, they will need to have a governance system in place to ensure that the organization has visibility of what software is being used, what software packages and specific versions are being used, and a way to track and manage that. The organization will need to set processes and standards to make sure they are interoperable as well.

Technical Debt in Data Science and ML

Technical debt is a term used in software development that is used to denote the long-term costs associated with software engineering. More specifically, it generally refers to the cost of "rework" by valuing quick wins over long-term robustness and longevity. If more time was taken by soft-

> Technical debt in software development increases both costs and risks to the organization.

ware developers up front, there would be less dependencies, more robust code, and thus, lower technical debit. There are several types of technical debt of which we will discuss a few below (Sculley et al., 2014).

Model Dependencies

Entangled abstraction layers – this essentially states that ML systems often mix signals together. Thus, if we want to change a feature in one system, it will change the feature in every system.

Cascading correlations – this is the notion that if you create a model to solve a specific problem and you have a slightly related but different problem and you use the same model or model with a tweak that can handle both problems. This makes it difficult to improve the model as it may have improved results on the original problem but not the related problem.

Unknown model consumers – when a model is run, its predictions may go to another system and it also will generate logs and metadata. Other systems may use the output or logs within the primary system owner knowing. This is an unknown model consumer. This comingles different parts of the ML system and creates a higher risk of breakage since they are linked.

Data Dependencies

Changing data inputs – this arises when the input of one model is fed from the output of the other model. If the original data changes over time or the raw input data changes, it may have a dramatic change on the model output.

Unneeded data – sometimes, data inputs are used that have little to know material effect on the model output. Having variables that have little discrimination power over your current model increases data-related technical debt.

Static data dependency analysis – tools to generate dependency graphs of data-related issues are not readily available which makes it difficult to understand which data is being used where.

Feedback

Direct feedback – this is where a model influences the selection of its future training data. The technical details of this are beyond the scope of this document but can be found in the reference cited above.

Hidden feedback – this occurs when two different systems actually influence each other when they are operating in the real world.

Anti-patterns or Poor Coding Habits

Glue code – this is the situation where there is a large amount of code in the job being run that is not really related to ML. It usually is supporting code to get data in an out of the package being used.

Data pipeline jungles – this situation arises when there are a variety of disparate data prep (joins, sampling, and other prep) steps that are inefficient and could be abstracted from the ML code.

Code dead ends – as one develops ML code, it is extremely iterative in nature. Thus, as you create an experiment and run it, you learn, optimize, and run another. What eventually happens is that the code begins to accumulate leftover code fragments from previous iterations and experiments that should be removed. Many times, they never are removed. "A famous example of the dangers here was Knight Capital's system losing $465 million in 45 minutes, apparently because of unexpected behavior from obsolete experimental codepaths (Sculley et al., 2014)".

Other types of technical debt include:

■ Lack of abstraction layers
■ "ML System Smells"
■ Configuration debt
■ Fixed thresholds
■ Testing and monitoring
■ Prediction bias
■ Action limits
■ Upstream producers
■ Data testing debt
■ Reproducibility debt
■ Cultural debt

As you can see, there are quite a few sources of technical debt. We encourage our readers to visit the paper from Sculley et al. (2014) to really understand more on the topic.

Summary

In this chapter we discussed:

■ Architectural considerations that data scientists will need to consider for each phase of the data science and ML process
■ Automation and ML

- How the real world is different than university
- Baking bread
- Architectural components and capabilities for a data science and ML process
- Features stores
- Cost considerations
- Technical debt

References

Amatriain, X., & Basilico, J. (2012, April 6). *Netflix Recommendations: Beyond the 5 stars (Part 1)*. Medium; Netflix Technology Blog. https://netflixtechblog.com/netflix-recommendations-beyond-the-5-stars-part-1-55838468f429.

Atul Gawande. (2017). *Finding Medicine's Hot Spots*. The New Yorker. https://www.newyorker.com/magazine/2011/01/24/the-hot-spotters.

Bock, R., Iansiti, M., & Lakhani, K. R. (2017, January 31). *What the Companies on the Right Side of the Digital Business Divide Have in Common*. Harvard Business Review. https://hbr.org/2017/01/what-the-companies-on-the-right-side-of-the-digital-business-divide-have-in-common.

Davenport, T. H., & Harris, J. G. (2017). *Competing on Analytics: The New Science of Winning*. Harvard Business Review Press, Brighton, MA.

Dowling, J. (2020, May 19). *What is a Feature Store for ML?* Medium. https://medium.com/data-for-ai/what-is-a-feature-store-for-ml-29b62580af5d.

Finkelstein, A., Zhou, A., Taubman, S., & Doyle, J. (2020). Health care hotspotting — A randomized, controlled trial. *New England Journal of Medicine, 382*(2), 152–162. https://doi.org/10.1056/nejmsa1906848.

Gilbert, M. E. (2020). The Evolution of Healthcare Consumer Engagement Hub Architecture. In *IBM.com*. Gartner, Inc. https://www.ibm.com/downloads/cas/YKNKQ9LO.

Hermann, J. (2017, September 5). *Meet Michelangelo: Uber's Machine Learning Platform*. Uber Engineering Blog. https://eng.uber.com/michelangelo-machine-learning-platform/.

IBM Cloud Education. (2019, August 6). *NoSQL Databases*. Ibm.com. https://www.ibm.com/cloud/learn/nosql-databases.

Indrayudh. (2020, August 31). *Feature Stores: The CEO's Guide*. Medium. https://medium.com/data-for-ai/feature-stores-the-ceos-guide-ce6182d7def2.

LF AI & Data Landscape. (n.d.). LF AI & Data Landscape. Retrieved December 6, 2020, from https://landscape.lfai.foundation.

Logan, V. (2020, November 10). *Webinar: 7 Ways To Build The Case For Data Literacy (And What If You Don't?!) - YouTube*. Www.youtube.com. https://www.youtube.com/watch?v=eQyhTsOnt2Y&feature=youtu.be.

logicalclocks/hopsworks. (2020, December 5). GitHub. https://github.com/logicalclocks/hopsworks.

Making Your Business Thrive With IoT. (2018). https://www.gartner.com/teamsiteanalytics/servePDF?g=/imagesrv/media-products/pdf/T-systems/T-Systems-Newsletters-Making-Your-Business-Thrive-With-IoT-featuring-Gartner-1-5DKCH9S,pdf.

Mayes, J. (2017, December). *Jason's Machine Learning 101*. Google Slides - Jason's Machine Learning 101. https://docs.google.com/presentation/d/1kSuQyW5DTnkVaZEjGYCkfOxvzCqGEFzWBy4e9Uedd9k/edit?imm_mid=0f9b7e&cmp=em-data-na-na-newsltr_20171213#slide=id.g168a3288f7_0_58.

Perry, M. J. (2016, December 13). *Fortune 500 firms 1955 v. 2016: Only 12% remain, thanks to the creative destruction that fuels economic prosperity.* American Enterprise Institute - AEI. https://www.aei.org/carpe-diem/fortune-500-firms-1955-v-2016-only-12-remain-thanks-to-the-creative-destruction-that-fuels-economic-prosperity/.

Robinson, J. (2019, February 3). *How Facebook Scales Artificial Intelligence & Machine Learning.* Medium. https://medium.com/@jamal.robinson/how-facebook-scales-artificial-intelligence-machine-learning-693706ae296f.

Schwab, K. (2016, January 14). *The Fourth Industrial Revolution: what it means and how to respond.* World Economic Forum. https://www.weforum.org/agenda/2016/01/the-fourth-industrial-revolution-what-it-means-and-how-to-respond/.

Schwartz, A. (2017, January 24). *The "Internet of cows" is taking over farms across the world.* Business Insider. https://www.businessinsider.com/bovcontrol-internet-of-cows-2017-1.

Sculley, D., Holt, G., Golovin, D., Davydov, E., Phillips, T., Ebner, D., Chaudhary, V., & Young, M. (2014). *SE4ML: Software Engineering for Machine Learning (NIPS 2014 Workshop).*

Serokell. (2020, April 27). *Artificial Intelligence vs. Machine Learning vs. Deep Learning: What's the Difference.* Medium. https://medium.com/ai-in-plain-english/artificial-intelligence-vs-machine-learning-vs-deep-learning-whats-the-difference-dccce18efe7f.

Shaikh, M., & Cornford, T. (2011). Total cost of ownership of open source software: a report for the UK Cabinet Office supported by OpenForum Europe. In *LSE Research Online*. https://eprints.lse.ac.uk/39826/1/Total_cost_of_ownership_of_open_source_software_(LSERO).pdf.

Stupakevich, B., Sweenor, D., & Swiderick, S. (2019). *Reporting, Predictive Analytics, and Everything in Between.* O'Reilly Media, Inc., Newton, MA.

Swanton, B. (2018, February 8). *You Can't Buy a Digital Business Technology Platform.* Bill Swanton; Gartner, Inc. https://blogs.gartner.com/bill-swanton/2018/02/08/you-cant-buy-a-digital-business-technology-platform/.

Sweenor, D., Hillion, S., Rope, D., Kannabiran, D., Hill, T., & O'Connell, M. (2020). *ML Ops: Operationalizing Data Science.* O'Reilly Media, Inc., Newton, MA. https://www.oreilly.com/library/view/ml-ops-operationalizing/9781492074663/.

Additional Resources

Blog, T. O. G. (2020, April 1). *Reference Architecture for Healthcare – Design Concepts*. The Open Group Blog. https://blog.opengroup.org/2020/04/01/reference-architecture-for-healthcare-design-concepts/

Facebook Engineering. (n.d.). Facebook Engineering. Retrieved December 7, 2020, from https://engineering.fb.com

Feature Store for ML. (n.d.). www.featurestore.org. Retrieved December 6, 2020, from https://www.featurestore.org

GDPR.eu. (2019). GDPR.eu. https://gdpr.eu/

Karthik Murugesan. (2018, June 28). *Facebook ML Infrastructure -2018 slides*. Slideshare.net. https://www.slideshare.net/KarthikMurugesan2/facebook-machine-learning-infrastructure-2018-slides

Nader, A. (2018, August 20). *The Internet of Cows: AI in Agriculture with SomaDetect*. Medium. https://medium.com/@alyssa.labelbox/the-internet-of-cows-ai-in-agriculture-with-somadetect-859593db9207

Netflix TechBlog. (n.d.). Netflix TechBlog. Retrieved December 7, 2020, from https://netflixtechblog.com

Publications - Facebook Research. (2019). Facebook Research. https://research.fb.com/publications/

Sourdough Baking | King Arthur Baking. (n.d.). www.kingarthurbaking.com. Retrieved December 6, 2020, from https://www.kingarthurbaking.com/learn/guides/sourdough

Uber Engineering Blog. (n.d.). Uber Engineering Blog. Retrieved December 7, 2020, from https://eng.uber.com

Some related terms – analytics architecture, feature store, technical debt, feature generation, streaming analytics, edge analytics, CRISP-DM, (IT) solution scaling,

Chapter 11

Technology to Communicate and Act Upon Analytics

ARTHUR: Camelot!

SIR GALAHAD: Camelot!

LANCELOT: Camelot!

PATSY: It's only a model.

Monty Python and the Holy Grail

Introduction

In the previous chapter, we discussed the architectural components required for data and analytics. We discussed considerations that the data scientist needs to think about when creating a workflow, capabilities required for data science and machine learning (ML) architectures, Auto ML, the increasing relevance of features stores, technical debt, and cost considerations when evaluating platforms.

Now that we understand the architectural components required to build data science and ML workflows, we now need to turn our attention to technology that will be needed to communicate and act upon analytics. To communicate and act upon analytics, there are a few essential factors to consider. Organizations need to be able to deploy and monitor analytic workflows, they need to be able to monitor the performance of models

DOI: 10.4324/9780429343957-14

using business, technical, and performance metrics, and they need to establish and adhere to an ethical and governance framework for analytics.

An Analytics Confluence

In Chapter 2, we discussed the notion of "composable apps" (Panetta, 2020) which are a grouping of data and analytics capabilities (e.g., data virtualization+ML+data visualization) assembled in a coherent manner to make a business decision (see Chapter 2) or solve a specific business problem. To assemble these applications, one can think of putting the various capabilities together like Lego bricks. How many different ways can you assemble these bricks to provide a unique solution and competitive advantage for *your* enterprise? According to Joseph Pine, the author of *The Experience Economy* published in 2019, if you take just six 2×4 Lego bricks, there are over 915,103,765 possible configuration combinations. Given the multitude of data and analytic capabilities involved in building business applications, the possibilities are limitless.

As discussed in previous chapters, the following capabilities are available for many businesses to work with. These include:

- Data capabilities
  - Data warehouses, lakes, and big data stores
  - Stream processing
  - Data virtualization (DV)
  - Master data management (MDM)
  - Data as a service (DaaS)
- Analytics capabilities
  - Reports, dashboards, and visualizations
  - Data science
    - Statistics
    - Forecasting
    - Machine learning
    - Optimization
    - Simulation
  - Feature stores
  - Analytics as a service (AaaS)
  - Model management

- Cross-cutting capabilities
- IoT platforms
- Cloud services and frameworks
- Open source languages and libraries

Through the confluence of these capabilities, organizations will assemble them in unique ways to build analytic applications to support digital decisions. These applications may be deployed as reports and dashboards, they may be embedded in custom apps, the output could feed other business systems and data sources, or the predictions could deliver results to other analytic systems.

However, simply creating and deploying the technical underpinnings of the analytics applications is not enough. Even though they may technically produce output that can be consumed and acted upon by other systems or people, more is needed. This is where an understanding of data storytelling can come in handy.

Data Storytelling

In many organizations, there are individuals who are comfortable interpreting the output of data and analytics which may take the form of reports, graphs, and other types of visualizations to make decisions, and there are also individuals who are more comfortable with making decisions by "gut feel", intuition, or other means. This is not to pass judgment on either group; it is just a fact that organizations need to understand.

To persuade or influence individuals with data and analytics for human-in-the-loop decisions (see Chapter 2, "Human vs. Automated Decisions"), it is important to present the analytic output in a way that "makes sense" to them on a personal level. Simply presenting information in the form of reports and graphs will not be sufficient for many people. In other words, we need to tell a good story using data and analytics. The usefulness and efficacy of storytelling extends far beyond data and analytics – it can be used for presentations, movies, songs, speeches, and many other activities. However, for our purposes, we will limit the scope of our discussion to data and analytics.

In the book *Resonate* by Nancy Duarte (2010), Duarate notes that there are several elements to telling a good story. Duarte suggests that all good stories follow similar patterns and best practices as outlined below. To tell a memorable good story, they need to contain the following elements.

- Stories convey meaning
- You are not the hero
- The audience is the hero
- Stories need
  - A repeatable and likable hero
  - Who encounters roadblocks
  - And emerges transformed

Similarly, the analyst firm Gartner suggests using the SIR (situation, impact, and resolution) framework (Barnes, 2013) which includes:

- **Lead with the outcome** – begin the story with the outcome in mind so readers will want to learn more
- **Situation** – describe the situation and the key pain point that the audience or prospect face
- **Impact** – describe how the situation is affecting the bottom line
- **Resolution** – describe how the problem is being solved

Now, looking at Duarate's advice, this may seem a bit odd to consider in the context of data and analytics output. Who is the hero for our purposes? In our context, the individual who needs to act on the analytic output is the hero. Oftentimes, they will need to convince others within the organization to take a different course of action that would otherwise occur without the influence of analytics so we will need to present the information in a compelling manner. Also, in our example, the hero can be thought of as the analytic output itself, and we need the information because the business has encountered a roadblock for which we will need the insight to overcome.

> To tell a good story using data and analytics, you will need contextualized information, personalized information, a narrative, and actionable insights.

For analytic storytelling, we will need to combine the following four elements:

Analytic StoryTelling = Contextualized Information + Personalized Information

+Narrative + Actionable Insights

Let's examine each of these attributes.

- **Contextualized information** – contextualized information is information that is presented in a way such that it relates to the surrounding environment and set of circumstances occurring.
- **Personalized information** – personalized information is presented in a way so that it is relevant and makes sense to the individual receiving the information.
- **Narrative** – a good narrative is presented or told in a way to maximize influence, persuasion, and memorability. In our case, we suggest using the techniques as outlined above by Nancy Duarte as well as the SIR framework.
- **Actionable insight** – actionable insight resulting from prescriptive analytics (see Chapter 10, "Analytics Maturity"), provides a tangible recommendation on what to do to achieve the desired outcome.

Now that we understand the formula for analytic storytelling, what can business leaders do to build an analytics culture?

ANALYTIC STORYTELLING FOR A PROCESS ENGINEER

For example, let's consider the example of a process engineer working in a semiconductor fabrication (fab) plant. For those who may be unfamiliar, semiconductors are the electronic components (aka chips) that power modern electronics. Just about everything you interact with these days, if it is electronic, it will have semiconductor chips within them. For example, a modern electric hybrid vehicle may contain up to 3,500 chips (Lawrence & VerWey, 2019)!

Semiconductor chips are manufactured on wafers which are about the size of a record (300 mm). There can be hundreds or thousands of chips on a single wafer (which are diced or cut up at the end of the process before final packaging). To manufacture a chip, the wafers undergo thousands of process steps over a period of 3–6 months. To say the wiring on the chips is miniscule is an understatement – currently, we are manufacturing chips at 5 nanometer (nm) scale! To put this in context, a typical sheet of paper is 100,000 nm thick, the width of a human hair may be 80,000 nm wide, and there are 25,400,000 nm in 1 in. (Size of the Nanoscale | Nano, 2019)!

As wafers proceed through the manufacturing process, there are thousands of measurements that are taken along the way. Since the wires and features (transistors) are so small, in the business of semiconductors, even the smallest of defects can cause the entire chip to become defective and unusable. As wafers are tested throughout the manufacturing process, visual patterns of the test data may emerge. For example, if measuring the thickness of thin films on the surface of the wafer, the thicknesses may be thinner or thicker at the edge (which looks like a ring) or one may see a pattern of failures that occurs in the center (which looks like a donut) if it is an electrical test (e.g., test for electrical shorts and opens). Oftentimes, these patterns may be indicative of a specific processing problem within the manufacturing process.

What does analytic storytelling look like for a semiconductor process engineer?

To answer this, let's look at what a semiconductor process engineer needs to do? Fundamentally, they need to optimize the process they are responsible for to maximize the yield (number of good chips/total chips tested) of the wafer. If we turn to our storytelling formula,

Analytic Story Telling = Contextualized Information + Personalized Information + Narrative + Actionable Insights

- **Contextualized information** – 15 of 100 wafers tested exhibit a donut failure pattern
- **Personalized information** – of these 15 wafers, 13 were processed in a specific set of tools in your sector and two were not.
- **Narrative** – after using an automated ML workflow, the system has correlated to a specific process step and a specific tool combination
- **Actionable insights** - the prescriptive analytics system recommends running a split lot (where ½ of the wafers go through an experimental process designed to fix the issue) and another go through the standard POR (plan of record process) to confirm the specific process and tool are causing the donut pattern

This storytelling formula provided the four attributes and a specific recommendation on what to do to confirm or deny that the process sector of interest caused the donut failure pattern.

Building an Analytics Culture

In Chapter 1, we discussed the importance of the organizational alignment that is needed for success with data and analytics projects. This included change management, the establishment of centers of excellence, and the project team. We also discussed the criticality of data literacy for organizations and strategies to improve the data literacy within businesses. What else can business leaders do to promote an analytics culture? Rather than rehash the aforementioned sections, we would like to provide a few other suggestions on what leaders can do to build an analytics culture within their organization.

As previously mentioned, there will be members of an organization that are comfortable using analytics for digital decision-making and others who are less comfortable. Analytics is more than the math! *Building and fostering a culture is paramount to success.* Building on the recommendations of Marr (2020) and Thompson (2020), we outline the following five recommendations for analytics leaders.

1. **A steady drumbeat** – starting from the senior executives, there needs to be a deliberate and continuous stream of communications from the team reaffirming the organizational commitment to analytics, how it aligns to strategic business objectives and OKRs (objectives and key results), and how analytics are critical to the long-term viability of the company.
2. **Assign a champion of champions** – the champion of champions is the project team's staunchest advocate for the analytics project team. They need to provide constant feedback to the Executive Leadership Team as well as the business. They are responsible for keeping the analytics team on track, forging alliances across the business, and removing any organizational barriers or impediments that may exist.
3. **Focus on the people** – as the Founder and CEO of SAS Jim Goodnight famously quipped, "You know, I guess 95% of my assets drive out the front gate every evening, It's my job to bring them back (Leung, 2003)". *Keeping the team interested, engaged, happy, and motivated is of the utmost importance.* This is the best investment a company and manager can make. After all, without the people, you don't have a project.
4. **Produce something, rather than nothing** – many teams can fall into the trap of planning, planning, and planning some more. They plan for every potential thing that could possibly occur and often-times, over-engineer the end solution. Endless planning cycles are the

death march of an analytics team. The analytics process is iterative and the organization should encourage experimentation and outcome over plans. In close partnership with the business, focus on producing usable results which you can refine and optimize in the quickest possible time rather than overplanning. As Dwight D. Eisenhower stated, "I have always found that plans are useless but planning is indispensable". Just don't wait for the "perfect" plan.

5. **Vision, learning, passion, and optimism** – there will be many roadblocks and obstacles along the analytic journey. The best analytics leaders we have seen exhibit a wide variety of attributes that make them successful. The four key ones that we see are vision, continual learning, passion, and optimism. Having a "Debbie Downer" (Debbie Downer, 2020) in charge will disenfranchise the project team and the organization from which the organization will never recover.

To summarize, the following quote from Deal and Pilcher seems appropriate: "Leaders must learn how to deal with the challenges of change, so they can successfully lead analytics initiatives with confidence, patience, and perseverance (Deal & Pilcher, 2016)".

Now that we have an understanding of data storytelling and the analytics culture, we will turn our discussion to technology that is absolutely necessary to deploy and monitor analytics workflows.

Model Ops

Analytics is different and deploying analytics workflows is very different than deploying any other type of business software.

How Is Analytics Different?

Typically, when organizations deploy software to the business, they can install the software, configure it, assign the appropriate permissions, and grant users entitlements so they can use the software. Increasingly, organizations are using software as a service, but this simply shifts the maintenance and operations of the software to a third party. This could be accounting software like Intuit QuickBooks, CRM software like SalesForce, or HR software like Workday. After the software is made available, barring any bugs or configuration issues, the software will work indefinitely. Now, there may be occasional bug fixes or upgrades, but the organization really doesn't have to think about it. They may of course monitor the number of users or transactions to make sure the usage doesn't exceed capacity but that's about it.

Now, analytic workflows are a completely different beast all together. If we recall from Chapter 10, your analytics workflow and architecture will consist of data sources, data operations, analytics, and deployment targets. At the core of this workflow, there is an analytic model that was built (trained) using a specific training set. The model was thoroughly validated, tested, and deployed to an operational business system.

All is well, *or is it?*

If we consider the model that was built, it generally provides a prediction or probability (see Figure 2.2) that something will occur. That prediction or probability is based on the underlying data that the model was trained on. Unfortunately, as soon as the model is deployed to production, it will start to decay. In other words, the predictions that are the model outputs are optimal when it is first deployed and will start to generate suboptimal results after that.

Why does this happen?

COVID-19 BROKE MY MODELS, NOW WHAT?

In 2020 the worldwide COVID-19 pandemic disrupted much of everyday life. The established norms and ways of doing business essentially changed overnight. No longer could we rely on traditional forecasting methods to predict future demand. No longer could we rely on same-store sales to understand what the projected sales would be next week. No longer could we expect our products ordered online to arrive on time. Retail, banking, and telco were the most impacted industries followed closely by transportation, media, insurance, and energy (Burkhardt et al., 2020). Whether it be lockdowns, travel bans, or shopping habits, just about everything was different.

To that end, many of the data science and ML models that were in place, no longer produced accurate or actionable results. In fact, some models were producing nonsensical results based on assumptions that were no longer valid. McKinsey reported that one energy company struggled with trading decisions because the models they were using had assumed that crude-oil prices always had to be positive and they happened to be negative (Burkhardt et al., 2020). Models used for customer segmentation, pricing, customer churn, forecasting, logistics, and all other models being used needed to be recalibrated (either retrained or completely remodeled).

Now, this may be an extreme example of change, but nonetheless, it occurred and something similar could occur again. The fact of the matter is, the world is constantly changing and the data changes. This is known as "data drift". Data drift is a phenomena which occurs by the dynamic nature of the real word. Data drift simply means that the new data has a different set of characteristics than the data the model was trained on.

Since we are aware that data is dynamic and is always changing, organizations need a way to continually monitor models to understand what is deployed and how they are performing. If the models are performing suboptimally, the organization may choose to retrain the model or create entirely new models. This is known as model Ops.

This happens because the new data (which the model has never seen before) that is being used to generate the predictions is different from the data used for testing. The new data comes from the real world and the real world is continually changing and evolving. As new conditions and events occur in the world, this may change the distribution (shape) or behavior of the data. Factors (variables) that were once important may no longer be important.

Model Ops "is a cross-functional, collaborative, continuous process that focuses on operationalizing data science by managing statistical, data science, and ML models as reusable, highly available software artifacts, via a repeatable deployment process" (Sweenor et al., 2020).

Why Does an Organization Need Model Ops?

Quite simply put, without it, your organizations' digital decision-making will be quite impaired. It's analogous to walking around with a blindfold on. If you walk far enough, you risk personal injury as you're likely to bump into something, walk into oncoming traffic, or fall off a cliff.

Many organizations are increasing their spending on data, analytics, and AI technology. To maximize the investment,

CAUTION ..... ***BEWARE***
If it takes an organization 6–9 months to deploy a model, what are you predicting? You're predicting what would have happened 6–9 months ago! Do you think your business has changed in the past 6 or 9 months?

organizations must correspondingly invest in model Ops. They need to have visibility on what models are deployed, they need to understand how the models perform, and they need to understand if the models are having the desired impact on their business.

"A good rule of thumb is that you should estimate that for every $1 you spend developing an algorithm, you must spend $100 to deploy and support it" (Redman & Davenport, 2020).

In addition to understanding what models are being used and how they are performing, model Ops provides a process and framework to allow data scientists, model Ops engineers, and DevOps professionals to deploy models in a repeatable manner using best practices. With the model Ops process, framework, and technology, organizations can deploy models faster than ever before. Many surveys suggest that about half of organizations take over 6 months to deploy models and there are about a quarter of organizations who take 9 months or longer to deploy.

Model Ops Capabilities

The following capabilities are required for a solid model Ops foundation.

Model Visibility

When organizations begin their data and analytics journey, they often think of having a handful of models in production. However, as they progress up the analytic maturity curve (see Figure 10.2), they may have hundreds or thousands of models in production. It is imperative that the business have a solid understanding of what models are being used where. Having a report or dashboard to understand what models are running within an organization are critical to model Ops.

Model Repository

A model repository is a centralized model that can be used across the entire organization. This promotes model reuse across the organization and also provides visibility for the business to understand how many models the organization may have and the specific versions associated with each. The model repository check-in and check-out capabilities are something one would expect in any well run organization. As a part of the model repository, there will be security and access controls on the models and project folders themselves. This will ensure that only the people who are entitled to see or access the model can do so.

Model Performance Metrics

As previously mentioned, when models are deployed in production their efficacy begins to degrade. Organizations need a way to understand how the models are performing. There are a wide variety of performance metrics to consider. These include:

- **Model accuracy** – how accurate are the models? They could be classification rates (confusion matrices), F1 scores, AUC–ROC (area under curve–receiver operating characteristic), and so forth.
- **Champion/challenger** – champion/challenger metrics occur when an organization periodically (often quite frequently) tests other models on the same live data that the production model is operating on. The production model is called the champion model and the other model is called the challenger model. If the challenger outperforms the champion model, the organization can decide if they want to replace the champion with the challenger.
- **Population stability index (PSI)** – this measures the "data drift" that was previously discussed. More specifically, it measures how much a variable has shifted when comparing the new data (population) that is being evaluated to the original data (population) that was used during the testing phase. There are also newer metrics that are related to prediction accuracy (Taplin & Hunt, 2019).
- **Performance metrics** – performance metrics include traditional IT metrics such as the number of records scored, input/output metrics, memory and CPU usage, and so forth. These are generally designed to understand the behavior and performance of the runtime environment.
- **Business metrics** – ultimately, you are deploying models to make digital decisions. This may be a recommendation system designed to cross-sell or up-sell products and services, churn prevention and customer retention, or fraud detection and prevention. It is important to define a set of business metrics so that the functional leaders can monitor the impact on the business resulting from the model. Ultimately, these should relate back to the OKRs and KPIs that the business defined.

Contextualized Collaboration Framework

To operationalize data science and ML workflows, a cross-functional team of data scientists, model Ops engineers, DevOps engineers, app developers, and business experts generally need to work together to deploy the workflows. The model Ops framework needs a contextualized collaboration framework that facilitates the seamless hand offs of the model and related assets between the different individuals who will operationalize the models. This collaboration framework provides the glue and connectivity between the data science environment and the corporate IT infrastructure.

Governance

Model Ops helps ensure that governance requirements are adhered to. Model Ops solutions generally have audit trails, approvals, and annotations which can help an organization or regulatory determine who changed what in a model, when they changed the model, and why the change was made. This is increasingly important for a variety of industries including finance, insurance, FDA regulated manufacturing, healthcare, and so forth. Bottom line: business, auditors, and increasingly citizens have a right to know why a specific algorithmic decision was made. Increasingly, organizations are also putting in checks and balances on data and model bias, model lineage, dependency tracking, and explainability and transparency.

Summary

In this chapter, we have examined several elements that are important to communicate and act upon analytics. These include:

- Creating analytic apps using various configurations and components of data and analytics functionality
- The importance of data storytelling and the elements required for memorable and good stories
- The five elements needed to build an analytic culture
- Model Ops and its capabilities

References

Barnes, H. (2013, August 28). *Messaging in Technology Marketing Stinks, But Improvement Is Possible.* Gartner.com; Gartner, Inc. https://blogs.gartner.com/hank-barnes/2013/08/28/messaging-in-technology-marketing-stinks-but-improvement-is-possible/.

Burkhardt, R., Naveria, C. F., Giovine, C., & Govindarajan, A. (2020, September 1). *Leadership's role in fixing the analytics models that COVID-19 broke.* Www.mckinsey.com. https://www.mckinsey.com/business-functions/mckinsey-analytics/our-insights/leaderships-role-in-fixing-the-analytics-models-that-covid-19-broke

Deal, J., & Pilcher, G. (2016). *Mining Your Own Business: A Primer for Executives on Understanding and Employing Data Mining and Predictive Analytics.* Data Science Publishing.

Debbie Downer. (2020, December 2). Wikipedia. https://en.wikipedia.org/wiki/Debbie_Downer.

Duarte, N. (2010). *Resonate: Present Visual Stories that Transform Audiences.* John Wiley & Sons, Cop., Hoboken, NJ.

Ethics guidelines for trustworthy AI. (2019, April 7). European Commission. https://ec.europa.eu/digital-single-market/en/news/ethics-guidelines-trustworthy-ai.

Lawrence, A., & VerWey, J. (2019). The Automotive Semiconductor Market - Key Determinants of U.S. Firm Competitiveness. In *United States International Trade Commission.* U.S. International Trade Commission (UTC). https://www.usitc.gov/publications/332/executive_briefings/ebot_amanda_lawrence_john_verwey_the_automotive_semiconductor_market_pdf.pdf.

Leung, R. (2003, April 18). *Working The Good Life.* Cbsnews.com. https://www.cbsnews.com/news/working-the-good-life/.

Marr, B. (2020). *The Intelligence Revolution: Transforming Your Business with AI.* Kogan Page, London.

Panetta, K. (2020, October 19). *Gartner Keynote: The Future of Business Is Composable.* Www.gartner.com. https://www.gartner.com/smarterwithgartner/gartner-keynote-the-future-of-business-is-composable.

Redman, T. C., & Davenport, T. H. (2020, September 8). *Getting Serious About Data and Data Science.* MIT Sloan Management Review. https://sloanreview.mit.edu/article/getting-serious-about-data-and-data-science/

Size of the Nanoscale | Nano. (2019). Nano.gov. https://www.nano.gov/nanotech-101/what/nano-size.

Sweenor, D., Hillion, S., Rope, D., Kannabiran, D., Hill, T., & O'Connell, M. (2020). *ML Ops: Operationalizing Data Science.* O'Reilly Media, Inc., Newton, MA. https://www.oreilly.com/library/view/ml-ops-operationalizing/9781492074663/.

Taplin, R., & Hunt, C. (2019). The population accuracy index: A new measure of population stability for model monitoring. *Risks*, 7, 53. doi:10.3390/risks7020053.

Thompson, J. K. (2020). *Building Analytics Teams: Harnessing Analytics and Artificial Intelligence for Business Improvement.* Packt Publishing Limited, Birmingham.

Additional Resources

Duarte, N. (2010). *Resonate: Present Visual Stories that Transform Audiences.* John Wiley & Sons, Cop.

McCarthy, B., McShea, C., & Roth, M. (2018, November 19). *Rebooting Analytics Leadership: Time to Move Beyond the Math | McKinsey.* www.mckinsey.com. https://www.mckinsey.com/business-functions/mckinsey-analytics/our-insights/rebooting-analytics-leadership-time-to-move-beyond-the-math.

Pine II, B. J., & Gilmore, J. H. (2011). *The Experience Economy: Vol.* (Updated edition). Harvard Business Review Press.

Keywords

Model Ops; Analytics Governance; Analytics Ethics

Chapter 12

To Build, Buy, or Outsource Analytics Platform

Rome was not built in 1 day.

John Heywood

Introduction

Before organizations embark on their analytics journey, business leaders need to clearly define their corporate strategy and understand what role data and analytics can play in achieving the strategy. Are data and analytics at the core of the strategy or on the periphery? We're hoping it's the former as every company needs to be a technology company fueled by data and analytics if they are not already.

For more specifics on using analytics to make digital decisions and how to align the organization, please see Chapter 1, "Analytics Technology Design for Success", which will cover this in more detail. Fundamentally, analytics leaders need to align strategic goals, business objectives, and key results, which are referred to as OKRs (objectives and key results). Each of the OKRs may give rise to one or more business initiatives that will be required to achieve the strategic objectives.

To build a sustainable competitive advantage, organizations need to embed analytics into critical business processes so that contextualized information can be delivered to the right person or system, at the right time, so

DOI: 10.4324/9780429343957-15

that the analytic output can change the behavior or actions of the business. Of course, the organization should keep ethics, fairness, and transparency in mind which is covered in Chapter 3.

To infuse analytics throughout the enterprise, organizations will need an analytics platform. Should organizations build or buy an analytics platform? Or perhaps outsource the analytics function all together? After all, there are a dizzying array of both commercial and open source technology components to choose from; so where does one begin?

To help answer the build vs. buy vs. outsource question, we first need to understand what components are required in an analytics infrastructure. We will then provide a set of considerations and questions that business leaders can use to help make an informed decision.

Analytics Infrastructure Components

In countless discussions with business leaders, when we discuss analytic strategies, many minds quickly race to the math. However, analytics is way more than the algorithms – the mathematical models are only a small (but very important essential) part of the end-to-end solution. Figure 12.1 illustrates the functional capabilities that are required for an analytics platform.

Functional capabilities for data and analytics architectures generally consist of data operations, analytics operations, and deployment systems. Please

Data and Analytics Functional Architecture

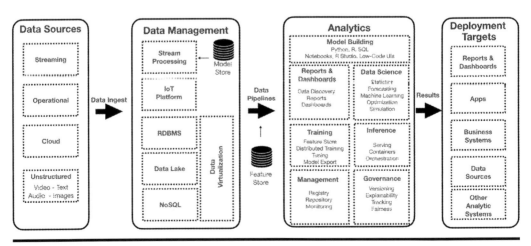

Figure 12.1   Functional capabilities for a data and analytics architecture.

note, the above architecture does not consider the security, computational, and collaboration frameworks that are needed for a complete data and analytics architecture. Chapter 10 covers the architecture in more detail. To review, a data and analytics infrastructure consists of:

- **Data operations** – consist of databases, data lakes, IoT platforms, feature stores, and stream processing components to ingest data from disparate sources and create data pipelines that analytics practitioners will use.
- **Analytics operations** – contain the elements and capabilities to create analytic workflows using statistics and machine learning, reports and dashboards, and model management capabilities. These will often use open source languages, libraries, and frameworks as well as cloud ecosystems.
- **Deployment systems** – are the target applications, business systems, and reports that the analytic outputs will manifest themselves to enable digital decisions.

It is interesting to note that machine learning (ML) code is only a small part of the overall infrastructure. This was identified in Google's seminal paper on technical debt in ML (Sculley et al., 2014) and is shown in Figure 12.2.

In addition to the functional capabilities identified in Figure 12.1, Figure 12.2 includes capabilities that are required to physically run the data science and ML workflows. These include configuration systems, computational machine resource management, process management tools, serving infrastructure, and IT infrastructure monitoring applications.

Machine Learning System Components

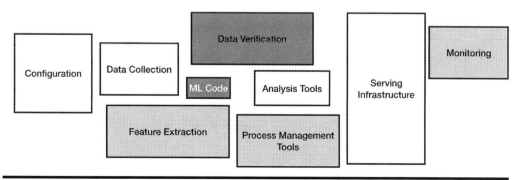

Figure 12.2 ML Code is only a small fraction of a real-world ML platform.

Now that we understand some of the components required for a data and analytics infrastructure, how can we evaluate if we should build, buy, or outsource platform development?

What Really Matters (In Your Business)?

In any business, there are core competencies that provide the foundation and essence of the business. These competencies are used to differentiate within the market and win more deals. This essence is often the basis for what we could call the "soul" of the business model. As an example, in *The Art of the Start*, by Guy Kawasaki, Guy discusses the difference between mission statements and mantra. The mantra that Mr. Kawasaki is referring to is the "soul" of the business. For example, in Table 12.1, Guy suggests the following mantras for a few companies (Kawasaki, 2004, 2006):

For businesses to live their mantra, there are things they need to be good at and then, there are things that are necessary to operate the business but are not critical to their differentiation. As an example, perhaps the human resources is not critical to Coca-Cola's core differentiation to "Refresh the world" or marketing is not as essential for FedEx to offer you "Peace of mind". But, I bet the marketing and distribution functions are critical for Coca-Cola while the Logistics function is paramount to Federal Express' business model! In other words, Coca-Cola and FedEx need to be experts at

Table 12.1 Hypothetical Mantras for Various Companies

Organization	Hypothetical Mantra
Southwest Airlines	Better than driving
Coca-Cola	Refresh the world
Wendy's	Healthy food fast
Red Cross	Stop suffering
United States Air Force	Kick butt in air and space
United Way (Hawaii)	Bring people together
March of Dimes	Save babies
Federal Express (FedEx)	Peace of mind
Nike	Authentic athletic performance
Target	Democratize design

the functions on which they compete and differentiate on but do not need to be experts at all corporate functions.

As technology matures, more and more businesses are looking to use data and analytics to differentiate their core traditional offerings. For example, Nike, a maker of athletic apparel, "released a new brand of smartphone-enabled self-lacing shoes, with plans to embed sensors that will allow the shoe to detect the wearer's blood pressure and adjust lace tightness accordingly" (Orad, 2020). As technology progresses, every company will need to become a data and analytics company; else they risk becoming irrelevant.

Build vs. Buy Considerations

There are a variety of factors that organizations need to consider when evaluating whether they should build, buy, or outsource an analytics platform. To summarize, Daneshgar et al. identified the following ten factors based on a literature review of build vs. buy decisions (Daneshgar et al., 2011).

Strategy and Competitive Advantage

Many business leaders would argue that organizations should build the systems that are core to their competitive differentiation and should purchase systems that are considered less strategic. This is exemplified by many of the Silicon Valley titans who have decided to build their analytics platforms including Facebook, Uber, AirBnb, Netflix, Apple, Amazon, and others. Since many of these companies had innovative business models fueled by technology at world-wide scale, commercial platforms simply did not exist.

Costs

These typically include both the direct and indirect costs associated with software systems. Chapter 10 (Table 10.4) has an in-depth table on evaluating open source software costs. For purchased systems, in addition to the initial implementation costs, organizations also need to include the ongoing maintenance, documentation, compliance, and customization costs that may be required. In general, purchased systems cost less than those developed in-house.

According to the analytics vendor *Algorithmia*, building a model management solution, one component of a complete end-to-end analytics platform, takes significant investment.

At a high level, you will need 18 technical resources, 28 months of time, and approximately $2.8 million to build a viable machine learning management solution on your own

Garrett (2020).

Scale and Complexity

As systems become more complex, some would argue that organizations should purchase these systems as they may benefit from economies of scale and built-in best practices that the vendor may provide. However, as the systems become large and more complex, there may be more integration, customization, and support costs that are also incurred. Additionally, vendor provided solutions may have features and components that are superfluous and not needed for your specific use case.

Commoditization, Flexibility, and Change

For organizations with unique and specific requirements, most businesses choose to build vs. buy a system (Daneshgar et al., 2011). This occurs because the customization required to modify COTS (commercial off the shelf) software package increases costs and risk to the organization. Furthermore, as more and more software packages are being offered "as a service", this customization may not even be possible.

Time

In general, systems that are built in-house take significantly more time to develop and implement compared to purchased systems. However, if the system is part of your core strategic strengths, it may be worthwhile in the long run to build. The business should also consider opportunity costs like what projects are being put on hold during the time the platform is being built.

However, building a solution takes years and headcount. Airbnb, for instance, took around three months figuring out what to build — and about four years to build it. By the end, they used numerous open source technologies and still had to fix the gaps in the path to production by defining their own services and user interface. This required expertise in supporting multiple frame-works, feature management, model and data transformation, multi-tenant training environments and much more. Similarly, Uber has been working for five years on its platform and Netflix started more than four years ago.

Parkey (2020).

Also, what is the risk to the organization if a competitive organization puts a system in place before you?

In-House Expertise

To be successful at building an in-house data and analytics platform, your organization will need to have significant experience and expertise. You will need subject matter expertise in data, analytics, visualization, cloud, APIs, DevOps, analytics, and application design to be successful. Does your organization have the expertise to build and maintain a system in the long run?

Risks

There are a myriad of risks for the organization who chooses to build a platform. As with any project, the organization will be at the mercy of the triple constraint (scope, costs, and time) when building quality software. For the buy option, is vendor lock-in and long-term vendor viability a concern?

Other common software development risks include (Ondov, 2001):

■ Inaccurate estimates and schedules
■ Scope creep
■ Employee churn
■ Vague requirements
■ Productivity issues
■ "Gold plating" (adding unnecessary features or using the latest and greatest tech that may be unproven)
■ Lack of clarity in responsibility and ownership
■ Technical risks
■ End user engagement
■ Poor quality code

Support Structure

For the build option, the organization will need to understand how much ongoing maintenance and support that the application will need. Is the organization willing to devote the resources necessary for long-term maintenance and support of the application? Will the organization keep the documentation up to date?

Operational Factors

Does your organization have a track record of building and delivering applications for the business? What is the organizational commitment to building and maintaining a system long term?

Intellectual Property

Organizations need to protect their IP so it may be best to buy if there is significant IP involved. If pursuing the build option, companies need to have a clear understanding of the various open source licenses that are available. If an organization is not careful, the software that is developed could become open source itself! For the buy option, long-term license and maintenance costs should be considered.

Outsourcing

For many organizations, if they lack the in-house skills necessary to build a solution they may consider an outsource arrangement. In some cases, very large and complex problems may require the expertise of global system integrators like Accenture, Deloitte, PwC, Tata Consultancy Services (TCS), and so forth.

Build vs. Buy vs. Outsource Guidelines

The analyst firm Gartner, Inc. put together a useful decision tree together on the subject which is summarized in Table 12.2 (Krensky & Linden, 2018).

Table 12.2 Build, Buy, or Outsource Guidelines

Criteria	Guideline
Is there a common use case for which a commoditized solution would be appropriate?	If so, consider a packaged application (i.e., Workday, Salesforce, etc.)
Can we use off the shelf-pretrained models from a cloud service provider? Do we have in-house expertise available?	If so, consider building using APis from AWS, Google, or Microsoft
Does the organization have in-house data science skills and expertise?	If so, consider using open source technology (R, Python, Google TensorFlow, Microsoft Cognitive Services) or a data science platform like SAS, IBM SPSS, Dataiku, Alteryx, or TIBCO Data Science.
Is the project global in scope and significantly complex? Do we have sufficient budget to fund the effort?	If so, consider outsourcing to a global consultancy, system integrator, or specialist.

Additionally, Gartner mentions that there are strengths and weaknesses associated with each approach. They recommend evaluating each of the options against the following criteria (Krensky & Linden, 2018):

■ Ease of use
■ Time to solution
■ Solution quality
■ Cost-effectiveness
■ Learning experience
■ Agility/granularity of control

Summary

In this chapter, we explored the ten factors that organizations should consider when thinking about building or buying an analytics platform and provided guidelines to help with the decision process. In the end, many organizations tend to use a hybrid approach and build the specific components that may be core to their strategic advantage and buy functionality (i.e., like reporting and dashboard software) that may be readily available off the shelf.

References

Daneshgar, F., Worasinchai, L., & Low, G. (2011). *An Investigation of "Build vs. Buy" Decision for Software Acquisition in Small to Medium Enterprises.* Papers.ssrn.com. https://papers.ssrn.com/sol3/papers.cfm?abstract_id=1867839.

Garrett, W. (2020, June 2). *The build versus buy decision for ML: A new Algorithmia whitepaper.* Algorithmia Blog. https://algorithmia.com/blog/the-build-versus-buy-decision-for-ml-a-new-algorithmia-whitepaper.

Kawasaki, G. (2004). *The Art of the Start: The Time-Tested, Battle-Hardened Guide for Anyone Starting Anything* (1st ed.). Portfolio, Brighton.

Kawasaki, G. (2006, January 2). *Mantras Versus Missions.* Guy Kawasaki. https://guykawasaki.com/mantras_versus_/.

Krensky, P., & Linden, A. (2018, October 30). *Data Science and Machine Learning Solutions: Buy, Build or Outsource?* www.gartner.com; Gartner, Inc. https://www.gartner.com/document/3892470.

Ondov, R. (2001, November). *Managing software projects at AT&T: common risks and pitfalls. Paper presented at Project Management Institute Annual Seminars & Symposium, Nashville, TN. Newtown Square, PA: Project Management Institute.* Pmi.org. https://www.pmi.org/learning/library/managing-software-projects-common-risk-pitfalls-7876.

Orad, A. (2020, February 14). *Council Post: Why Every Company Is A Data Company.* Forbes. https://www.forbes.com/sites/forbestechcouncil/2020/02/14/why-every-company-is-a-data-company/?sh=5acb90e817a4.

Parkey, C. (2020, November 23). *Machine Learning Platforms: Should You Buy Commercial or Build In-House?* Built In. https://builtin.com/machine-learning/building-ML-platforms-artificial-intelligence.

Sculley, D., Holt, G., Golovin, D., Davydov, E., Phillips, T., Ebner, D., Chaudhary, V., & Young, M. (2014). *SE4ML: Software Engineering for Machine Learning (NIPS 2014 Workshop).*

Additional Resources

This article by IEEE (Institute of Electrical and Electronics Engineers) applies to the 'Build vs Buy' decision for software, but applies in many ways to larger applications and platforms: https://ieeexplore.ieee.org/stamp/stamp.jsp?arnumber=8085093.

Index

Note: **Bold** page numbers refer to tables and *italic* page numbers refer to figures.

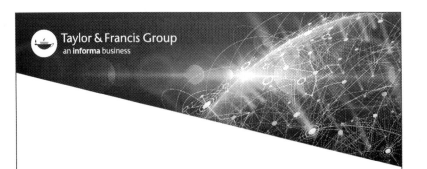